T0342372

Elementary School Wellness Education

Elementary School Wellness Education

An Integrated Approach to Teaching the Whole Child

Matthew Cummiskey, PhD

West Chester University

Frances Cleland Donnelly, PED

West Chester University

HUMAN KINETICS

Library of Congress Cataloging-in-Publication Data

Names: Cummiskey, Matthew, 1974- author. | Cleland, Frances E., author.
Title: Elementary school wellness education : an integrated approach to
  teaching the whole child / Matthew Cummiskey, Frances Cleland Donnelly.
Description: Champaign, IL : Human Kinetics, [2023] | Includes
  bibliographical references and index.
Identifiers: LCCN 2021062544 (print) | LCCN 2021062545 (ebook) | ISBN
  9781718203426 (paperback) | ISBN 9781718203433 (epub) | ISBN
  9781718203440 (pdf)
Subjects: MESH: School Health Services | Health Education | Health
  Promotion | Physical Education and Training
Classification: LCC RA440.5 (print) | LCC RA440.5 (ebook) | NLM WA 350 |
  DDC 613.071/2--dc23/eng/20220323
LC record available at https://lccn.loc.gov/2021062544
LC ebook record available at https://lccn.loc.gov/2021062545

ISBN: 978-1-7182-0342-6 (print)

Copyright © 2023 by Human Kinetics, Inc.

Human Kinetics supports copyright. Copyright fuels scientific and artistic endeavor, encourages authors to create new works, and promotes free speech. Thank you for buying an authorized edition of this work and for complying with copyright laws by not reproducing, scanning, or distributing any part of it in any form without written permission from the publisher. You are supporting authors and allowing Human Kinetics to continue to publish works that increase the knowledge, enhance the performance, and improve the lives of people all over the world.

The online learning content that accompanies this product is delivered on HK*Propel*, **HKPropel.HumanKinetics.com.** You agree that you will not use HK*Propel* if you do not accept the site's Privacy Policy and Terms and Conditions, which detail approved uses of the online content.

To report suspected copyright infringement of content published by Human Kinetics, contact us at **permissions@hkusa.com**. To request permission to legally reuse content published by Human Kinetics, please refer to the information at **https://US.Human Kinetics.com/pages/permissions-information**.

Permission notices for material reprinted in this book from other sources can be found on page xiii.

The web addresses cited in this text were current as of January 2022, unless otherwise noted.

Acquisitions Editor: Scott Wikgren; **Developmental and Managing Editor:** Amanda S. Ewing; **Copyeditor:** Annette Pierce; **Proofreader:** Librum Artis Editorial Services; **Indexer:** Ferreira Indexing; **Permissions Manager:** Dalene Reeder; **Graphic Designer:** Julie L. Denzer; **Cover Designer:** Keri Evans; **Cover Design Specialist:** Susan Rothermel Allen; **Photographs (cover):** FatCamera/Getty Images; © Human Kinetics; **Photographs (interior):** © Human Kinetics, unless otherwise noted; **Photo Asset Manager:** Laura Fitch; **Photo Production Manager:** Jason Allen; **Senior Art Manager:** Kelly Hendren; **Illustrations:** © Human Kinetics, unless otherwise noted; **Printer:** Versa Press

Printed in the United States of America   10 9 8 7 6 5 4 3 2 1

The paper in this book is certified under a sustainable forestry program.

Human Kinetics
1607 N. Market Street
Champaign, IL 61820
USA

United States and International
Website: **US.HumanKinetics.com**
Email: info@hkusa.com
Phone: 1-800-747-4457

Canada
Website: **Canada.HumanKinetics.com**
Email: info@hkcanada.com

E8301

Tell us what you think!
Human Kinetics would love to hear what we can do to improve the customer experience. Use this QR code to take our brief survey.

Contents

Preface

The time has come for elementary health education and physical education to evolve to a new style of instruction called school wellness education (SWE). SWE combines physical activity and health-enhancing skills into the same lesson. In doing so, students are educated in a more holistic fashion across the multiple domains of wellness. SWE meets multiple learning standards simultaneously and better uses the limited class time afforded to health and physical education. Because SWE lessons take place in the gymnasium, there is no need for a separate health education classroom. The transition to SWE is easier and more comfortable for traditional PE teachers because half of wellness education is physical education. Finally, SWE better reflects the nature of well-being, which is interdisciplinary and multifaceted.

A typical wellness education lesson combines classroom-based learning activities such as discussions, worksheets, and videos with physical activity. For example, consider a lesson on hockey passing and tooth brushing. The lesson starts with a basic discussion about teeth and why they are important. In pairs, students complete a geography of the teeth activity, in which they draw a map of the teeth in their partner's lower jaw. Using the map, students arrange 14 cones in the shape of the teeth on the gym floor. Next, students watch a video on how to correctly brush their teeth. Students are given hockey sticks and pretend to brush the teeth (cones) using the correct technique. Next, the teacher demonstrates how to properly pass and receive a hockey ball or puck, and students practice this in pairs. Finally, students play a game called dental defenders, where both teams attempt to pass the ball, called plaque, past the center dividing line toward the teeth models on the other side. Students demonstrate correct hockey-passing technique while the dental defenders attempt to receive or block passes that will damage their side's teeth.

The example lesson highlights several key aspects of a SWE approach:

1. Students are meeting health and physical activity standards at the same time.

2. SWE lessons are learning focused, with each activity carefully aligned to the standards and objectives.

3. Lessons are fun, which better promotes learning and students' enjoyment of class. Students aren't sitting in a traditional classroom learning about health, but instead are doing it in the gymnasium.

4. SWE uses traditional PE equipment and the gymnasium in new and creative ways. This is especially important in schools that lack a separate health education classroom.

Our hope is that this book will become a seminal resource and that the school wellness education approach will become the predominant mode of instruction in elementary schools. All current and future undergraduate teacher education majors should learn to teach using this model. For current teachers, the good news is that SWE is not a dramatic departure from existing instruction. Students are still moving and being taught in the gymnasium, but now health content and skills are being infused into all lessons. The book is also suitable for use by classroom teachers who want to promote wellness or incorporate additional physical activity into their students' days.

The book introduces the school wellness educator. This person is the cornerstone of the whole-school model, charged with promoting wellness through school, community, and family interventions. That means collaborating with many people to promote wellness:

- Classroom teachers
- Administrators
- School nurses
- School counselors
- Custodians (environmental health)
- Security officers (safety)
- Social workers
- Food service employees (nutrition)
- Transportation (walking and active transport)

Countless studies have shown that healthy and active students

- score better academically,
- attend school more frequently, and
- are more on task.

The school wellness education approach is aligned with several models. Principal among them is the CDC's Whole School, Whole Community, Whole Child (WSCC) model (CDC, 2021). The curriculum can be incorporated throughout the school in a way that reflects the needs and resources of the community.

Organization

The book is organized into two parts. The first portion contains four chapters:

- Chapter 1 defines SWE, justifies its place in schools today, discusses its benefits and challenges, explores its historical context, and presents an overall vision of SWE.
- Chapter 2 presents the Whole School, Whole Community, Whole Child (WSCC) model and explores in detail each of its 10 components along with action steps for implementing the model in schools.
- Chapter 3 focuses on emergent pedagogies such as skill-based wellness education, universal design for learning, social and emotional learning, and social justice.
- Chapter 4 addresses teaching school wellness education online in a manner commensurate with face-to-face instruction. The chapter shows teachers how to prepare for online classes, showcases effective pedagogies, and presents practical activities for selected domains of wellness.

The second part of the book provides SWE lesson plans broken into grade bands: K-2 and 3-5. The lessons are designed to be turnkey, meaning they can be easily implemented in most elementary schools. The lessons provide teachers with formative and summative assessments aligned to specific learning objectives and WSCC components. The assessments are age appropriate and include checklists, rating scales, and qualitative rubrics. The assessments and lesson plan handouts are available online at *HKPropel* for ease of use. See page ix to learn how to access the lesson plan supplemental materials.

Instructor Ancillaries

Instructors using this resource in the higher education setting have access to several ancillaries to help facilitate teaching the material.

- *Presentation package.* The presentation package includes more than 60 PowerPoint slides for chapters 1 through 4 that instructors can use for class discussion and demonstration. The slides in the presentation package can be used directly in PowerPoint or printed for use as transparencies or handouts to distribute to students. Instructors can easily add, modify, and rearrange the order of the slides as well as search for images based on key words.
- *Instructor guide.* The instructor guide contains big ideas, objectives, lecture topics, and teaching activities for chapters 1 through 4.
- *Test package.* The test package contains questions in multiple-choice, true-false, and matching formats for chapters 1 through 4. The files may be downloaded for integration with a learning management system or printed for use as paper-based tests.

Instructor ancillaries are free to adopting instructors, including an ebook version of the text that allows instructors to add highlights, annotations, and bookmarks. Please contact your sales manager for details about how to access instructor resources in *HKPropel*.

How to Access the Lesson Plan Resource Handouts

Throughout *Elementary School Wellness Education* you will notice references to HK*Propel* online content. This online content is available to you for free upon purchase of a new print book or an ebook. HK*Propel* provides you with access to all of the lesson plan resource handouts in convenient PDF format. Select resource handouts are also available as Word documents for ease of filling out the information electronically.

Follow these steps to access the HK*Propel* online content. If you need help at any point in the process, you can contact us via email at HKPropelCustSer@hkusa.com.

If it's your first time using HK*Propel*:

1. Visit HKPropel.HumanKinetics.com.
2. Click the "New user? Register here" link on the opening screen.
3. Follow the onscreen prompts to create your HK*Propel* account.
4. Enter the access code exactly as shown in the next column, including hyphens. You will not need to re-enter this access code on subsequent visits.
5. After your first visit, simply log in to HKPropel .HumanKinetics.com to access your digital product.

If you already have an HK*Propel* account:

1. Visit HKPropel.HumanKinetics.com and log in with your username (email address) and password.
2. Once you are logged in, navigate to Account in the top right corner.
3. Under "Add Access Code" enter the access code exactly as shown below, including hyphens.
4. Once your code is redeemed, navigate to your Library on the Dashboard to access your digital content.

Access code: CUMMISKEY1E-5UGH-D8JP-C38L

Once you have signed in to HK*Propel* and redeemed the access code, navigate to your Library to access your digital content. Your license to this digital product will expire seven years after the date you redeem the access code. You can check the expiration dates of all your HK*Propel* products at any time in My Account.

For technical support, contact us via email at HKPropelCustSer@hkusa.com. **Helpful tip:** You may reset your password from the log-in screen at any time if you forget it.

Acknowledgments

Countless thanks go out to my wonderful wife and three beautiful boys for their patience throughout the development of this book. Their selfless support means the world to me. I'm looking forward to more family time in the years ahead. I would also like to acknowledge my coauthor, Dr. Fran Cleland. It is a true testament to her dedication to our shared field that she has embarked upon such an undertaking in the twilight of her career. Finally, I would like to thank the faculty at Slippery Rock University for inspiring our school wellness education journey.

—Matthew Cummiskey

I thank my colleague Dr. Matthew Cummiskey for his vision of creating a school wellness textbook and for including me in the project. It is always great to be academically challenged! I also thank Dr. Monica Lepore for her insight and expertise in revising sample lesson plans using universal design for learning. I thank my teacher candidates at West Chester University, who always encourage and support my scholarship and creative ideas. Finally, I thank my husband, Jim Donnelly, for his willingness to let me bounce ideas off of him and for his support in all my scholarly pursuits.

—Frances Cleland Donnelly

Credits

The SHAPE America Outcomes listed in the lesson plans are reprinted by permission from SHAPE America, *National Standards & Grade-Level Outcomes for K-12 Physical Education* (Champaign, IL: Human Kinetics, 2014).

The National Health Education Indicators listed in the lesson plans are copyright 2007, SHAPE America—Society of Health and Physical Educators, PO Box 225, Annapolis Junction, MD 20701, www.shapeamerica.org. All rights reserved. Used with permission.

Page 7 Christopher Futcher/Getty Images/iStockphoto
Page 15 FatCamera/iStock/Getty Images
Page 29 Drazen Zigic/istock/Getty Images
Page 31 Halfpoint Images/Moment/Getty Images
Page 38 Christopher Futcher/iStock/Getty Images
Page 43 Drazen Zigic/istock/Getty Images
Page 45 Images By Tang Ming Tung/Digital Vision/Getty Images
Page 47 Yulkapopkova/E+/Getty Images
Page 51 da-kuk/E+/Getty Images
Page 62 Amir Mukhtar/Moment/Getty Images
Page 149 Andy Cross/The Denver Post via Getty Images
Page 188 Eyewire
Page 188 Stockdisc Royalty Free Photos

PART I

Introduction to School Wellness Education

School Wellness Education (SWE) is a unique and comprehensive approach to promoting wellness at the elementary level. The goal is to positively affect wellness throughout the lifespan.

Chapter 1 reconceptualizes the role of traditional health and physical education into a new form of instruction called SWE. In the past, physical education focused principally on the physical domain of wellness, while health education focused on content knowledge. In an SWE approach, students achieve the SHAPE America Standards and National Health Education Standards at the same time. Students learn about health-enhancing skills and movement-based skills simultaneously, courtesy of engaging, fun, and creative instruction. SWE makes excellent use of available instructional time and can be used by both existing teachers and preservice teachers. The chapter also discusses challenges to SWE, the historical processes culminating in SWE, and a vision for future instruction.

Chapter 2 focuses on the Whole School, Whole Community, Whole Child Model and the multiple dimensions of wellness, including emotional, spiritual, intellectual, physical, environmental, occupational, and social wellness. This acknowledges and celebrates the interconnected nature of wellness, where each dimension affects other dimensions. Only through focusing on the whole child can optimal levels of wellness be achieved. The school wellness educator coordinates interventions both in school and the community. They work with diverse stakeholders, including parents, bus drivers, cafeteria workers, school counselors, and others to promote wellness. This aligns with the CDC's whole school model and reinforces the idea that practicing wellness is a daily and ongoing commitment.

Chapter 3 orients readers toward effective instructional practices in health education and physical education but goes a step further by postulating emergent pedagogies in school wellness education. These pedagogies are aligned with developmental characteristics of K-5 learners. Special attention is given to meeting the needs of all learners through universal design for learning, which includes multiple means of expression and multiple means of engagement. Social justice also plays a pivotal role in chapter 3 by positioning the school wellness educator to actively teach diversity, equity, and inclusion concepts, often through physical activities.

Chapter 4 describes how school wellness educators can deliver online instruction at a level commensurate with face-to-face instruction. The chapter explores the many advantages and challenges of online education. Ultimately, if teachers are able to adequately prepare for online instruction, develop competence in communication technologies, and master common pedagogical tools, they will be successful. Teachers will learn to plan for standards-based instruction, build a positive learning environment, and deliver robust instruction. Specific instructional practices and activities are aligned with multiple domains of wellness. In addition, best-practice technology platforms are presented along with multiple means of assessing student learning.

Chapter 1

The School Wellness Approach

The future is not health education or physical education; it is wellness education. The goal of wellness education is to develop the knowledge and skills to practice wellness throughout the lifespan (Brewer et al., 2017). Health education and physical education have traditionally been taught as two separate and distinct subjects.

- Physical education exists in its own silo and principally teaches movement skills and fitness concepts in the gymnasium.
- Health education exists in its own silo and principally teaches content knowledge in a traditional classroom.

Yet adults aren't concerned with these arbitrary distinctions; they simply want to be well in body, mind, and spirit. So, instead of teaching health-enhancing skills separately, they should be fused into a new style of instruction called *school wellness education* (SWE) (figure 1.1).

In doing so, students would be educated in a more holistic manner that includes components of both traditional health education and physical education. The key is to integrate health-enhancing knowledge and skills while also being physically active. For example, in a wellness education approach, students would learn about the cardiovascular system by creating a model of the heart from physical education equipment and then exploring and physically traveling through the model. Students are learning physical activity skills and health skills in the same lesson. This model of instruction engages students in active learning. Properly executed,

a school wellness education program constantly challenges students to be moving and learning.

School wellness education is about more than just fusing health education and physical education content in the gymnasium. It incorporates an interdisciplinary approach to promoting comprehensive well-being through family, school, and community interventions. (CDC & ASCD, 2014)

The wellness educator is the cornerstone of this strategy. Their intent is to imbue students with the knowledge, skills, and dispositions to lead a healthy and physically active lifestyle that carries forward into adulthood.

Making the Case for School Wellness Education

In traditional health and physical education, content overlaps to the point it is difficult to discern where one subject ends and the other begins. Consider the lesson previously mentioned on the cardiovascular system. In traditional health education, one could expect the following topics:

1. Structure (e.g., left ventricle, right semilunar valve)
2. Pumping action
3. Pulmonary and systemic circulation
4. Common afflictions (e.g., heart attack, aneurysm)
5. Risk factors
6. Treatments
7. Maintenance of health

Students in a traditional physical education setting might complete an aerobic capacity test such as the PACER, record their heart rates, measure step counts, calculate their target heart rate, and perform a series of activities designed to improve cardiovascular endurance.

In a single school wellness education lesson, the teacher can present the learning objectives simultaneously in a more coherent, holistic, and time-sensitive fashion. Imagine students creating an obstacle course based on the structures of the heart using PE equipment and collaborating to learn about heart structures. By moving through the course, students travel the

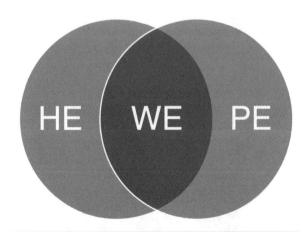

FIGURE 1.1 Wellness education (WE) is a holistic combination of health education (HE) and physical education (PE).

same path as the blood, stopping at heart valves and changing speed to mimic the effects of physical activity. At the same time, students practice psychomotor skills such as leaping, jumping, and transfer of weight while moving (SHAPE Standard 1). At the conclusion of the lesson, the teacher discusses how effectively each group communicated and functioned as a team (SHAPE Standards 4 and 5). This combined approach more naturally approximates wellness, its dimensions, and the attributes toward which adults strive.

Traditional health education lessons are by their nature more sedentary. Students are seated in desks, the arrangement of which limits movement and open space for activities. Reducing sedentary behaviors and incorporating more physical activity has been shown to enhance academic performance (Michael et al., 2015; Donnelly et al., 2016). In the SWE approach, physical activity doesn't come on a separate day in a separate location; it is part of every class. SWE lessons take place in the gymnasium, not a classroom. Students spread out and learn health-enhancing skills and physical activity skills simultaneously in an active, enjoyable, learning-focused format. There is no need for physi-

cal activity breaks because activity is germane to the design of each lesson plan.

The process of transitioning from a traditional approach to a robust SWE approach is achievable. This is important because the amount and quality of traditional health education varies tremendously. Many elementary schools hire teachers whose principal training is in physical education. They may have little or no training in traditional health education. Therefore, they lack the educational background critical to implementing school wellness education. According to the 2014 School Health Policies and Practices Study (SHPPS), only 23.5 percent of elementary schools had a certified health educator teaching health education (CDC, 2015). In 65.6 percent of schools, the physical educator taught health education. It is likely therefore that the amount of health education taught at the elementary level is grossly insufficient. Many physical educators focus more on physical activity and fitness because of a lack of health education content knowledge and pedagogy. This tendency is heightened by the fact that only 38.5 percent of school districts require schools to assess student achievement of health education standards, and only 32 percent of districts have specific time requirements for health education. SWE can ameliorate these challenges by scaffolding health skills atop the best practices physical educators are already using.

SWE is even more practical in states where the elementary classroom teacher teaches physical education. To a classroom teacher, the gymnasium is often a foreign and intimidating environment. There are no desks, no seats, and few, if any, whiteboards. Students are moving vigorously, often using equipment. Sometimes these teachers have little or no formal wellness training (Evans & Sims, 2015). In some states, preservice teachers must complete one course on health or physical education before graduation. Elementary classroom teachers often lack the resources and know-how to effectively teach a wellness-based curriculum. For these teachers, SWE is less of a leap because it combines elements of traditional classroom instruction (videos, worksheets, projects) with physical activity. SWE can also make the gymnasium less intimidating because teachers can use many of the same management and instructional strategies.

From a student perspective, SWE is more enjoyable. Using a SWE model, students will spend more time in the gymnasium being physically active while learning health-enhancing knowledge and skills. Imagine telling students they will learn about tooth brushing seated in a classroom. Then imagine telling students they will learn about tooth brushing, create models of their teeth using PE equipment, learn how to execute a pass in hockey, and defend their teeth using hockey sticks against plaque. Which lesson would students prefer? The answer is obvious, as is the case for using a SWE in elementary school. The learning activities and environment serve as a primer to internally motivate students to lead healthy and active lifestyles outside of class (DeLong & Winters, 2002).

A focus on wellness will also enhance the credibility of the discipline (SHAPE America, 2017). Physical educators have long complained of feeling marginalized in their school communities and stigmatized as "just a gym teacher" (Beale, 2015, p. 4). This is borne out of poor practice on the part of some teachers but most often stems from outdated perceptions of physical educators from parents and administrators. Transitioning to SWE makes a break from past perceptions while also aligning the pedagogy toward more focused, tangible, and publicly endorsed goals (Gray et al., 2015, p. 165). Parents and administrators can more clearly identify the purposes of wellness education just from its title. Terms like *physical education* or *health education* tend to trigger stereotypes and garner less support.

Benefits of School Wellness Education

Transitioning from a traditional health education or traditional physical education model to SWE best supports the health and well-being of students. According to Murray and colleagues (2007), students who received health instruction

- were absent fewer days,
- stayed in school more frequently,
- were less apt to experiment with drugs and alcohol,
- had improved behavior, and
- scored better academically.

Equally important are student grades. There is a perception that devoting additional instructional time to student well-being will lower student grades in other subjects (CDC, 2014). This has not proven true; in fact, when students' health improves, grades also improve.

SWE positively affects students' physical activity levels. Students in school should accumulate a minimum of 60 minutes per day of moderate to vigorous physical activity (Kohl & Cook, 2013). Students accrue a multitude of benefits through regular, ongoing physical activity, the kind that is promoted both in and out of class (USDHHS, 2018). Physical activity has been shown to reduce chronic diseases such as cancer, obesity, diabetes, and cardiovascular disease (CDC, n.d.).

Physical activity results in many mental and emotional benefits (CDC, 2014). Too often, parents and students associate physical activity only with physical benefits. Yet it has also been shown to reduce depression, anxiety, stress, and sleep problems while improving overall energy, vitality, and mood (Lavizzo-Mourey et al., 2012). Many Americans experience excessive amounts of stress and anxiety. Learning to reduce those negative emotions can improve well-being. The COVID-19 pandemic created additional burdens on mental health, including loss of some freedoms, disrupted personal lives, financial difficulties, and worries related to personal or family health (Holmes et al., 2020).

Physical activity and fitness have been shown to improve academic performance (Michael et al., 2015; Donnelly et al., 2016; Rasberry et al., 2011). Bartee

and colleagues (2018) found that cardiovascular training significantly improved students' math percentile ranking, especially for students with lower academic performance and fitness levels. Another study (Amin et al., 2017) found that low-income students in schools with a supportive physical activity environment performed better on academic tests. Promoting school wellness can serve as an equalizer by offering programs and services that benefit all students (Kohl & Cook, 2013), particularly those in underrepresented groups and with lower socioeconomic status.

Bartee and colleagues (2018) found that elementary students who improved their cardiovascular fitness also significantly improved their math percentile ranking. This effect was most pronounced for less fit students and lower academic performers, populations for whom improvement is most needed. Sullivan and colleagues (2017) conducted a review of 218 journal articles related to physical activity and academic performance and concluded that there is a positive association between the two. In 2014, the Centers for Disease Control and Prevention (CDC) stated the following:

- Physically active students are more likely to have better grades, attendance, memory concentration, and on-task behaviors.
- Increased time spent in physical education does not adversely affect academic performance.
- Eleven of the fourteen studies examined found one or more positive association with physical activity.

Physical activity has been shown to increase resilience factors (Moljord et al., 2014). Developing resilience is an important life skill that allows individuals to persist and overcome challenges. A lack of resilience can mean failing to achieve goals an individual could and should achieve. Wellness education can be a microcosm for the world, one in which planning, preparation, hard work, success, and failure teach life skills.

SWE lends itself well to fusing physical activity with social and emotional learning. Lessons can be geared toward improving collaborative skills, communication, personal responsibility, decision-making, goal setting, confidence, empathy, problem-solving, perseverance, and emotional control, among others (Ciotto & Gagnon, 2018). Again, students are learning health-enhancing skills while moving. Physical activity has been shown to improve on-task behaviors and foster a more positive classroom climate (Mahar et al., 2006). Consistent levels of physical activity have proven effective for managing stress and anxiety while also reducing symptoms of depression (Brewer et al., 2017).

Challenges Confronting School Wellness Education

The rationale, benefits, and teaching strategies for SWE are strong. However, it is a newer approach, so those making the switch will experience a period of adjustment. This book is structured to provide a theoretical foundation for SWE but with a heavy emphasis on practical, easy-to-use, standards-based lesson plans. The aim is to make the transition from being a traditional health and physical educator to being a wellness educator as seamless and painless as possible.

Gray and colleagues (2015) found that teachers using a school wellness approach were often too narrowly focused. They emphasized physical health (fitness, psychomotor skills) to the detriment of the whole child, specifically mental and emotional well-being. Another challenge confronting SWE is the dearth of instructional time allocated by schools. The lack of state- or district-mandated instructional time negatively affects the amount of SWE that can be implemented. According to the 2016 SHAPE of the Nation Report (SHAPE America, 2016), only 18 states specify a required amount of instructional time for physical education. The amount ranges from 40 minutes per week (Arkansas) to 150 minutes per week (Florida, Louisiana, New Jersey, and Oregon). The average amount of time required among those states is 103.2 minutes per week. According to Kohl and Cook (2013), only 10 percent of elementary schools achieve the recommended 150 minutes of weekly physical education, and only 20 percent require daily recess. There is no accurate data about the required amount of instruction in health education. The only reference to required health education instruction comes from New Jersey, which requires 150 minutes of health, safety, and physical education. Twenty-three states require physical education at the elementary level, but they do not specify a duration; that decision is left up to local school districts. This often results in insufficient instructional time as administrators funnel resources and time into tested subjects. Eight states do not require any health or physical education in elementary school. SWE can somewhat compensate for these shortcomings by addressing both sets of national standards simultaneously, thus making instruction more efficient.

The wellness educator must work effectively with administration to promote a healthy school. Administrative input is necessary to effectively implement the Whole School, Whole Community, Whole Child (WSCC) model and the Comprehensive School Physical Activity Program (CSPAP). This relationship is critical because there are relatively few fixed requirements for wellness education. One way administrators can assist wellness education is by providing additional instructional time. The importance of wellness education cannot be overstated; in fact, at the elementary level, instruction should be provided every day. Unfortunately, this is rarely the case. Nevertheless, teachers should lobby for increased time and avail themselves of the many advocacy tools available through SHAPE America. In some schools, physical activity time has been decreased in favor of additional classroom time in other subjects, principally to increase test scores and meet academic standards (Kohl & Cook, 2013). This trend persists despite the fact that Trudeau and Shephard (2008) found that a one-hour increase in physical activity did not adversely affect achievement and in some cases improved it.

The current health status of the nation's youth represents both a challenge and an opportunity. A great deal of progress needs to be made. According to the United States Report Card on Physical Activity (National Physical Activity Plan Alliance, 2018), the United States received an overall physical activity grade of D- with school-based physical activity also receiving a D-. Following are key findings from the report:

- Only 24 percent of children and youth meet the recommended 60 minutes per day.
- Women, people in underrepresented groups, and low-income individuals are less physically active.
- Fewer than 15 percent of elementary schools require PE three days per week.
- Twenty-nine percent of elementary PE teachers do not need undergraduate training to teach physical education.

The lack of emphasis on our children's well-being is quite literally making them sick. The frequency of lifestyle-related diseases has increased substantially in the past 30 years (Kohl & Cook, 2013). A lack of physical activity is associated with heart disease, hypertension, osteoporosis, anxiety, diabetes, depression, and other diseases. SWE is not a panacea for these problems, but it can absolutely be part of the solution. Inactivity increases the risk of heart disease, colon and breast cancer, diabetes mellitus, hyperten-

sion, osteoporosis, anxiety and depression, and other diseases (Kohl & Cook, 2013). Studies have found that, in terms of mortality, the global health burden of physical inactivity approaches that of cigarette smoking and obesity. In addition to physical ailments, children and youth can experience a range of social and emotional problems (Brewer et al., 2017). These challenges include "low self-esteem, depression, anxiety and, even more concerning, suicide" (19).

Part of the American dream is predicated on the notion that all people can improve their station in life. However, if individuals believe the system discriminates against them, it creates a disincentive for improvement and limits potential. Students living at risk for physical inactivity, in poverty, or with a disability have a greater likelihood of experiencing health issues (Basch, 2011; Cheak-Zamora & Thullen, 2016). Approximately 30 percent of students with disabilities have two or more health issues. Furthermore, students with an intellectual disability are more likely to be obese (Hinckson et al., 2013).

The Journey Here

Traditional physical education and traditional health education have for most of their histories been separate and distinct fields. However, the past several years has seen a more coordinated, symbiotic, and forward-thinking approach to overall well-being.

The history of physical education in the United States began with an emphasis on physical training and gymnastic systems (Shimon, 2020). In time, sports such as basketball and baseball were added to the curriculum. In 1885, the Association for the Advancement of Physical Education (AAPE), the forerunner to SHAPE America, was formed (SHAPE America, n.d.a). More states began to require physical education, and a more formalized curriculum began to take hold. In 1937, the association changed its name to the American Association for Health and Physical Education. The R for recreation and D for dance were added later. Fitness became an emphasis in the years following World War II, especially with the advent of the President's Council on Youth Fitness established under President Eisenhower (Shimon, 2020). Today, many goals and objectives of the President's Council are reflected in the Presidential Youth Fitness Program. Throughout the 1960s and 1970s, physical education continued to diversify by incorporating adventure programming, lifetime activities, and outdoor pursuits. Additional instructional models were implemented such as tactical games, sport education, and personal and social responsibility. National standards were first published in 1995. The alliance officially changed its name to SHAPE America, Society of Health and Physical Educators in 2014.

- SHAPE's vison: A nation where all children are prepared to lead healthy, physically active lives (SHAPE America, n.d.b).
- SHAPE's mission: To advance professional practice and promote research related to health and physical education, physical activity, dance, and sport.

Although SHAPE America has officially included health since 1937, the organization has throughout most of its history focused more on physical education. This was evident in the overall membership, conference presentation topics, national standards, and resource allocations. In many ways, the disciplines were thought of as separate silos, each with its own distinct and separate goals.

The history of health education progressed in a less linear fashion than that of physical education. Early on, health education focused principally on hygiene and personal health. School health was initially composed of three parts: health education, health services, and healthy school environment (Allensworth & Kolbe, 1987). A major change occurred with the introduction of the comprehensive school health (CSH) model in 1987. This model included the following components: health education, physical education, health environment, health nurse services, family and community involvement, counseling psychological and social services, character education, and nutrition. CSH introduced the idea of a coordinated effort to promote health. Although it did not promote the fusion of health and physical education espoused in this book, it brought the two disciplines closer together and began the breakdown of the silos. Other goals of CSH included eliminating overlap, addressing oversights, and using resources more effectively. During the late 1990s, the CDC began to emphasize the achievement of measurable outcomes but continued to support CSH (Lohrmann et al., 2011). The American Cancer Society promoted the integration of a health coordinator, a CSH council, and school-level teams.

The Association for Supervision and Curriculum Development (ASCD) entered the field with the publication of the Healthy School Report Card. The report card added the role that school principals and administrators play in CSH (Lohrmann et al., 2011). Shortly thereafter ASCD formed the Commission on the Whole Child, which produced the Whole School, Whole Community, Whole Child (WSCC) model (Rasberry et al., 2015). This model focused on the holistic development of the child through the interplay and support of multiple stakeholders. It continues to be widely employed today. According to Brewer and colleagues (2017), WSCC is more encompassing and interconnected than CSH. In higher education, Slippery Rock University amended their program to focus on SWE and published a related article on teacher preparation in 2017.

It is evident when examining the history of physical education and health education that these two disciplines have been slowly moving toward one another for some time. The natural next step in this evolution is SWE within the context of the whole child movement.

Wellness as a word is a natural fit. According to the Global Wellness Institute (n.d.), wellness is the "active pursuit of activities, choices and lifestyles that lead to a state of holistic health." Several salient points are made in the definition. First, wellness is an active process focused on building health-enhancing skills. It should not entail sitting in class and having information poured into one's head. The word *pursuit* implies the longevity of the process.

There is not an endgame or finish line; the pursuit of wellness is ongoing throughout one's lifetime. The word *activities* implies physical activities, which are part of the wellness equation, but also cognitive activities in which students actively build health-enhancing skills. Finally, the word *holistic* directly links to the dimensions of wellness (figure 1.2). Dictionary.com (2020) defines wellness as "the quality or state of being healthy in body and mind, especially as the result of deliberate effort." Merriam-Webster (n.d.) defines it as "the quality or state of being in good health especially as an actively sought goal." Although the second definition is less encompassing than the first, both stress the importance of deliberate effort and actively seeking a goal.

SWE ties in well with the pivotal role educators play in public health (Corbin et al., 2014). Make no mistake, wellness educators are part of public health. According to Charles Winslow, public health is "the science and art of preventing disease, prolonging life, and promoting health through the organized efforts and informed choices of society, organizations, public and private communities, and individuals" (Rosner & Fried, 2010, pp. 4-5). The federal government has seen fit to publicly promote the role of SWE through the passage of multiple laws. The Child Nutrition and WIC Reauthorization Act of 2004 mandated that schools create a local school wellness policy (Buns & Thomas, 2015). The Every Student Succeeds Act of

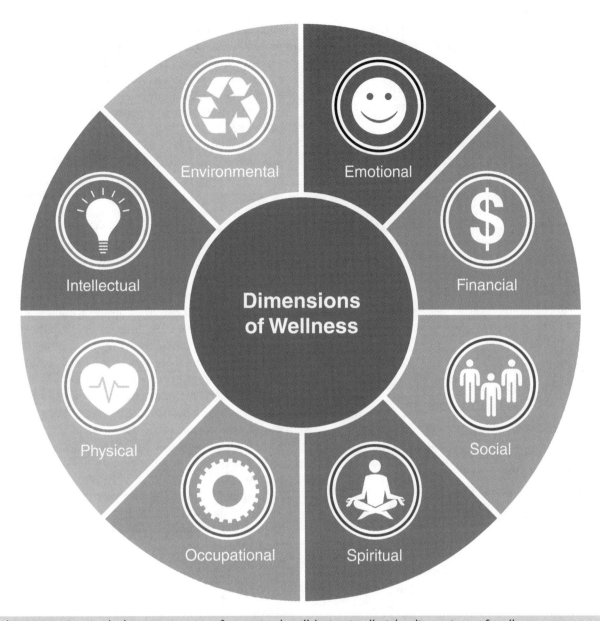

FIGURE 1.2   A whole person strives for optimal well-being in all eight dimensions of wellness.

2015 replaced the concept of core academic subjects with a well-rounded education. Wellness educators can therefore be seen as one of the most effective agents for public health, *preventing* disease and disorders from occurring in the first place.

Vision for School Wellness Education

Schools have been critical to promoting health, wellness, and physical activity for decades. They have conducted education, screenings, immunizations, nutri-

tion services, and substance abuse programs (Kohl & Cook, 2013). Over 50 million students spend a portion of their day in schools (Michael et al., 2015) for up to seven hours. Schools therefore have a tremendous capacity for affecting wellness. Given this fact and the growing body of evidence cited earlier that student well-being positively affects academic achievement and other variables, school wellness education should be a *priority* for schools. SWE can be a pervasive and powerful force that positively affects health outcomes for the next generation (Basch, 2011; CDC & ASCD, 2014).

In SWE, the wellness educator functions as both the instructor in the wellness classroom and coordinator of the WSCC model (see figure 2.1). The wellness educator is the person best suited for this responsibility for three reasons:

1. They are trained educators with experience meeting standards and implementing effective instruction.
2. They see students weekly.
3. Their undergraduate coursework directly aligns with most components of the whole child model more than any other school employee.

According to Westrich and colleagues (2015), most whole school research has examined individual components of the model. O'Brien and colleagues (2010) found that a school coordinator helped promote the goals of health education outside the classroom. The following attributes were identified as critical to implementing a coordinated approach (Valois & Hoyle, 2000; Weiler et al., 2003):

- Administrative support and buy-in
- A school-based health promotion team
- A program champion
- A staff wellness coordinator
- Long-term commitment of resources

Having a school-level wellness coordinator is critical to the success of wellness policies. Currently, however, that responsibility is performed by a range of individuals. In a study by Westrich and colleagues (2015), the implementation of wellness policies was examined in four school districts and eight schools. Each of the school districts had a district-level wellness coordinator, but at the school level, one or multiple staff members functioned as the unofficial "wellness champion" (p. 263). These individuals informally and to varying degrees supported the wellness goals of the district-level coordinator. In one school, the role was fulfilled by the school counselor, who also performed their normal duties. This scenario is not ideal because school counselors lack training in health, physical activity, and most aspects of the whole school model. School wellness educators are best suited to coordinate and implement the whole school model. In addition, wellness educators can use their teaching role to extend and reinforce wellness goals throughout the entire school, not just the gymnasium (O'Brien et al., 2010).

The state of Maine implemented a series of wellness organizational practices. They created a position called the school health coordinator (SHC) (O'Brien et al., 2010), charged with implementing the wellness plan.

Each school in the study had its own SHC. The plan promoted wellness through divergent yet coordinated practices involving staff, nutrition, school policy, and classroom policies. Overall, the study found that schools with SHCs improved their wellness programs more and decreased risky behavior more than schools without a SHC.

It is vital that school wellness educators view their role within the context of the entire school and community (Brewer et al., 2017). Their responsibility is no longer simply the physical education classroom or the health education classroom. Rather, they operate within the whole school and the whole community as what Brewer and colleagues called the "quarterback of the WSCC model" (p. 17). The new approach includes morning walking clubs, active transport to school, partnerships with community groups, nutritious school lunches, an emphasis on social and emotional learning, family outreach, brain boosters in the classroom, peer mediators, bullying prevention, family wellness nights at school, presentations by community groups, and a host of other wellness-centric interventions. This will entail momentous changes for teacher education, involving not just pedagogy but also real-world, practical experiences and assessments aligned with different components of the whole school model. Wellness education teacher education (WETE) should address public policy (Beale, 2015), coalition building, community partnerships, and parent outreach.

One of the barriers Hivner and colleagues (2019) identified was finding a starting point for making changes. An important first step is becoming involved with the school district's wellness policy and committee. These steps will be discussed in greater detail in chapter 2. Schools and school districts are often large, complex structures that are resistant to change. It is important therefore to get the support of stakeholders and involve other constituents identified in the whole school model, such as the school nurse, school psychologist, custodian, cafeteria staff, and others.

School Wellness Education in the Classroom

What would SWE look like in practice? An ideal way to explore this is by deconstructing a lesson plan. For the purposes of the succeeding paragraphs, refer to the lesson Handwashing, Overhand Throw, and Locomotor Skills found in chapter 5. All lesson plans align with and meet both SHAPE America Outcomes and National Health Education Performance Indicators.

Again, this dual approach is more holistic in nature and allows wellness educators to best use valuable but limited instructional time while meeting academic standards. The lesson introduction will address three important questions:

1. **WHAT** are we learning today?
2. **WHY** are we learning this?
3. **HOW** will learning be measured?

These questions will be repeated in all lesson plans. First, the *what* addresses that eternal question many elementary students ask upon arriving at the gymnasium, "What are we doing (learning) today?" The *why* communicates why the information is important. Finally, the *how* focuses on measuring student learning, specifically how teachers and students will know the learning objectives have been met.

Following the lesson introduction, teachers will typically lead a general discussion or explanation of a learning task aligned with the lesson objectives. Each activity section is clearly labeled and may or may not be subdivided into parts. The inflated chicken activity is meant to showcase areas commonly missed during

handwashing. Because students are in the gymnasium, they will be able to spread out and work independently. This activity could also be done in groups of two. It requires higher-order thinking and involves students in the learning process, hallmarks of the SWE approach. Moreover, what elementary student wouldn't love a glove masquerading as a chicken?

Germ crusaders is a classic wellness education activity. It uses physical education equipment, ample space, student learning groups, physical activity, and health skills. The setup of the fictitious bathroom is accomplished by student groups, which in itself is a cooperative activity. The teacher can observe soft skills (affective traits) such as communication (clear, concise, supportive, positive), teamwork (working together, contributing), and problem-solving (making adjustments, answering unknown questions). Once the "bathroom" is set up, students apply the information in a fun way with support from classmates. Other students complete a peer assessment, which requires them to *analyze and evaluate* performances. The peer assessment uses higher-order skills and engages all students, not just the one washing their hands. The assessment may also be used in a formative manner to provide feedback or a grade. The lesson features high engagement throughout, minimal wait time, and repetition to promote long-term retention.

Pass the soap tag combines physical activity skills (fundamental movement patterns, overhand throwing, and catching) with health skills (handwashing technique). It again exemplifies the idea of learning health-enhancing skills along with physical activity skills in a fun, educational format. The closure directly involves students by having them apply concepts in a social format.

A unique feature of the SWE lessons presented in this book is the inclusion of an assessment for each lesson plan. Assessment data provide critical evidence documenting student learning. It drives program improvement and enhances the profession's standing among administrators, legislators, school boards, parents, and students (Sundaresan et al., 2017). Unfortunately, there is an overemphasis on grading based on effort and participation rather than learning, which serves to reinforce negative stereotypes (Baghurst, 2014). It is critical that teachers use the assessments provided in this book and communicate the results to students and parents.

Summary

Ultimately, SWE is about living well throughout the lifespan (Brewer et al., 2017, p. 20). It is a new approach that scaffolds well with existing practices while reflecting the reality of time constraints and a more holistic approach to well-being. It cannot eliminate educational achievement gaps or health disparities (Sanetti, 2017), but it can and will make significant inroads for student well-being. This is important because no matter how much progress is made with testing, standards, and technology, students will fail to meet their potential if their health needs are not adequately met.

Chapter 2

Whole School, Whole Community, Whole Child Model

The Whole School, Whole Community, Whole Child (WSCC) model combines and builds on elements of the traditional coordinated school health approach proposed by the Centers for Disease Control and Prevention (Allensworth & Kolbe, 1987) and the whole child model (ASCD & CDC, 2014). The WSCC model is a collaborative approach to learning and health that answers the call for greater alignment, integration, and collaboration between education and health to improve each child's cognitive, physical, social, and emotional development.

The WSCC model recognizes the symbiotic relationship between learning and health and considers students as active participants in their development. The WSCC model incorporates the five tenets of the Whole Child Model (Lewallen et al., 2015):

1. Each student enters school healthy and learns about and practices a healthy lifestyle.

2. Each student learns in an environment that is physically and emotionally safe for students and adults.

3. Each student is actively engaged in learning and is connected to the school and broader community.

4. Each student has access to personalized learning and is supported by qualified, caring adults.

5. Each student is challenged academically and prepared for success in college or further study and for employment and participation in a global society.

Similarly, the WSCC model incorporates the components of the coordinated school health (CSH) approach. CSH was first conceptualized by Allensworth and Kolbe (1987) and was supported by the Centers for Disease Control and Prevention (2015). CSH was a system-based approach addressing eight components of the school as a venue for health promotion and disease prevention:

1. Health education
2. Physical education
3. School health services
4. Healthy and safe school environment
5. Counseling, psychological, and social services
6. Family and community involvement
7. Health promotion for staff
8. Nutrition services

The WSCC model launched by the ASCD in 2014 combines and builds on the elements of the whole child model and the CSH approach to create a unified model that supports a systematic, integrated, and collaborative approach to health and learning (Lewallen et al., 2015). The WSCC model strives to ensure that all students are healthy, safe, engaged, supported, and challenged. It provides a framework for collaboration devoted to improving student learning and health in schools (ASCD, CDC 2014).

In figure 2.1, the comprehensive scope of the WSCC model is illustrated. The inner ring of the model stresses the need for coordination among policy, process, and practice. The outer ring reflects greater integration and alignment between health and education. It incorporates the components of the CSH approach while emphasizing the school as an integral part of the community. It also stresses the importance of sectors and individuals working together to implement policies and practices in an integrated approach to addressing health and learning (Lewallen et al., 2015).

WSCC Components

Each of the 10 components of the WSCC model are described in the following sections. It is important to note that the WSCC model is a schoolwide approach. The WSCC model acknowledges the position of learning and health, and most importantly views the school as being a reflection of the local community. It is not an initiative owned by one teacher, one nurse, or one department. Instead, this model outlines the whole school approach, with every adult and every student playing a role in the growth and development of self, peers, and the school overall. The school is the hub, but it remains a focal reflection of its community and requires community input, resources, and collaboration in order to support its students (Lewallen, et al., 2015).

Health Education

Schools play a vital role in promoting students' health and well-being. The U.S. Department of Health and Human Services (2021) released Healthy People 2030, which sets objectives to improve the health and well-being of the United States. Increasing the number of schools that provide comprehensive health education is one objective described by Healthy People 2030 as necessary for improving the health of the nation. Comprehensive school health education encompasses

FIGURE 2.1 Whole School, Whole Community, Whole Child model.

Reprinted from Centers for Disease Control and Prevention, *The Whole School, Whole Community, Whole Child*. https://www.cdc.gov/healthyyouth/wscc/pdf/wscc_fact_sheet_508c.pdf?s_cid=tw-zaza-1081

planned, sequential, developmentally appropriate, and culturally inclusive educational experiences taught by certified health education teachers (Rooney et al. 2015). A comprehensive health education curriculum helps students recognize how personal choice affects their short-term and long-term goals and how responsible decision-making can lead to risk reduction and an improved quality of life.

Physical Education and Physical Activity

Physical education provides students with a planned, sequential, standards-based program of curriculum and instruction designed to develop motor skills, knowledge, and behaviors for active living. The goal is to develop physically literate individuals who have the knowledge, skills, and confidence to enjoy a lifetime of healthful physical activity (SHAPE America, 2014). A Comprehensive School Physical Activity Program

(CSPAP) is a national framework for physical education and physical activity in schools today. CSPAP includes high-quality physical education as the foundation of a program that offers physical activity before, during, and after school and that promotes staff involvement and family and community engagement (CDC, 2013). CSPAP provides a framework for students to perform the recommended 60 minutes of moderate to vigorous physical activity per day (USDHHS, 2018).

Nutrition Environment and Services

A school's nutrition plan focuses on creating an environment that supports proper nutrition for students by teaching, modeling, and providing opportunities for healthy eating in schools. The nutrition plan should follow the Dietary Guidelines for Americans, 2015-2020 (USDHHS & USDA, 2015). WSCC emphasizes the importance of giving students opportunities to learn about and practice eating healthy foods based on the foods provided in schools. Schools should provide messages about healthy eating, including how proper nutrition plays a critical role in health and academic achievement.

Health Services

School-based health services are designed to ensure access to primary health care services and to prevent and control communicable diseases. School health services also provide emergency care in case of illness or injury and promote and provide the best possible sanitary conditions for ensuring a safe school facility and school environment. Last, a school's health services provide education-based opportunities for promoting healthy children, healthy families, and a healthy community.

Social and Emotional Climate

A school's social and emotional climate encompasses the psychosocial aspects of students' school experiences that affect their social and emotional development (CASEL, 2020). A positive social and emotional environment is one that provides a supportive culture for learning that is inclusive and allows all students, families, and staff members to feel safe, secure, accepted, and valued. CASEL provides a plethora of programs designed for implementation in the elementary school.

Counseling, Psychological, and Social Services

Provided by professionals such as certified school counselors, school psychologists, and school social workers, these services support students' social and emotional development and promote success in the learning processes. Services include individual and group assessments, interventions, and referrals to school and community support services. Mental health professionals within the school can provide consultations with school staff and community stakeholders and ensure that school services and community interventions reinforce learning. Systems-level approaches, such as conducting needs assessments, also contribute to students' health and the school environment (ASCD, CDC 2014).

Physical Environment

Schools promote learning by ensuring the health and safety of students and staff across the physical environment, which encompasses the school building and the areas surrounding it. A healthy physical environment protects students and staff from physical threats, including violence, traffic, and injuries, and from exposure to chemical and biological hazards, including pesticides, mold, and corrosives, and it ensures proper ventilation and lighting, among other factors (ASCD, CDC 2014).

Employee Wellness

Schools are places of learning, but they also are worksites for teachers, administrators, and staff. Supporting the physical, emotional, and social health and wellness of employees who work with students, either directly or indirectly, contributes to greater productivity in schools. Healthy school employees help foster an environment in which students can be healthy. Employee wellness includes a coordinated set of programs, policies, benefits, and environmental supports designed to meet the needs of all employees, both instructional and noninstructional.

Family Engagement

Family engagement within the school setting plays a powerful role in supporting the whole child, with school staff and families working together to support students' learning, development, and health (ASCD, CDC 2014). Engaging families is a shared responsibility in which schools provide opportunities for families to engage with purpose and intent, and families commit to participating in their children's learning and development.

Community Involvement

Schools by themselves cannot solve the health and social problems that plague children and families. Families, health care workers, religious organizations, organizations that serve children and adolescents, and young people themselves also must participate in the process. Community engagement is a call to action for local businesses, grocery stores, social service agencies, colleges, faith-based organizations, nonprofit organizations, medical organizations, and government agencies to work with schools to develop strategies that promote students' health and success.

Implementing the WSCC Model

The steps suggested for implementing the WSCC model within a school reflects

> a socioecological approach that is directed at the whole school, with the school in turn, drawing its resources and influences from the whole community and serving to address the needs of the whole child. ASCD and CDC encourage use of the model as a framework for improving students' learning and health. (Lewallen, et al., 2015, p. 734)

The implementation of the WSCC model brings together all stakeholders to engage with the education and health issues present in the community. Community agencies, educators, families, policymakers, children, and youth all play a role. It is a model, not an intervention (Lewallen et al., 2015). The key to moving from model to action is collaborative development of local school policies, processes, and practices. The day-to-day practices within each WSCC component require examination and planning so that they work in tandem with appropriate complementary processes guiding each decision and action. Developing joint and collaborative policy is half the challenge; putting it into action and making it routine completes the task. To develop joint or collaborative policies, processes, and practices, all parties involved should start with a common understanding of the interrelatedness of learning and health. From this understanding, current and future systems and actions can be adjusted, adapted, or crafted to achieve both learning and health outcomes.

Hunt and colleagues (2015) provided a sequence of steps helpful in establishing the WSCC model within a school. Those steps are outlined here.

Form a Committee

The first step involves forming a committee of individuals who are interested and passionate about improving the health and academic outcomes of students. Establishment of a committee should include a clear statement about the authority given to the committee and which decisions will require approval from an administrator or school board. When determining committee membership, keep all 10 WSCC components in mind. Some staff members are clearly associated with specific WSCC components. Creativity may be needed to identify individuals who can represent the needs and interests of other components that might not have staff assigned to them. For example, the committee may need to contact community experts to provide beneficial services such as mindfulness classes. It is more important to identify dedicated, passionate, and knowledgeable individuals who can represent the components as they relate to the whole child than to focus only on officially appointed individuals.

Conduct a Needs Assessment

Before designing a WSCC plan, conduct a needs assessment. This assessment determines the health-risking and health-promoting behaviors that are prevalent among students and how these behaviors are related to academic achievement. A variety of sources and tools

can be used to identify the priority health problems and health-risk behaviors of students in a district or school. The Youth Risk Behavior Surveillance System (YRBSS) monitors six types of health-risk behaviors that contribute to the leading causes of death and disability among youth and adults (CDC, 2019). Existing YRBSS data can be used to highlight priority health-risk behaviors among middle and high school students. The identified risks may then be addressed through targeted programming earlier in the elementary grades. For example, local data might show that students are not meeting physical activity recommendations. Students who are physically active tend to have better grades and classroom behaviors (CDC, 2014). County health departments may have other data about health problems and health risks experienced by young people in their community or even neighborhoods that make up a school cluster. Staff within the school or district might have access to additional useful data. For example, the nutrition services director has data on breakfast and lunch meal counts and might have information concerning the specific foods students eat

from school meals. The school counselor and school psychologist might have data from school climate surveys (Hunt et al., 2015).

Prioritize Outcomes

Committee members should review the results of the needs assessment and identify priority health-related areas that need improvement. It is desirable to narrow the list of priorities to a manageable number of health problems or risk behaviors. In addition, it is important to set specific and realistic outcome expectations with clear indicators that will demonstrate what success will look like when the outcomes are achieved.

Determine Health Outcomes and Academic Achievement

The next suggested step is to determine the relationship between the selected health outcome and academic achievement. It is practical for the committee to choose priorities that have both clear health and academic outcomes. The Centers for Disease Control and Prevention provides several resources linking alcohol use, sedentary behavior, and tobacco use and academic grades. Please search the CDC website for these sources.

Identify Interventions

This step involves identifying promising or effective interventions that have the greatest potential for affecting the chosen health outcomes. Use evidence-based programs that target health problems or risk behaviors of the children. CDC provides an array of evidence programing, including, but not limited to, a program that targets oral health and one that addresses asthma. Please search the CDC website for relevant sources.

Determine Collaboration

Determine how staff and other committee members will collaborate and align to maximize success in achieving priority health and academic outcomes. Engage the key individuals representing or working within the WSCC components who will be involved in implementing the recommendations. Determining how interventions or actions will be coordinated requires concrete steps, including establishing schedules, timelines, milestones, and deliverables; establishing effective communications; holding periodic meetings to identify problems and effective solutions to those problems; and reporting progress as a form of accountability.

Engage Community Agencies and Organizations

Invite community agencies and organizations that have a mission or similar interest in addressing the identified priority health and academic outcomes. Expand the committee's membership beyond school or district staff to include neighborhood and community members who can focus school and community resources on achieving the priority health and education outcomes. Volunteers or public health agencies frequently have health expertise and resources that can help districts or schools successfully reach their goals. For example, the Chester County Health Department serves the county in which the authors live. This agency provides information on their website on chronic diseases, food protection, disease, and maternal and child health.

This step also challenges community members to identify strategies they can implement outside of the school setting, thus reinforcing, or even improving, the impact of school programs.

Create an Action Plan

Create an action plan to affect the chosen health outcome. Make concrete plans with timelines and all actions assigned to specific people, such as those responsible for implementing interventions, completing committee tasks, and monitoring progress in meeting expected outcomes.

Implement the Action Plan

Implement and monitor the results of the action plan. During implementation, the committee should meet regularly to ensure that all tasks are being completed on time and to troubleshoot any problems that arise. Plans are not static and might need to be changed during the implementation process. Evaluation should be a regular part of committee meetings to monitor implementation and look for barriers and unexpected difficulties. Collection of information throughout the implementation process will help ensure that the committee is able to understand the implementation of new interventions or practices.

Monitor the Action Plan

Develop a plan to monitor the implementation and outcomes of interventions. An action plan is only effective if people act on it, if it is implemented as intended, and if there is a way to discern whether it made a real difference. Districts and schools rarely have the resources to conduct full-scale outcome evaluations, but using interventions with evidence of effectiveness minimizes the need for this type of evaluation. Instead, districts and schools can determine how they will use their evaluation findings and shape their monitoring and evaluation plan around these goals. The committee can collect and analyze simple monitoring data to determine how, when, and where activities are conducted and who participates in each activity. In terms of outcomes, the committee can determine the level of changes they wish to explore. Some might decide to document changes observed in the classroom, school environment, or provision of services. Others might want to identify the strengths and weaknesses of their policies or practices and make a plan for improvement.

WSCC in Action

School District 49 in Peyton, Colorado, drafted School Wellness Policy Guidelines providing resources for implementing the WSCC model within a school. The guidelines are intended to be easy to use and are based on best practices and experience by WSCC leaders in Colorado. Their plan includes the following categories:

- Nutrition
- Wellness education
- Physical activity

The guidelines are depicted in table 2.1. School District 49 also developed an issue brief addressing various components of the WSCC model. Figure 2.2 on page 30 is an issue brief about bullying, which addresses WSCC component 5.

TABLE 2.1 School District 49 School Wellness Policy Guidelines

Part 1—Nutrition Goal: The District will support and promote nutrition education, healthy nutrition choices, and proper dietary habits contributing to student's health status and academic performance to include the federal government guidelines.

Items sent from home for student's personal consumption are exempt from the District guidelines except in the case of classroom and school allergies.

Nutrition category	Federal law	State law

School meals and a la carte operated by D49 Nutrition Services Department	Must comply with all laws that govern the National School Lunch and Breakfast Programs.	• Must comply with all laws that govern the National School Lunch and Breakfast Programs.
		• SB12-068* prohibits public schools from making foods with industrial trans fats available to students. This includes all food and beverages made available to a student on school grounds during each school day and extended school day, including:
		  – School cafeteria a la carte items
		  – School stores
		  – Vending machines
		  – Other food service entity existing upon school grounds
		  – Food or candy handed out by teachers in the classroom

Vending machines accessible to students during the school day (midnight to 30 minutes after last bell)	All vended foods and beverages sold in schools must comply with HHFKA Smart Snack Regulations.	• All vended foods and beverages sold in schools must comply with the Colorado SB12-068*.
Fundraisers after school day	All fundraisers after the school day (30 minutes after the bell until midnight) are exempt from competitive food standards and Smart Snack requirements (see resources)	

Board policy	Best practice
	Schools will aspire to: • Give adequate time for students to sit and eat for breakfast (10 min) and lunch (15 min) • Provide a dining area that is clean, orderly, and inviting. • Provide seating to accommodate all students served during each meal period. • Provide supervision in the dining area. • Allow students to converse in a reasonable manner with one another while they eat their meals. **Entire silent lunch periods are not allowed;** however, brief no-talking periods are allowed for safety and to accommodate students through the lunchroom procedure.
All vended beverages and foods must meet Board Policy EFEA.	
	Notification of fundraisers occurring after the school day is allowable on school campus to students through posters, social media, website, and emails.

(continued)

TABLE 2.1 *(continued)*

Nutrition category	Federal law	State law
Fundraisers during school day	All fundraisers during the school day (midnight to 30 minutes after the bell) available for sale to students for immediate consumption must meet the Smart Snack Regulation under the HHFKA.	• Each school is allowed 3 fundraisers that are exempt from the Smart Snack Regulation per school year. The school must maintain documentation of the fundraiser along with all nutritional labels. See the Nutrition Services web page for CDE exemption tracker. Exempt fundraisers are to be determined by School Administration. Learn more at www.cde.state.co.us/nutrition/smartsnackscolopolicyexemptfundraisers. • The sale of all food or beverages outside of the Nutrition Department will not take place from 30 minutes before through 30 minutes after the last meal period to follow the Colorado State Competitive Food Service Policy 2202-R-20300. • SB12-068*
Marketing of food and beverages	Marketing of food and beverage on district property during the school day to students (midnight to 30 minutes after the last bell) must meet competitive food standards and be Smart Snack compliant (see resources).	
Classroom parties, celebrations, classroom rewards		SB12-068*
After-school programs	Snacks served under the USDA afterschool snack program must comply with all applicable federal regulations and state policies if they are receiving funding from federal sources.	

Board policy	Best practice
	Plan ahead with school administrators for the 3 school-wide food-exempt fundraisers to get the best ROI.
	Food and beverages may be marketed 30 minutes after the bell. Examples: banners that are placed 30 minutes after the bell and removed after a game or vendors who provide food at games 30 minutes after the bell.
	• Foods offered during the school day will be store-bought items of **100 calories or less, 0 grams of trans fa**t, with recommendations of less than 4 grams of fat and less than 9 grams of sugar with the exception of fresh fruit. • No candy or sodas will be allowed. • Items are to be store bought with nutritional information visible. • Food prepared in a private home may not be served at school to students because knowledge of ingredients, sanitation, preparation, and temperature of food in storage or transit is not available. In addition, quality and sanitation standards cannot be controlled. • Exceptions can be made by the principal for grade-level and school-wide curriculum-related events. A sample form can be found at www. d49.org/wellness. Administrators will keep on file. • One day per quarter will be allowed for school-wide celebrations. These days are exempt from the district wellness policy nutritional values, but food needs to be store bought for food safety. • Birthday celebrations with treats will follow Wellness Policy Guidelines and school-level policies. • Parents, teachers, and organizations are informed about the guidelines and encouraged to follow them during the school day. • School administrators may allow teachers to set their own guidelines for students' personal snacks in classrooms. • Reward and incentive programs that provide coupon cards for food not available for immediate consumption are allowable. Examples: coupon card.
Snacks served under the USDA afterschool snack program must comply with all applicable federal regulations and state policies.	

(continued)

TABLE 2.1 (continued)

Part 2—Wellness Education Goal: The District will provide a comprehensive learning environment for developing and practicing lifelong wellness behaviors, including nutrition, physical activity, and mental health for staff and students.

All students in grades PreK-12, including students with disabilities and special health care needs and in alternative education settings have the opportunity to participate in a variety of learning experiences that support development of healthful habits to encourage total-body wellness.

Wellness education category	Federal law	State law
Comprehensive health education and physical education		SB 08-212 created comprehensive health education and updated physical education standards.
Family and community		
Staff wellness		

Part 3—Physical Activity Goal: The District will provide opportunities for staff and students to engage in physical activity.

Physical activity category	Federal law	State law/practice
Physical education class		• HB 11-1069 requires all public elementary schools to provide students with a minimum of 600 minutes of physical activity per month (30 minutes per school day). • The physical education curriculum is sequential and consistent with Colorado Board of Education–approved physical education teaching standards for pre-kindergarten through grade 12. • Physical education teachers are licensed by the Colorado Department of Education.

Board policy	Best practice
	• Teachers are encouraged to secure recommended wellness education resources.
• Teachers are encouraged to incorporate wellness topics in lesson plans throughout the school year.
• School administrators inform teachers about opportunities to attend training on wellness and the importance of role modeling healthful habits for students.
• Staff development will be offered inside and outside the district to support staff and student wellness. District will support the use of buildings for staff development opportunities by not charging facilities usage fees for staff and school wellness activities during regular building hours. If a school needs to utilize the facilities for wellness staff/student activities on the weekend or any days the district is closed, the school will incur the expense of any custodial staff needed on site.
• Instruction encourages hands-on activities that engage students in developmentally appropriate, culturally sensitive, participatory activities.
	• Parents are invited to join students for school meals.
• Schools are encouraged to provide families with information that encourages them to teach their children about physical and mental health.
• Family and community members are encouraged to become actively involved in programs that provide wellness education, including school wellness teams.
• Opportunities are available for the WSCC team and for individuals to share their healthful practices with the school and community.
	• The school encourages each member of the staff to serve as a healthy role model for students.
• The WSCC team will support/encourage at least one school-wide activity each year that promotes staff wellness.

Board policy/district practice	Best practice
• IFK Graduation Requirements require that high school students demonstrate mastery in health and physical education to graduate.
• All District 49 PE teachers must hold an endorsement in PE.	• Middle school students are encouraged to take more than one semester of physical education.
• High school students are encouraged to take more than two semesters of physical education.
• The school provides a physical and social environment that encourages safe and enjoyable physical activity for all students, including those who are not athletically gifted. Students have the opportunity to participate in lifetime physical activities (e.g., walking, Pilates, swimming, golf, tennis).
• Adequate age-appropriate equipment is available for all students to participate in physical activity.
• Physical activity facilities on school
• grounds are safe.

(continued)

TABLE 2.1   *(continued)*

Physical activity category	Federal law	State law/practice
Throughout the day		
Punishment		
Recess		HB 11-1069 requires all public elementary schools to provide students with a minimum of 600 minutes of physical activity per month (30 minutes per school day).
Before and after school		

Resources

Nutrition
    www.cde.state.co.us/nutrition
    www.actionforhealthykids.org
    www.schoolnutrition.org
    www.sneb.org
    www.healthiergeneration.org

Wellness Education
    www.aap.org
    https://healthychildren.org/English/Pages/default.aspx
    www.cde.state.co.us/cohealth/statestandards
    www.heart.org

Physical Activity
    www.fueluptoplay60.com
    www.shapeamerica.org
    http://www.shapeco.org

Reprinted from School District 49, *Wellness Policy Guidelines* (Peyton, Colorado, 2020). https://go.boarddocs.com/co/d49/Board.nsf/files/BPMR9N6CEB7A/$file/ADF-R-wellnesspolicyguidelines.pdf

Board policy/district practice	Best practice
	• Classroom health education reinforces the knowledge and self-management skills needed to maintain a physically active lifestyle and to reduce time spent on sedentary activities such as watching television. • When circumstances make it necessary for students to remain indoors and inactive for two or more hours, the students are given periodic breaks during which they stand and be moderately active. • Physical activity breaks and brain boosters should be provided in all courses. • Staff are allowed to take their break in an active way.
	• Strenuous physical activity is not used (e.g. running laps, push-ups) as punishment. • Students should not be required to "sit out" any part of recess as punishment. • A student's recess time can be replaced with a focused physical activity or community service. This guideline does not apply to extracurricular sports teams or office referrals.
	• Elementary school students will have a minimum of 30 minutes daily supervised.
	• All elementary, middle, and high schools offer extracurricular physical activity programs, such as physical activity clubs or intramural programs.

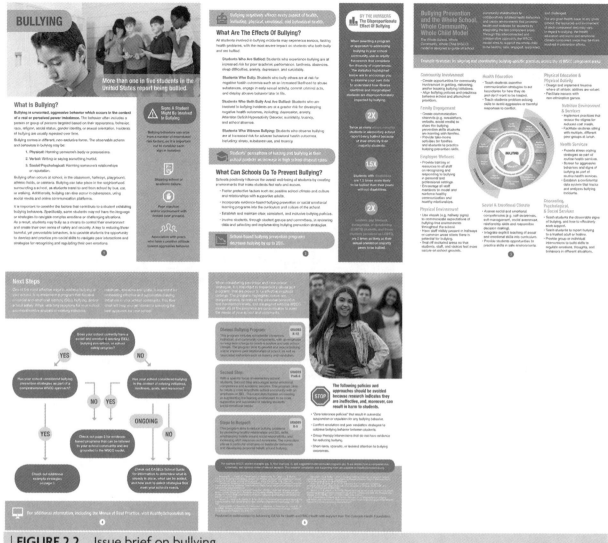

FIGURE 2.2 Issue brief on bullying.

Reprinted by permission from RMC Health. Produced in collaboration by Advancing IDEAS for Health and RMC Health with support from The Colorado Health Foundation.

Summary

In this chapter we have focused on the Whole School, Whole Child, Whole Community (WSCC) model, which recognizes the symbiotic relationship between learning and health and considers students as active participants in their development. The WSCC model strives to ensure that all students are healthy, safe, engaged, supported, and challenged. It provides a framework for collaboration devoted to improving student learning and health in schools (ASCD, CDC 2014). The model places the student as the focal point and emphasizes the alignment, integration, and collaboration required among the school, health, and community sectors. Multiple school components provide the full learning and health support systems critical to each student (e.g., community involvement, physical education and physical activity, health education, health services, nutrition, and environmental services). Although the school is the hub of the WSCC model, the community is also a valuable resource for augmenting the model.

Chapter 3

Emergent Education Pedagogies

School wellness education embraces both physical literacy and health literacy. Physical education develops the physically literate individual through deliberate practice of well-designed learning tasks that allow for skill acquisition in an instructional climate focused on achieving one's personal best. Physical education addresses the three domains of learning: cognitive or mental skills related to the knowledge of movement; affective, which addresses growth in feelings or attitudes; and psychomotor, which relates to the manual or physical skills related to movement literacy (SHAPE America, 2014). A well-designed physical education program does the following (CDC, 2013):

- Meets the needs of all students
- Keeps students active for most of the physical education class time
- Teaches self-management
- Emphasizes knowledge and skills for a lifetime of physical activity
- Provides an enjoyable experience for all students

SHAPE America defines health literacy as "An individual's capacity to access information, resources and services necessary to maintaining and promoting health" (SHAPE America, 2021). Sorenson and col-

SOCIAL AND EMOTIONAL LEARNING

Social and emotional learning (SEL) is not a pedagogical or teaching approach; rather it is a framework with competencies (self-awareness, self-management, relationship skills, social awareness, and responsible decision-making). In this chapter, we address children's motor, cognitive, and social development so that teachers can design developmentally appropriate lessons. We also address universal design for learning, active learning, and a skill-based approach to health education. These are the teaching methods or strategies used in our K-5 lesson plans. In addition, several of our sample K-5 lesson plans address one or more of the SEL competencies. The Collaborative for Academic, Social, and Emotional Learning (2022) defines SEL as follows:

> We define social and emotional learning (SEL) as an integral part of education and human development. SEL is the process through which all young people and adults acquire and apply the knowledge, skills, and attitudes to develop healthy identities, manage emotions and achieve personal and collective goals, feel and show empathy for others, establish and maintain supportive relationships, and make responsible and caring decisions.

It is certainly important to promote SEL in school wellness education. Here is one example of how that can be done.

Head, Shoulders, Knees, Toes

- ○ **SEL component:** self-management
- ○ **Directions:** Have students in your class find a partner and get a dome cone. All partner groups line up (facing each other on a center floor line) and place the dome cone between them on the floor. Explain that students are to touch the body part as you say head, shoulders, waist, knees, toes, or cone. When you yell out, "cone," the object is for students to try to grab the dome cone as quickly as possible. Students do this about three times and then shift one space down the line so students get a new partner. Do this until students have had three or four different partners.
- ○ **Debrief:**
  1. How many people won their matches? How many people lost a match or two?
  2. How did it make you feel when you lost? When you won?

leagues (2012) provide a bit more specificity in their definition:

> Health literacy is linked to literacy and entails people's knowledge, motivation and competencies to access, understand, appraise, and apply health information in order to make judgments and make decisions in everyday life concerning healthcare, disease prevention and health promotion to maintain or improve quality of life during the life course. (p. 3)

According to *Characteristics of Effective Health Education Curricula* (CDC 2015), effective health education does the following:

- Provides functional health knowledge that is basic and accurate and directly contributes to health-promoting decisions and behaviors.
- Builds personal competence, social competence, and self-efficacy by addressing skills.
- Provides opportunities to reinforce skills and positive health behaviors.

School wellness educators strive to address both physical literacy and health literacy within interdisciplinary lessons that, as stated in chapter 1, imbue students with the knowledge, skills, and dispositions to lead a healthy and physically active lifestyle that carries forward into adulthood.

Developmental Characteristics of the K-5 Learner

Understanding the K-5 learner is critical to the design of developmentally appropriate school wellness lessons, the hallmark of which is active learning. School wellness educators must consider children's psychomotor, cognitive, and social development when designing K-5 learning experiences.

In grades K-2, the focus is on children's acquisition of locomotor, manipulative, and stability movement skills within the fundamental movement phase. During this phase, children display initial stage movement characteristics or their first observable and purposeful attempts at performing fundamental movement skills. With encouragement, instruction, and practice, children progress to the emerging elementary stage, during which they gain greater control of their movements and can increase the range of motion during skill performance, and eventually children achieve the mature stage, characterized by progress in gaining a well-coordinated and biomechanically efficient movement performance (Cleland Donnelly et al., 2017).

In grades 3-5, children enter the specialized phase of motor skill development. Mature-stage fundamental movement skills are now combined with the movement concepts of space, effort, and relationships to form the specialized movement skills children use to engage in cooperative and competitive skill

and tactic practice in gamelike activities as well as in developmental dance and gymnastic- and fitness-based activities (Cleland Donnelly et al., 2017).

Cleland Donnelly and colleagues (2017) provided a detailed account of preK-5 children's cognitive and social development. These are depicted in tables 3.1 and 3.2. We are advocating that school wellness learning experiences be based on children's psychomotor, cognitive, and social development.

TABLE 3.1 Cognitive Development of PreK-5 Children

	Pre-K	Grades K-2	Grades 3-5
Stage of cognitive development and learner characteristics	In the preoperational stage, children are egocentric and unable to view the world from another's perspective. Children are curious and imaginative and enjoy exploring their environment and testing their limits.	In the preoperational stage, children use elementary logic and use symbols to represent objects in their environment (learning to read), and reasoning reflects past experiences.	In the concrete operational stage, children can mentally represent objects or a series of probable events, can think logically about events they have personally experienced, and are less egocentric and capable of considering others' perspectives.
Teaching implications	Use simple instructions and task cards with pictures, activities of short duration, and a variety of tasks; move into activity quickly; use of whole-class format should be brief (3-5 minutes) with small bits of information provided at one time; format station with a single focus; use activities that stimulate imagination and creativity.	Use simple instructions and task cards with few words and with pictures; whole-class format can be used for increasingly longer periods of time; format stations with a single focus; use activities that stimulate imagination and creativity; elementary logic enables children to look for one movement cue when observing a peer; students can correct their own performance based on feedback; students can design or vary a short movement combination and follow simple rules; children begin to develop a movement vocabulary.	More complex task cards and worksheets can be used to facilitate the understanding and acquisition of movement skills; whole-class format can be used for an entire class period; stations can focus on multiple tasks; students can follow more complex rules, can observe and use critical elements to help others, can use feedback to improve performance, and can understand and apply simple game strategies and principles of movement.

Adapted by permission from F. Cleland Donnelly, S. Mueller, D. Gallahue, *Developmental Physical Education for All Children—Theory Into Practice*, 5th ed. (Champaign, IL: Human Kinetics, 2017), 23.

TABLE 3.2   Social Development of PreK-5 Children

	Components	Pre-K	Grades K-2	Grades 3-5
Learner characteristics	Self-concept	Self-concept is highly influenced by the actions, thoughts, and feelings expressed about them by caregivers.	Self-concept is less differentiated and centered on concrete characteristics such as physical attributes, possessions, and skills.	Self-concept becomes more abstract and based on internal, psychological characteristics and feelings of self-worth; one's peers can influence self-concept.
	Self-esteem	n/a	Parents and teachers influence self-esteem.	Self-esteem is now influenced not only by what others value but also by what the child deems important.
	Personal and social responsibility	Children are egocentric and engage in solitary and then parallel play.	Children are less egocentric and able to engage in associative and some cooperative play.	Children are more self-directed and begin to develop empathy for others; they engage in cooperative and competitive play.

Adapted by permission from F. Cleland Donnelly, S. Mueller, D. Gallahue, *Developmental Physical Education for All Children—Theory Into Practice*, 5th ed. (Champaign, IL: Human Kinetics, 2017), 23.

Universal Design for Learning

In today's society, diversity plays a large role in the foundation of instructional decision-making and the development of effective instructional practices. There is no longer a clear-cut expectation of the student body that will represent a typical classroom environment. Diversity initiatives in education today comprise an even wider range of categories and practices, which initially were recognized as including race, gender, ethnicity, sexual orientation, and socioeconomic status (Cleland Donnelly et al., 2017). One effective means of catering to students with different abilities, preferences, or cultural norms in the classroom is to incorporate differentiated instructional strategies.

One means of differentiating instruction is using universal design for learning (UDL). UDL is not a method in which the teacher writes a lesson and then subsequently determines what modifications should be made for students with disabilities (CAST, 2018; Rose & Meyer, 2002). Rather, UDL is a proactive approach in which teachers gather information about diverse learners (i.e., students' learning needs are unique to them, thus creating diversity within the classroom) before planning the lesson (Lieberman, 2017). Therefore, the lesson content, instructional processes, and expected outcomes are embedded into the lesson as the lesson is created. The core principles of UDL reflect inclusionary practices and include the need for knowledge (Rose & Meyer, 2002).

- Provide multiple means of presentation to allow varied ways of gaining information and knowledge.
- Provide multiple means of action and expression to allow alternatives for demonstrating knowledge.
- Provide multiple means of engagement to challenge appropriately, to motivate, and to allow learners to express and participate in their interests.

Using these principles, modifications could include

- providing verbal directions as well as sign language to students,
- providing directions on a whiteboard or on a handout in braille,

- providing directions via video on a tablet or providing an auditory version of the directions saved on an MP3 player so the directions can be viewed or listened to several times, and
- creating a quiet zone in the gymnasium.

Such modifications would be available to all students, not just a specific individual (Cleland Donnelly & Millar, 2019). The lesson plans in this textbook offer an array of modifications to meet the needs of students with different abilities.

Social Justice in Elementary School Wellness Education

Social justice "strives to create a society in which all members, without exception, are psychologically safe and secure, recognized and treated with respect" (Bell 2016, p. 3). Lynch and colleagues (2020) offer five tips for a socially just physical education program:

1. Get to know your students, their identity, their cultural background, and their overall biographies.
2. Provide an opportunity for students to be engaged in designing their learning experiences, thus gaining ownership of their learning.

3. Include students in creating class expectations.
4. Provide opportunities for students to debrief, reflect, and evaluate their learning experiences, similar to Hellison's model of teaching personal and social responsibility (Hellison, 2011).
5. Be a guide on the side instead of a sage on the stage. In other words, be a facilitator of learning.

The two-part journal article "The A-Z of Social Justice Physical Education" (Lynch et al., 2020; Landi et al., 2020) provides an in-depth social justice glossary. We urge readers to study both of these readings. We will highlight a few of these important and relevant considerations when designing school wellness learning experiences.

Ability Awareness

A is for ability awareness, a critical concept to understand as school wellness educators. Describing students as able or not abled is not socially just. We must recognize that all students have unique abilities and frame our instruction to highlight our students' strengths versus what they cannot do. That is why it is critical to understand developmental phases and stages in all domains of learning (e.g., psychomotor, cognitive, and affective and social). Development is age related, not age dependent (Goodway et al., 2019).

Lynch and colleagues (2020) emphasize that physical ability is most valued in physical education, resulting in classifying students as low ability or high ability. A social justice approach, with a focus on ability, would describe what a student can do—for example, "Tien can demonstrate the preparation and execution parts of the overhand throw and is developing the complete follow-through action." As teachers, we need to provide positive, descriptive feedback about what students can do and what aspects of the movement skill they can continue to develop.

Diverse Forms of Assessment

D is for providing diverse forms of assessment (Lynch et al., 2020). Process assessments that focus on the critical cues and the form of how a movement skill is performed provide learners with descriptive feedback and are more helpful for skill development than product assessments (e.g., how high, how fast, how far). Showing students how they move through videos, having a peer mold their body into the proper preparation stance, or having students draw a picture of their peer performing a movement skill are all viable process assessment tools. The affective domain should also be assessed in school wellness education; students can assess their feelings about a manipulative activity using things like an exit ticket for enjoyment (figure 3.1).

Knowledge of Minority Groups

K is for knowledge of minority groups (Lynch et al., 2020). Schools in the 21st century are quite diverse. In a school in southeast Pennsylvania, 53 languages are spoken by the student population. "As the social justice educator, you should seek to become informed of cultural norms circulating each minority group, along with understanding a group's history" (Lynch et al., 2020, p. 12). Teachers need to be sensitive to their students' cultural celebrations, practices, and beliefs. Lynch and colleagues (2020) highlight how requiring a Muslim student to engage in a learning activity with a Christmas celebration theme may be uncomfortable for this student. The student may be unfamiliar with the holiday traditions and thus be less able to see the learning experience as relevant. Understanding cultural norms may assist teachers in more valuable exchanges with students as well as in the design of appropriate learning experiences.

Queering Physical Education

Q is for queering physical education. Landi and colleagues (2020) discuss how physical education is a "straight" place and promotes gender binaries. We agree that many traditional teaching practices must be modified to respect all individuals' perspectives and needs. We recommend no longer addressing children as boys and girls, but as fifth or first graders. In addition, Landi and colleagues (2020) suggest not using the terms *leaders* and *followers* within a dance unit, nor pairing students by creating boy/girl partners, but instead encouraging students to choose their own partners.

Standards-Based Education

S is for standards-based education. Landi and colleagues (2020) question the equity of implementing standards-based education. They suggest that because outcomes-based education is based on behaviorist theory, it treats all students the same and therefore is not socially just and leads to precarity. Butler (2004) defines precarity as a state experienced by marginalized, poor, and disenfranchised members of society because of their status as alienated. A socially just curriculum recognizes that precarity—such as an underresourced school, ramifications of gender

I like _____ (name of manipulative activity).

It is fun to _____ (name of manipulative activity).

FIGURE 3.1   Sample exit ticket for enjoyment of a manipulative activity.

identity, and acceptance of one's ethnicity—may affect peer interactions, curricular decisions, and teaching practices. The authors of this textbook recognize the validity of this supposition; however, grade-level outcomes in physical education (SHAPE America, 2014) and health performance indicators (CDC, 2019c) do not necessarily lead to a one-size-fits-all model.

We suggest grade-level outcomes and performance indicators be used as guidelines. A school wellness curriculum must be relevant to the student population being served. Such a curricular approach recognizes students' needs, gender identify, cultural background, and so forth. In agreement with letter Y, youth-centered and empowering, we agree that students should be engaged in making choices about their curriculum, be offered opportunities to reflect on their learning, and be involved in discussion relevant to acceptance and understanding of all individuals' ability and worth. It can begin with creating class contracts and involving students in establishing norms for their classroom culture. Overall, "The A-Z of Social Justice Physical Education" provides profound considerations for all physical educators.

Social Justice Standards

Teaching Tolerance, now called Learning for Justice, an organization associated with the Southern Poverty Law Center, established social justice standards in 2016 (Teaching Tolerance, 2016). These anchor standards

and age-appropriate learning outcomes are divided into four domains:

1. Identity
2. Diversity
3. Justice
4. Action

The standards provide a common language and organizational structure; teachers can use them to guide curriculum development, and administrators can use them to make schools more just, equitable, and safe. The standards are leveled for every stage of K-12 education and include school-based scenarios to show what antibias attitudes and behavior may look like in the classroom. K-2 and 3-5 grade-level standards are provided for each of the four domains. Here are examples:

Anchor Standard Identity Code ID.K-2.1 (Grade K-2)

- *Grade-level outcome:* I know and like who I am and can talk about my family and myself and name some of my group identities.

- *Antibias scenario:* For show and tell, Joi brings in a picture of her family on a church camping trip. "My family goes camping a lot. I like camping. I'm a Christian, and sometimes my family goes camping with the church. I'm also a big sister, so I have to help my parents take care of my little brother, especially when we go camping."

Anchor Standard Diversity Code DI.K-2.10

- *Grade-level outcome:* I find it interesting that groups of people believe different things and live their daily lives in different ways.

- *Antibias scenario:* "You have two moms? Do you call both of them Mom?" "I call them Mamma Kendra and Mamma Sam," Lisa says.

Anchor Standard Justice 11 Code JU.3-5.11 (Grade 3-5)

- *Grade-level outcome:* I try to get to know people as individuals because I know it is unfair to think all people in a shared identity group are the same.

- *Antibias scenario:* A class is discussing Cesar Chavez and the American labor movement. Kelly mentions seeing on TV that most of the clothes sold in the United States are made in other countries where workers aren't protected the way U.S. laborers are. She notes that even though worker conditions have improved in the United States, it doesn't mean that we should ignore injustice elsewhere. She and several other students are inspired to go home and talk to their parents about purchasing clothes from companies that practice ethical manufacturing. They also plan to set up a clothes swap to help reduce wastefulness.

Anchor Standard Action 16 Code AC.3-5.16 (Grade 3-5)

- *Grade-level outcome:* I pay attention to how people (including myself) are treated, and I try to treat others how I like to be treated.

- *Antibias scenario:* In physical education students are engaged in a creative movement lesson. The task is to make different shapes with a partner using different levels and different body parts. One student in the class has an intellectual disability, and another student with a physical disability uses a wheelchair. The teacher creates partner groups. Before beginning the activity, the teacher discusses with the class how we are all similar but different and has the students contribute their ideas while writing them on a whiteboard. Of course, the teacher may supplement these ideas. Students then are reminded that there is no one correct way to create these partner shapes, and they should provide positive feedback to their partner. Partner groups are combined to make groups of four. Groups are now challenged to create a quilt or collage of four different types of shapes. Students are reminded to accept other's ideas and to treat each other using kind and positive words.

Skills-Based Pedagogical Approach and Active Learning

Dewey thought that schools and classrooms should be representative of real-life situations, allowing children to participate in learning activities interchangeably and flexibly in a variety of social settings, thus engaging in active learning (Dewey, 1938; Gutek, 2014). Active learning has been defined as

> a process that has student learning at its center. Active learning focuses on *how* students learn, not just on *what* they learn. Students are encouraged to think hard, rather than passively receive information from the teacher. (Teaching and Learning Team International, 2020)

Approaches that promote active learning focus more on developing students' skills than on transmitting information and require that students do something—read, discuss, write, or demonstrate (Brame, 2016). In this chapter we examine how active learning or skills-based learning can be achieved in the school wellness setting and how this pedagogical approach facilitates students' achievement of both physical and health literacy.

Benes and Alperin (2019) make a strong case for a skills-based teaching approach in health education. They explain that in a skills-based approach,

> there is a shift from the more traditional approach in which curricular units are determined by topics such as drugs and alcohol, nutrition, and healthy relationships to one where the skills become the units and the emphasis shifts from knowledge acquisition to skill development. In a skills-based approach traditional topics and information provide a context for skill development. (p. 31)

Functional or factual knowledge is described in NHES Standard 1: "Students will comprehend concepts related to health promotion and disease prevention to enhance health" (CDC, 2019a). However, that is simply not enough. Knowledge does not automatically lead to behavior change. Benes and Alperin (2019)

suggest that health education programs are more effective when students develop skills that contribute to behavior change and do not solely focus on knowledge acquisition. "In order for health programs to be the most effective, time needs to be spent on factors that will contribute to behavior change and that is not through knowledge acquisition" (Benes & Alperin, 2019, p.34). Behaviors such as analyzing influences and accessing reliable information are among two of the seven skills students should develop (CDC, 2019c).

We are espousing Benes and Alperin's (2019) approach to the design of health education learning experiences and agree that school wellness learning experiences must extend beyond functional knowledge. In the National Health Education Standards (CDC, 2019c), Standards 2 through 8 describe these health behavior skills as follows:

Standard 2: analyzing influences

Standard 3: accessing valid and reliable information, products, and services

Standard 4: interpersonal communication

Standard 5: decision-making

Standard 6: goal setting

Standard 7: self-management

Standard 8: advocacy

Developing children's skills instead of limiting the school wellness curriculum to the regurgitation of facts is at the heart of the skills-based school wellness education.

Schools are a place of learning and self-exploration. A skills-based approach in the health education classroom challenges students to go beyond knowing to applying. They must critically analyze their own health and then consider the tools, strategies, and information that will help them to maintain and enhance their own health or the health of those around them. (Benes & Alperin, 2019, p. 36)

Let's examine one example of the school wellness curricular approach for children in grades K-1 through the CDC's Healthy Schools standards. NHES Standard 7 states that students will demonstrate the ability to practice health-enhancing behaviors and avoid or reduce health risks (CDC, 2019b). A traditional approach to teaching about health-enhancing behaviors might be to watch an age-appropriate video about bike safety.

The traditional assessment of student learning about such practices might be to have children complete a worksheet, checking off inappropriate versus appropriate pictures of the safety practices. Many schools have bicycle safety programs. In one of SHAPE America's success stories, a bike-riding program was initiated for all second graders in public schools in Washington, D.C. (Chandler, 2015). To engage children in a more active learning experience, the school wellness educator could design bike safety lesson conducted on the school playground or in the gymnasium. The student-learning outcome would be not only to know that wearing a bike helmet is important but also to be able to properly put on a bike helmet and navigate a bicycle course during which the student must stop at a stop sign and cross the street when no cars are coming within a pretend neighborhood.

The skills-based pedagogical approach is illustrated in tables 3.3 and 3.4.

TABLE 3.3 Designing Active School Wellness Learning Experiences

Teaching tasks	Lesson content development grades K-2
1. Determine standards and grade-level outcomes.	• *NHES grade-level outcome:* 7.2.1 Demonstrate healthy practices and behaviors to maintain or improve personal health. • *SHAPE America Standard 1 (2014):* The physically literate individual demonstrates competency in a variety of motor skills and movement patterns. • *Proposed grade-level outcome:* Can balance and coordinate upper- and lower-body actions on a bicycle with or without wheels. • *Social justice teaching strategy:* Provide balance bikes, bikes with training wheels, and standard properly sized bikes to accommodate students with differing abilities. Provide diverse forms of assessment (e.g., use a tablet to record the child to provide feedback). Do not use binary gender terms such as boy's bikes and girl's bikes.
2. Design learning objectives	• Students will be able to demonstrate how to properly put on a bicycle helmet and safely navigate a bicycle course that simulates riding through a neighborhood. • *Social justice teaching strategy:* Discuss with students and their families where safe neighborhoods and parks are located; if students do not live in safe environments, riding paths need to be created in and around the school.
3. Introduce the lesson.	**WHAT** are we learning today? Students will learn how to control their bodies and balance while riding a bicycle. **WHY** are we learning this? Riding a bicycle is a skill that can be used throughout one's life. **HOW** will learning be measured? The teacher will take videos of the children as they are practicing various tasks throughout the lesson and share the video with the students.
4. Demonstrate the skill.	The teacher, using a flipped classroom, could make an instructional video of a child learning how to ride a bicycle. Students view video before engaging in step 5.
5. Design practice task progressions and provide ample practice time.	• Put on a bicycle helmet. • Ride a balance bike or bike without pedals and walk while sitting on the bike while feet push bike forward. • Start gliding by taking feet slightly off the ground for brief periods. • Put the pedals on the bike and use the same progression but glide with the feet on the pedals. • Pedal on the bicycle with an adult or older student's assistance. • Pedal bicycle on own.
6. Provide instructional feedback.	"Keep your head up so you can see where you are going." "Try not to shake the bicycle handles."
7. Assess student learning.	Take a video clip of each child properly putting on their bicycle helmet and a short clip of them riding through the bicycle course. Have child view the video and write a sentence or color a picture about one safe practice they demonstrated.

TABLE 3.4 Designing K-5 Students in Active School Wellness Learning Experiences

Teaching tasks	Lesson content development grades 3-5
1. Determine standards and grade-level outcomes.	NHES 1.5.1. Describe the relationship between healthy behaviors and personal health. SHAPE America: • S1.E1.4 Uses various locomotor skills in a variety of small-sided practice tasks, dance, and educational gymnastics experiences. • S1.E8.3 Transfers weight from feet to hands with momentary weight support • S1.E3.4 Uses spring and step takeoffs and landings specific to gymnastics • S3.E3.3 Describes the concept of fitness and provides examples of physical activity to enhance fitness.
2. Design learning objectives.	• Students will leap and jump over low obstacles using correct form and while increasing their heart rate. • Students will transfer weight from feet to hands to feet (wheeling action) to go over foam trapezoid shapes with control. • Students will travel on hands and feet to move under obstacles with control. • Students will be able to identify the major structures of the heart and describe the blood flow pathways. • Students will be able to complete a weeklong journal, recording how they have demonstrated a minimum of three heart-healthy habits from a larger list generated by the students through online research and classroom discussion. • *Social justice teaching strategy:* Discuss with students how important heart health is. Ask student to share information they may have about their family's heart health.
3. Introduce the lesson.	**WHAT** are we learning today? Explain that students will practice the fundamental movement skills of running, leaping, jumping, and transferring weight from hands to feet within an obstacle course designed to simulate the heart and the pathway of blood through the heart. **WHY** are we learning this? To improve the form of their locomotor skills, to develop their cardiovascular fitness, and to identify how blood flows through the heart. **HOW** will learning be measured? Students' performance can be measured through a formative assessment of their fundamental movement skills. In addition, students will successfully complete the heart parts worksheet and complete a weekly heart health journal.
4. Demonstrate the skill.	The teacher will demonstrate how to move through the heart obstacle course on a scooter and using legs to push the scooter.
5. Design practice task progressions and provide ample practice time.	Learning teams will design their heart obstacle courses and then move through it using a leap, jump, and transfer of weight from hands to feet.
6. Provide instructional feedback.	"Be sure to push off of two feet and land on two feet while jumping!"
7. Assess student learning.	1. Self-assessment: Set up a tablet to be able to record the entire obstacle course. After students have completed the obstacle course using the prescribed fundamental movement skills, play back the video multiple times so that students can observe themselves and complete the self-assessment. 2. Peer assessment: Pairs of students assess each other, switching roles after each fundamental movement skill is completed. 3. Teacher-administered assessment: Observe the class moving through the obstacle courses and indicate which students performed a critical element incorrectly.

Summary

As noted in chapter 1, the overall goal in wellness education is for students to be physically active while learning health concepts and practicing health skills within the same lesson. This model of instruction engages students in active learning by infusing health concepts into the physical education setting. It is important to understand the developmental charac-teristics of your learners across all three domains of learning and to employ universal design for learning in your lesson design and practice. Social justice concepts also make significant contributions to culturally relevant pedagogies, while skills-based health education emphasizes going beyond teaching only functional knowledge to also helping students apply content knowledge in purposeful and meaningful ways.

Chapter 4
Online School Wellness Education

Online education was perceived as a distant change on the horizon. However, the COVID-19 pandemic greatly accelerated the timeline and forced abrupt changes upon teachers, students, parents, and administrators. In the spring of 2020, teachers were forced to adapt content and instructional practice from a face-to-face format to an online format overnight. For classroom-oriented subjects like history and mathematics, the transition was undoubtedly challenging. Yet wellness education was uniquely vulnerable due to its focus on the whole child. Wellness standards span psychomotor, cognitive, and affective outcomes (SHAPE America, 2013) and performance indicators (JCNHES, 2007).

Online physical education (OPE) may have been perceived as an "oxymoron" (Buschner, 2006, p. 3), but it has undoubtedly arrived. It will also have staying power because administrators have seen firsthand that it can be an adequate substitution for traditional education. In the event of future pandemics, snow days, or other school closures, instruction can be provided online (Williams & Ritter, 2020). The COVID-19 pandemic accelerated a shift toward online learning that was already occurring. Henceforth, undergraduate programs should provide comprehensive pedagogy for online wellness education.

During the pandemic, many teachers came to realize that online wellness education was not only possible but also could be successful. Given the whirlwind conditions under which most teachers adapted, the product that resulted was inspiring. The SHAPE America Google Drive filled with gigabytes of shared videos, activities, PowerPoint slides, and worksheets. It was heartening to see educators coming forward to support their colleagues and student learning.

These efforts demonstrate how teachers must adapt to an ever-changing world. Online education is but one change in a long line of seismic shifts, including coeducation, racial integration, inclusion of students with disabilities, and high-stakes testing, to name a few. Ultimately, it is the skill of the educator leading class that matters most. As Buschner said, online wellness education "needs an effective, reflective, qualified teacher," otherwise it is just "wires and lights in a box" (2006, p.3).

The purpose of this chapter is to empower wellness educators to be highly effective online educators. Readers will be able to identify the unique challenges and advantages associated with online education, develop curricula to harness its strengths, examine online pedagogy, and study meaningful activities aligned with selected components of wellness.

The focus of this chapter is on online wellness education at the elementary level. The age range is challenging because developmentally, a kindergartener is vastly different from a fifth grader. The latter can typically function more independently, has more advanced technology skills, and can use a traditional and robust learning management system (LMS) such as Schoology, Canvas, or Blackboard. A younger student (grades K-2) needs more guidance, is less self-directed, and requires a simpler technology interface such as Seesaw.

There are four primary modes of instruction:

1. Face-to-face (F2F) occurs when students physically gather in the same location for synchronous instruction.

2. Online takes place at a distance through the computer via the Internet (Digital Learning Collaborative, 2019).

3. Blended coursework is a combination of F2F and online, with the important distinction that online materials are not meant to replace traditional instruction but to supplement it (Siegelman, 2019). For example, a teacher posts online materials, activities, and quizzes that students complete outside of class.

4. Hybrid is not the same as blended. The important distinction is that online modalities are meant to replace some F2F instruction. For example, a wellness education class is scheduled for 80 minutes per week, half of which takes place face-to-face, and the remainder occurs online.

This chapter primarily focuses on online wellness education because that mode of instruction is the most unfamiliar to practicing and prospective teachers. Hybrid learning will be discussed secondarily because many of the modalities used in online education can also be used in a hybrid mode.

This chapter assumes that elementary students learning online have a one-to-one school-issued technology device. The most employed devices are Chromebooks by Google (60 percent), personal computers (PC) running Windows (22 percent), and iPads by Apple (14 percent) (Molnar, 2019). Mobile apps are discussed because Chromebooks and iPads use mobile operating systems (Android, iOS) that can run apps.

- Smartphones are not discussed because most elementary students do not have a smartphone.

- Most social media platforms such as Facebook, Instagram, Twitter, Snapchat, WhatsApp, and TikTok are excluded because many elementary students do not use these services. Parents may also object because of privacy and data collection concerns.

- Fitness technology such as heart rate monitors, accelerometers, and Fitbits are not included because of the cost.

- Exergames that require the use of a gaming console such as an Xbox, PlayStation, or Nintendo are also excluded because of cost, complexity, and home availability.

Growth of Online Education

Before the COVID-19 pandemic, online education was steadily growing in the United States. According to the Digital Learning Collaborative (2019), enrollment in online K-12 schools increased at 6 percent per year between 2009 and 2019. In the United States, statewide online K-12 schools operated in 31 states and had an enrollment of 310,000. Enrollment in state virtual schools that offered coursework to supplement F2F instruction was 420,000.

The 2006 Shape of the Nation Report indicated that 12 states allowed for online physical education credits (NASPE, 2006). That number grew to 22 states in 2010 (NASPE & AHA, 2010), 30 states in 2012 (NASPE, 2012) and 31 states in 2016 (SHAPE America, 2016). According to Gemin and Pape (2016), over two million students in the 2015-2016 school year completed four million courses. Of those, 10 percent were courses related to health and fitness. Unfortunately, accurately tracking the growth of online physical education is challenging "due to the complexity of hybrid and online course options" (SHAPE America, 2018, p. 4). These options include statewide online public schools, blended schools, career academies, charter schools, private schools, and online cyber academies run within a school district (Schroeder, 2019).

The COVID-19 pandemic dramatically changed the enrollment landscape. According to the United States Census Bureau, 93 percent of households with school-age children received all or part of their education through distance learning in 2020 (McElrath, 2020). Previously, that figure was 1 percent (Digital Learning Collaborative, 2019). In the fall of 2020, there were approximately 50.7 million public schools. That means that slightly over 47 million students learned through distance education. In the aftermath of the pandemic, the percentage of students who participate in distance education will fall precipitously but will likely not

return to pre-COVID levels. In essence, the genie is out of the bottle.

Challenges of Online Education

Teaching online is a monumental challenge, yet the obstacles are not insurmountable. The first step to creating solutions is identifying the challenges. Then the goal can become creating learning experiences commensurate with F2F instruction (Goad & Jones, 2017).

What makes wellness education unique is the emphasis on the whole child, including outcomes derived from all three domains: psychomotor, cognitive, and affective (CDC & ASCD, 2014). However, this distinction also makes wellness education challenging to deliver, especially in the psychomotor domain (Daum & Buschner, 2012). Consider the challenges faced when teaching one of the most fundamental elementary school skills: the overhand throw. First is the actual thrown object. In school, students would choose from objects of different sizes and difficulty levels, thus allowing for differentiation. At home, students may not have a suitable or safe object. A common solution is to use a sock ball or stuffed animal instead. Normally a teacher would demonstrate the movement from multiple angles and at different speeds using the whole-part-whole method. However, online students view a small video demonstration, making it harder to glean essential cues. The look, feel, and sound of demonstrations do not completely translate. The flight of the ball may not be viewable as it sails outside the margins of the screen. The teacher may struggle to provide frequent, specific, and meaningful feedback from observing small Zoom tiles. That is of course assuming students are even visible! Often students fall outside the camera's range when they back up to perform skills.

OPE forces teachers to focus more on discrete skills to the detriment of skill combinations, strategy, and small-sided games (Daum & Woods, 2015). For example, students may not have a throwing and catching partner. Students could throw the ball off the wall, but the speed and trajectory of the rebound would not approximate one thrown from another person. More-complex skills such as throwing to a moving target, finding open space, or executing a give-and-go are challenging, if not impossible, without a partner.

Motor skills and movement patterns were assessed less frequently in OPE compared to F2F instruction

(Harris, 2009). There is more emphasis on fitness because those activities are less complex, easier to demonstrate, and more individual in nature. Daum and Buschner (2012) surveyed 45 schools and noted how many times the following content topics were taught: fitness for life (24 times), weight training (13), aerobics (10), tennis (5), soccer (5), volleyball (5), and step aerobics (5). This narrowing of the curriculum does not promote competence "in a variety of settings" (SHAPE America, 2009, p. 17). Curriculum should offer a diverse selection of activities, thus allowing students multiple avenues for success. Elementary school focuses on fundamental movement patterns and basic sport skills (SHAPE America, 2013). However, Daum and Buschner (2012), found an overemphasis on cognitive learning to the detriment of physical activity. In fact, six courses in the study required no physical activity at all. According to SHAPE America (2018), it is simply easier to disseminate cognitive material.

This data reflects one of the greatest concerns about OPE: an overall lack of physical activity. SHAPE America recommends that students be enrolled in physical education for at least 225 minutes per week at the elementary level (NASPE, 2004). Of that time, a generally accepted recommendation is that students be physically active for a majority of class (Daum & Buschner, 2018). Measuring compliance with those recommendations is difficult. Physical activity logs are subject to concerns about accuracy (Daum & Buschner, 2012). Students may falsify information or provide erroneous information. These shortcomings call into question the rigor of OPE (NASPE, 2007). There are also concerns that psychomotor skills are not being assessed properly (Trent, 2016).

It is challenging for elementary school students to sit in front of a computer for hours and remain focused. K-2 students are not sufficiently able to independently use their device, monitor their schedule, complete assignments, submit work, and remain on task. For that reason, the great majority of teachers in Daum and Wood's (2015) study believed that online education was appropriate for secondary-level students but not elementary students. For example, one study participant said, "I think foundational skills at the elementary school require more face-to-face contact, and those kids aren't as self-directed [as older kids]" (p. 721). Younger students also have a limited capacity to communicate. "For somebody that is very young, they are not even able to read and write at that point, so I think online usage would be a challenge" (p. 721). For this reason, the initial SHAPE America position statement included recommendations only for second-

ary schools, not elementary (NASPE, 2007). SHAPE America "believes there should always be a face-to-face option for physical education because online learning is not appropriate for all students" (2018, p.1). It is SHAPE's contention that online instruction should supplement traditional instruction, not replace it.

Teachers may be resistant to online education because of how dramatically different it is from F2F. Some have expressed that online wellness education is "counterintuitive" (Daum, 2020, p. 42) or simply not what they signed up for. Resistance to change is natural. Part of it stems from the notion that teaching will simply return to the way it was before the pandemic. The future is hard to predict, but most likely, online wellness education (OWE) will be more prevalent. Adapting F2F instruction to online methodology is a tremendous amount of work (Hastie et al., 2010). Most teachers underestimate the time, commitment, and effort needed to effectively teach online (Daum & Buschner, 2012; Mohnsen, 2012). Compounding the challenge is the fact that many teachers have not been trained to provide online instruction. Only recently have teacher training programs begun to include online education in required coursework. Even so,

many programs are struggling with how to integrate a comprehensive strategy toward online instruction (Juniu, 2011). Therefore, most teachers rely on on-the-job professional development. Essentially, they are flying a plane as it is being built. If training is provided by districts, it is often not specific to wellness education (Daum & Buschner, 2012). Teachers compensate by relying on the Internet and colleagues for training. However, this is not ideal and will result in uneven growth.

Advantages of Online Education

Arguably the greatest advantage of online instruction is flexibility. Students can learn from anywhere, provided they have a device, an Internet connection, appropriate equipment, and proper supervision (Bakia et al., 2012). These advantages extend to teachers as well (Williams, 2013). Instruction can still be differentiated based on learning needs, academic performance, and disability status (Gemin et al., 2015). Flexible scheduling allows students to participate more readily in extracurricular activities and in some cases graduate on time (Harris, 2009).

Wellness educators have traditionally been disadvantaged by the amount of allocated instructional time (SHAPE America, 2016). When online, class time is no longer bound by a traditional school schedule (Hastie et al., 2010). Teachers may expand learning opportunities beyond predetermined levels to better meet the academic standards.

Students can access online materials at an individualized pace and frequency (Bakia et al. 2012). Students having trouble learning to skip, for example, might replay the demonstration and activity repeatedly until mastery. Teachers can use the inclusion teaching style by recording a range of videos and allowing students to pick their level of challenge depending on perceived competence.

Online education allows for greater success by individuals or groups traditionally marginalized in physical education (Bryan & Solmon, 2012; Rhea, 2011). Students with lower skill levels can participate in a more private setting with less fear of ridicule. There is less of a "fishbowl effect" in which students perceive other students are watching them. Casey and Jones (2011) reported previously uninterested students were more confident online and participated more frequently. For some students, just being able to participate at home in a familiar setting made them more comfortable. Technophiles enjoyed being able to use their computer to fulfill PE requirements (Buschner, 2006).

Teachers can easily share materials and collaborate. The SHAPE America Google Drive referenced earlier includes many resources teachers can adapt and use. Never in the history of the field has so much information been shared so readily. For example, teachers in the West Chester Area School District in Pennsylvania developed and shared online lessons in response to COVID-19 school closures. One teacher developed K-5 striking lessons that included video demonstrations, activities, and lesson plans. Another developed a K-5 dance unit and another a fitness unit. Once all materials were created, they were shared among the elementary teachers. Therefore, students in one school might watch another teacher's videos and perform related activities while their assigned teacher supervised class. This strategy reduced the considerable amount of work needed to develop online lessons and allowed teachers to select instructional units in which they had a high degree of expertise.

Online wellness can be a great advocacy tool. Too often parents or family members view wellness education through the outdated lens of their own negative experiences and stereotypes. Negative stereotypes of gym class include roll-out-the-ball teachers, highly competitive activities, play dominated by athletes, curriculum oriented toward team sports, and toxic conditions for low-skilled students (Gaudreault, 2014). Parents who have not stepped inside a physical education classroom recently are exposed to an updated version of PE through online instruction. Ideally, parents will see an educator working hard to promote mastery of the standards through fun, engaging best practices. They will see an inclusive environment regardless of skill level and high levels of activity. In short, online wellness education provides a real opportunity to positively move the needle of perception.

Instructional Prerequisites

The following are the steps for preparing online instruction:

1. Create a website.
2. Develop a toolbox of supplies.
3. Set rules and expectations.
4. Prepare a welcome video.
5. Prepare and distribute a syllabus.
6. Determine students' technology proficiency.
7. Communicate clearly.

Create a Website

It is challenging for parents and students to keep track of what equipment is needed, what assignments are due, what students should wear, and when class starts and ends. Teachers should make it easier on caregivers by creating a website where all information can be readily found. A variety of free, easy-to-use website builders are available including Wix, Weebly, and Google Sites. The website could be as simple as one page with a listing of classes for the week, times, and equipment needed. Take the opportunity to provide additional information such as program philosophy, standards, a teacher biography, and links to health and physical activity options; the choices are endless.

Develop a Toolbox of Supplies

Develop a PE toolbox of supplies that students must have available for each class (Niedzwiecki, 2020a). Possible items include a small ball for bouncing and rolling, 3 sock balls, 3 plastic grocery bags, 12 numbered paper plates, 1 water bottle (one-third filled), 2 bath-sized towels, 1 gallon milk jug with the bottom cut off, 12 plastic cups, 1 paper towel tube or pool noodle, 3 balloons, 3 beanbags or bean socks, 1 pencil, 1 roll of painter's tape, writing paper, and a large target basket (laundry basket) or cardboard box (figure 4.1). The basket or box can double as a place to store all the equipment. If students will need an item that is not on the list, email students and post an announcement at least two days before the item is needed. Be prepared, because despite ample communication, some students will not have the proper equipment. Be flexible and creative in adapting equipment needs on the spot.

Set Rules and Expectations

Because students are taking classes from home, they might not feel like they are in school. Students may be in their bedroom, at a desk, at the kitchen table, or on the TV room couch. "It may not always be obvious to students that joining a Zoom meeting is functionally

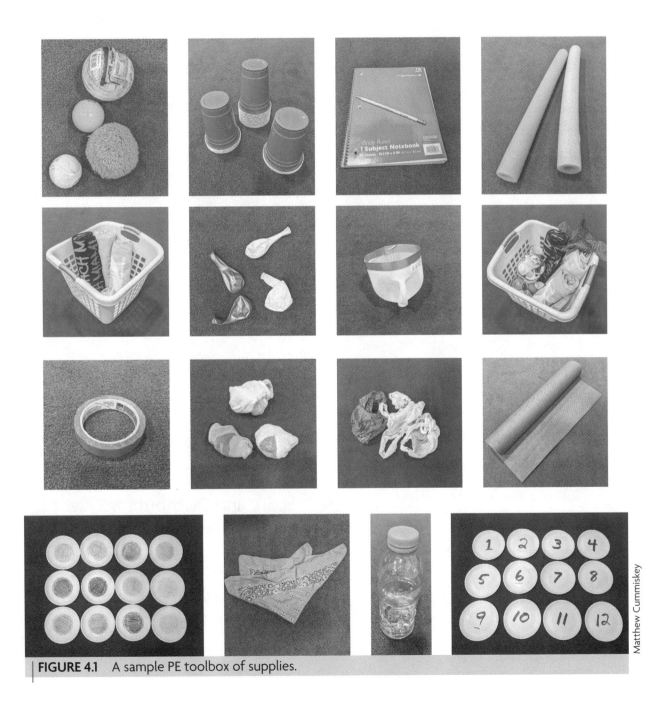

FIGURE 4.1   A sample PE toolbox of supplies.

Matthew Cummiskey

equivalent to walking into a classroom" (Dartmouth, n.d.). Therefore, use the concept of *student mode* (Harvard, n.d.) to trigger a set of expectations students uphold while in class. Enforce these consistently so students know what to expect (Goad & Jones, 2017). It also helps counter the notion that it is acceptable to be passive and uninvolved.

Provide a set of rules and expectations customized for online delivery. To build the rules collaboratively, put students in breakout rooms and ask them to develop rules that would allow everyone to feel supported and be successful. Back in the main room, groups share their responses. Distill the rules into a classroom code of conduct. Post the code on Google Forms and have all students sign the document.

Consider incorporating some aspects of *netiquette* into the classroom (Albion, 2011). Netiquette is a prevailing set of principles that govern online communication and civility. Below are examples of netiquette:

- Choose a quiet location away from distractions; avoid joining class while riding in a car (Goad & Jones, 2017).

- Use school-issued devices. Put away other devices.

- Remain seated, present, and engaged throughout the lesson. Avoid lying down or putting one's head down.

- "Remember the human" and accept that the medium has limitations (Albion, 2011). Computer screens poorly convey subtlety, nonverbal communication, gestures, and tone. Be mindful that communications can be easily misinterpreted and avoid actions that do not translate well online such as sarcasm (UOTP Marketing, 2020). This is especially true in chat rooms and discussions where users only have "lonely written words" (Albion, 2011). Be precise and selective in word usage to avoid misinterpretation. Always remember that on the other end of the Ethernet wire is another human, one with feelings and emotions.

- Use age-appropriate sentence structure and grammar (Mosier & Lynn, 2012). Avoid texting speech and informal jargon. Setting this expectation reinforces proper grammar and promotes cross-curricular learning (UOTP Marketing, 2020).

- Avoid typing in ALL CAPS because this is generally interpreted as shouting. Use alternative means to convey emphasis such as italic or bold text (Solano, n.d.).

- A good rule of thumb is to avoid saying or typing things that would be uncomfortable if spoken face-to-face (Solano, n.d.; UTEP Connect, n.d.). Do not use the separation afforded by the Internet as a shield to insulate oneself from the effects of words and actions (UOTP Marketing, 2020).

- Be mindful to respect students' privacy; do not divulge personal information such as addresses, phone numbers, or medical information (UTEP Connect, n.d.). Do not allow students to take pictures of other students or record the lesson in any form.

Before using digital videos or pictures featuring students, check the district's policy (Laughlin et al., 2019). According to the Family Educational Rights and Privacy Act of 1974, student records must remain confidential unless access is permitted by the parents or guardians. Do not share or forward confidential material; use it strictly for educational purposes.

Prepare a Welcome Video

Prepare a welcome video for students that includes the information normally presented on day one of face-to-face classes. Replicate the look and feel of F2F classes online. Be enthusiastic and welcoming; let your personality show through the computer screen. A welcome video is also an excellent opportunity to talk about the overarching goal of wellness education, which broadly defined is to promote wellness throughout the lifespan. Include information about learning goals and the whole child model. Relate the course back to the national standards, how those standards will be met, and how they will be assessed.

Prepare and Distribute a Syllabus

The syllabus may include the following:

- Teacher name and contact information (work phone, email, and address)
- Wellness program philosophy or teacher philosophy
- Course objectives with links to the standards
- Tentative topics

- Grading
- Assignments
- Makeup policy
- Class expectations and netiquette
- Keys to success
- Safety when participating at home
- Proper physical activity attire

Keep it as simple and straightforward as possible, especially because it is geared to elementary school students. By creating a syllabus, all parties are informed of expectations and policies and the "I didn't know" excuse cannot be used. Furthermore, a syllabus provides protection to the teacher. For example, if a student inadvertently shares personal information, you could reference the course policies. If a student is injured because they lack proper attire, you could again point to the course policies. Provide availability times such as 8:00 to 4:00 for meeting online (Mosier & Lynn, 2012; NASPE, 2007). Include possible mediums such as videoconference, phone calls, and text messages. If using a personal phone and you'd like to keep the number private, dial *67 first. Another solution is to use an application like Cisco Jabber where messages and voice calls display work contact information. Set a reply time for all communications, which is typically 24 or 48 hours.

Determine Students' Technology Proficiency

Students have varying levels of technology proficiency and comfort levels (Laughlin et al., 2019). Therefore, verify that students have the prerequisite technology skills to participate in the planned activities. Most likely the classroom teacher will have explained how to use the learning management system (LMS) and video communication service (e.g., Zoom, Google Meet, Microsoft Teams). However, that may not be the case with other applications such as Google Docs, Google Slides, Nearpod, Kahoot!, Flipgrid, Google Drive, Quizlet, Jamboard, and others. If using an application for the first time, plan to demonstrate it synchronously, or post an instructional video for students to watch beforehand.

Communicate Clearly

Organization, clarity, and redundancy are pivotal in online classes. For example, if fourth- and fifth-grade students are developing home escape plans in the event

of a fire, explain the assignment as clearly and concisely as possible. Develop a Word document and perhaps a video. In physical education, a good demonstration is said to be worth a thousand words. In online teaching, a good video is likewise worth a thousand words. Post the assignment in the LMS and post an announcement; include a due date and time in both. The two most common times are the start of class or 11:59 p.m.; to avoid possible confusion, don't select 12:00. Check in at least once before the assignment is due to ascertain progress, answer questions, or provide hints. Consider making larger assignments due in stages. This is especially helpful for younger students or those with poor time management or organizational skills.

Core Communication Infrastructure

There are two essential platforms online educators must operate seamlessly: the learning management systems (LMS) and the video communication service (VCS). The LMS is the heart of an online course because of the myriad functions it provides. A typical LMS is capable of

- posting announcements and content files;
- uploading student files;
- tracking attendance and involvement;
- calculating grades;
- delivering quizzes, tests, and surveys; and
- organizing discussions.

Common providers include Google Classroom, Canvas, Schoology, Blackboard, D2L, Edmodo, and Moodle (Bouchrika, 2021). Teachers must be able to operate all major LMS functions.

Unlike the LMS, teachers and students use the VCS synchronously. Therefore, the stakes are higher! If something goes wrong, students are left waiting for the teacher. There are fewer VCS providers; Zoom, Google Meet, and Microsoft Teams are the dominant three as of 2021. As of October 2020, Zoom had roughly 300 million global users compared to 100 million for Google Meet and 44 million for Microsoft Teams (Hughes, 2020). For that reason, Zoom will be presented with an emphasis on functions suited to wellness educators. These features may change slightly over time or be conveyed differently by another provider but will likely not be removed.

In many cases, teachers will need to create videos, especially when implementing unique activities or lessons. Therefore, it's important to master basic editing functions such as trimming, cutting, slow motion, inserting title screens, overlaying audio, and adding transitions. The slow-motion effect is especially useful when demonstrating skills. For Mac users, iMovie is the program of choice. For PC users, Windows 10 and higher includes Video Editor, which is a basic but effective program. Other free PC options include VSDC Free Video Editor, Shotcut, VideoPad, HitFilm Express, and Filmora. Cloud-based video editing platforms include Vimeo and Kizoa. Video editing may seem challenging, but the process becomes easier with each attempt. Videos can be shown on the school website and used for open houses, parent nights, year-end highlight videos, and makeup assignments.

Zoom Teaching Tips

Here are some basic considerations to follow when using Zoom:

- Find a quiet, uncluttered space, preferably with a hardwired Internet connection for the most reliable service. If that is not possible, find a spot close to the Wi-Fi router.
- Position the laptop so the top of the monitor is at approximately eye level.
- Use a headset with a microphone to better hear students and produce higher quality audio. In addition, you won't have to speak louder or yell when distant from the computer. Bluetooth-enabled headsets allow you to roam freely and demonstrate skills more easily.
- The background should be uncluttered and free of distractions. An easy solution is to blur the background or find a wall with minimal distraction. Position a table or desk away from the wall and face the laptop toward it.
- Be mindful to turn off a virtual or blurred background when stepping back from the computer to perform demonstrations.
- Have good lighting; this makes nonverbal communication clearer and your appearance more inviting. Use a lamp to illuminate your face if necessary and avoid being backlit.
- Beforehand, check for lighting and audio.

Take time to personalize various Zoom settings, some of which may be managed by administration or the school district.

- Mute participants upon entry to eliminate background noise and conversation at the outset. They may choose to unmute themselves if that function is enabled.

- *Zoombombing* is the appearance of uninvited individuals who interrupt class (Gunnell, 2020). To guard against this, do the following:

  - Enable the waiting room feature so you must approve entry into class.

  - Disable the "join before host" feature.

  - Disallow removed participants from rejoining.

  - Require a password or limit users to a specified domain or both. Do not share the meeting link on a public website or social media platform.

  - Once all students are in attendance, lock the meeting to prevent additional entrants.

  - Allow only the host to share the screen.

- Have Zoom play a sound when students enter or exit a meeting to better keep track of attendance.

- Consider disabling private chats so messages not originated by the host are visible to everyone. This can be turned off when the teacher wants students to answer questions via private chat messages. Set Zoom to save the chat automatically.

- If a class is particularly challenging, consider functions that maximize teacher control so that students cannot chat, rename themselves, share a screen, or unmute.

Once inside the meeting, students join the main room, characterized by a gallery view of participants visible in small tiles. This is also called The Brady Bunch view (Raygoza et al., 2020). Teachers can move student tiles. This feature is useful for monitoring specific students or arranging them in a desired order. Whenever possible, look directly at the camera so viewers perceive you are looking at them. Encourage students to share their video feed because this makes the class more personable and better resembles F2F instruction.

Become familiar with the participant window and its communications functions such as "yes," "no," "go faster," "go slower," "thumbs-up," "thumbs-down," and "more." A useful feature in this window is the "mute all" button to silence audio emanating from an unknown live microphone.

An often-used feature of Zoom is "share screen." Teachers can share individual windows or their entire screen. Be mindful that when using the latter, viewers see whatever is on the instructor's screen. Here are screen-sharing tips:

- Be vigilant about keeping personal information, emails, and other sensitive material from showing on the screen. This includes student information, family photos, personal health information, and controversial or nonprofessional applications.

- If sharing a video, click "share computer sound" and "optimize screen sharing for video clips." Otherwise, students will see the video but not be able to hear the audio.

- One of the biggest challenges with screen sharing is not being able to see students. To overcome this, share only the portion of the screen with the desired content and leave the gallery view in the unshared portion. Another solution is to have a separate monitor and to share the content on one monitor but not the other.

- Sharing can include only audio. A common use of this feature is playing music during an activity or before class. To do so, click "share screen," then "advanced," and then "music or computer sound only."

Breakout rooms are ideal for small-group projects and activities. The greatest disadvantage of breakout rooms is that the teacher cannot see what is happening in individual rooms. For that reason, some schools disallow breakout rooms. If your district allows breakout rooms, circulate between the rooms to answer questions and check status. It is possible to record breakout rooms to improve accountability (Surdin, 2018) and to communicate with students in all breakout rooms.

Online Teaching Tools

The LMS and the VCS are used by virtually all online wellness educators. Other technologies should be selected based on their effectiveness in promoting mastery of the standards. There are myriad choices. The sidebar on technology used in online teaching lists some of the most common technologies along with a description of useful functions. Later in the chapter these technologies will be paired with specific learning activities.

COMMON TECHNOLOGIES USED IN ONLINE TEACHING

- *Blogger* allows teachers to create short, informal, and frequent discussion posts called *blogs*. Students can blog about an experience, post questions for a guest speaker, summarize a just-completed class (best summary), and submit a post for the current health blog.

- *EdPuzzle* allows students to view interactive, self-paced videos with embedded assessment questions. Teachers can upload or create their own videos and add voice-over narration. Analytics includes the number of views and by whom, student scores, and question statistics.

- *Flipgrid* is a video discussion board. Teachers create topics, and students record short video responses that are arranged into a grid. Teachers and students can comment on other videos.

- *Google Forms* enables teachers to create, share, and administer surveys capable of collecting virtually any kind of information. It can be used to create traditional quizzes. Responses are organized into a downloadable spreadsheet.

- *Google Workspace* includes Google Docs, Sheets, and Slides. These tools approximate Microsoft Office but with enhanced real-time collaboration and sharing so that multiple students and teachers can work together in the cloud.

- *Homemade videos* in which teachers record videos using their smartphone, laptop, or other device can be edited using software such as Microsoft Video Editor or iMovie. Editing software includes basic functions such as title screens, trimming, and narration.

- *Jamboard* is similar to the Zoom whiteboard but has more functionality and flexibility. Teachers and students can collaborate in real time using notes, pictures, text, drawing, and other tools.

- *Kahoot!* is a game-based platform where students compete for points by answering multiple-choice questions. After each question, point totals are updated. Students can play as individuals or in teams. Teachers can access student scores and basic question statistics.

Planning and Pedagogy

According to SHAPE America, online instruction "can be a viable alternative to face-to-face instruction if the course: a) is standards-based; b) follows appropriate practices; and c) is taught by a state-licensed physical educator" (2018, p. 24). Online wellness education uses different methods but ultimately hopes to achieve the same goals—for students to demonstrate achievement of the standards. A temptation when teaching online is to focus on the technologies first and the learning second (Kennedy & Archambault, 2012). The outcomes (SHAPE America, 2013) and the performance indicators (JCNHES, 2007) should drive instruction (Goad & Jones, 2017). As Mohnsen succinctly stated, the difference "lies in the instructional approach, the standards, the curriculum and the assessment remain the same" as F2F (2012, p. 45).

Building Connections and a Positive Classroom Climate

Take time when a class starts to build connections and create a positive learning climate. These efforts make a classroom feel warmer and more comfortable (Raygoza et al., 2020). Students in turn are more likely to attend, ask questions, voice an opinion, be successful, and remain satisfied with the class.

As emphasized previously, teachers should try to replicate the friendly banter, conversations, and human connection that occurs face-to-face. Here are tips:

- Arrive early, enable your video feed, and play music to engage students but not so loud that it hampers conversation.

- Strike up a dialogue with students in the room to build rapport.

- *Nearpod* delivers online, self-paced interactive presentations with embedded assessments. Formative assessment options include open-ended questions, multiple choice, true or false, fill in, and matching pairs. Students can draw, answer polls, and collaborate in real time. Teachers can embed videos and links. Nearpod generates real-time statistics and reports.

- *Poll Everywhere* is an online, audience-response system used to promote engagement and monitor comprehension. It includes traditional formative assessment options such as multiple-choice and open-ended questions and offers other functions such as word cloud, clickable image, icebreaker, upvote, leaderboard, brainstorm, and ranking.

- *Popular websites:*
  - *Wheel of Names* is a spinner with customizable text on pie wedges.
  - *Random number generators* randomly forms groups or groups with a predetermined number of students. There are several available online.
  - *GoNoodle* provides fun, interactive videos that get kids moving.
  - *BrainPop* offers short, animated educational videos for kids.
  - *Classsroomscreen* provides a range of technology tools all on one website, including dice, sound level, QR code, text, timer, stopwatch, and clock.

- *Search engines* that are kid friendly such Kiddle, KidRex, and Wackysafe minimize the chance students will see inappropriate content.

- *Screen recorders* enable teachers to video record lessons, demonstrations, or assignments. They offer a video-centric mode of communication to improve clarity. Common screen recorders include Camtasia, FlashBack Express, OBS Studio, and QuickTime.

- *YouTube* has an incredible assortment of videos that teachers can use. However, videos can be removed or play with poor quality. To compensate, download YouTube videos and store them locally.

- Encourage students as they join to enable their video feed; it makes online class feel more like sitting in a classroom (Raygoza et al., 2020).

- Create a bitmoji avatar (figure 4.2) and customize it for different uses.

- Take attendance before class starts to reduce lost instructional time.

- Welcome students by name as they enter (Krause, 2020).

- Continually communicate in a supportive, present, and welcoming fashion; this helps students see you as a real person who wishes them success (Quality Matters and Virtual Learning Leadership Alliance, 2019).

- Share a portion of your screen that lists the day's learning objectives and the equipment needed from the student toolbox.

Use purpose-designed activities at the start of class to build a positive climate. Here are examples:

- Before the first class, record a Flipgrid introducing yourself and the course. That way students can be more familiar with you and at ease on the first day. Students respond by recording their own Flipgrid introductions that include their name, nickname, and responses to three "get to know you" questions. Students must comment on two videos, and no one video can have more than two comments.

- In a whip around, all students start with live microphones (mics). The teacher begins by saying someone's name and something positive related to that person and then mutes their mic. That person in turns says something positive to anyone whose mic is live, and then mutes their own mic. This continues until all mics

Matthew Cummiskey

FIGURE 4.2   Bitmoji of one of the authors.

are muted, meaning everyone has participated (Friedrick, 2020).

- A temperature check tells others how individuals in class are doing. For example, students may share a *rose* (something positive) and a *thorn* (something challenging), represent their week with an emoji or weather icon, or hold up one to five fingers. Ask selected students why they made their selection (Raygoza et al., 2020).

- Ask meaningful open-ended questions that build community and spark conversation (Friedrick, 2020). We! Connect Cards feature 60 question cards divided into three categories: fun and light, a bit deeper, and encourage self-reflection (We and Me, 2020). For example, What is the most adventurous thing you have ever done? What has been the highlight of your week so far? What things hold you back from doing what you really want to do?

- Begin class with quotes, poetry, or mindfulness activities (Krause, 2020). Mindfulness activities include deep breathing, tensing and relaxing portions of the body, meditation, and static stretching.

- Play casual games:
  - Picnic: Students bring a pretend item that corresponds to the first letter of their first name. For example, William could bring watermelon. Another option is for students to bring an object that equals the number of letters in their first name. For example, Maria could bring salad.
  - Two truths and a lie: Give students one minute to formulate two true statements and one lie

about themselves. Create breakout rooms with two students in each room. Once in the rooms, students take turns saying their three statements; the partner must guess which statement is the lie. Upon returning to the main room, ask students who was able to guess the lie correctly. Recreate the breakout rooms so students have a new partner and repeat.

- Whose side are you on: Share a Google Jamboard with two vertical lines. Upon entry, students create a sticky note with their name on it and position it between the two lines (figure 4.3). The teacher reads off two sides of an issue (vanilla vs. chocolate, loud vs. quiet) and each student moves their name to the corresponding side (Miller, 2020). After each round, discuss. When sharing the Jamboard, set the permissions so that students can view and edit the document. Otherwise, students will not be able to create and move their sticky note.

- Have you ever: A student asks whether the other students have done something they have done. For example, "Have you ever played on a sports team?" Students who have done this show the thumbs-up symbol in the Zoom participants window. After each round, the

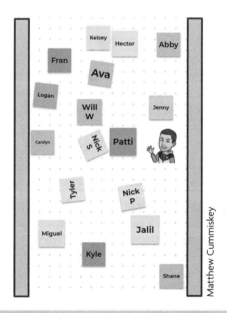

Matthew Cummiskey

FIGURE 4.3   Whose side are you on activity.

teacher picks a new student or uses the wheel of names spinner.

- – Human bingo: Distribute a bingo board to students via the LMS or as a chat attachment in Zoom. Put students in breakout rooms of two and give them 30 seconds to quickly say, "Hi!" and ask a question on the bingo board. Repeat until there is a winner and then discuss who has done some of the tiles on the board.

Purposely create student-to-student collaborations using required course assignments. For example, fifth-grade students are researching dental care, brushing technique, and flossing in pairs using a kid-friendly search engine. They create a Google Slides presentation and embed a video of themselves brushing and flossing. Choose pairings to acquaint students with someone new or outside their circle of friends. A type of collaboration is the peer critique. This can be done with projects (healthy snack assignment) and physical activities. Put students in breakout rooms and have one perform a skill correctly, the forearm pass in volleyball with a balloon for example, while the partner rates the performance using a Google Form.

Use breakout rooms copiously. This is especially helpful for students reticent to speak up in the main room (Dartmouth, n.d.). Breakout rooms improve the likelihood that students will contribute (Krause, 2020). Before opening the rooms, be clear about expectations and allow students time to ask questions (Harvard, n.d.). Remind students they can use the "Ask for help" button if they encounter difficulties or have questions.

End class the way it began, on a positive note. Have students share appreciations for anything big or small (Raygoza et al., 2020). Share announcements, celebrations, and upcoming events. Ask students to share three words that represent what they took away from class or a sentence representing how their thinking changed (Harvard, n.d.). Invite students to share one word expressing how they are feeling. Thank students for attending and stay afterward for additional questions, casual conversation, or a one-on-one chat (Darby, 2019). If a student has something personal to discuss, move them into a breakout room and follow them.

Generalized Online Pedagogy

Many effective teaching practices used face-to-face are effective online. Consult the SHAPE America Appropriate Instructional Practice Guidelines, (SHAPE America, 2009). Some appropriate practices may need to be modified or the spirit of a practice employed differently. This section focuses on pedagogy differences between online and F2F, not what is already codified as appropriate practice.

Effective online teaching presupposes that a teacher already has the requisite skills and competencies to teach F2F. A teacher who lacks professional knowledge, progressions, and skill development expertise will be a "marginal online teacher no matter what" (Goad & Jones, 2017, p. 7). Teachers should avoid assuming that what works F2F will automatically work online. A hallmark of good teaching is flexibility and creativity, both of which will be summoned extensively when transitioning to or preparing for online classes (Daum, 2020).

Most physical educators move through lessons without referencing a lesson plan or other documentation. The lesson introduction, activities, transitions, and critical elements are implemented from memory. Doing this online is more challenging because of the variety of materials employed. For example, YouTube videos have long URLs (website address), and documents may be stored in different locations. To combat confusion, use an organizational medium such as PowerPoint or Google Slides and embed links, pictures, videos, and activities into the presentation. Lessons will be more cohesive, and students will be kept waiting less. Additionally, students can access the lesson asynchronously if they were absent or would like additional practice.

Wellness educators are accustomed to varying instructional activities throughout the lesson. A good rule of thumb is to spend no longer than 15 minutes per activity. However, there are differences online. Students may not be required to share their video feed depending on the school or district; all that is visible is a black box with the student's name. To check on engagement, do the following:

- Use cold calling and have students periodically respond in the chat.
- Have students use "yes" (green check) or "no" (red circle) for quick true and false questions.
- Check for pacing by having all students use the "go faster," "go slower," or "clap" prompts.
- Require all students to interact at least once in a lesson. Keep track of interactions using a pen

and paper checklist or a cloud document where students put a check next to their own name. The latter strategies are effective for fourth and fifth grades, but not earlier grades.

- If students have been sitting for too long or need a changeup, incorporate a brain booster (energizer). A popular brain booster website is GoNoodle.

Effective teachers use a mixture of teacher-centered (direct) and student-centered (indirect) teaching styles (SHAPE America, 2009). Use different types of interactions, including teacher-to-student, student-to-student, and student-to-content/world. If possible, have students talk and interact with one another at least once during a lesson. This reduces solitary silence, which is especially challenging for elementary school students. Incorporate health-enhancing skills and physical activity skills together in the same lesson using the wellness approach. That way, there is less need to incorporate brain boosters. The activity *is* the lesson, not a break from the learning.

Feedback is vital to helping students master motor skills and movement patterns. However, providing specific, frequent, and immediate feedback is more difficult online (Ransdell et al., 2008). Here are tips to make feedback more successful:

- If one or more students are struggling, move their tile to the top so their performance can be better monitored.

- If one student needs specialized attention, switch Zoom from "gallery view" to "speaker view" so that student's tile is enlarged.

- Use "mute all" to silence all other microphones.

- Play recorded demonstrations instead of performing them live.

- Loop the playback during physical activity so students can be reminded of the desired performance, freeing you to provide more feedback.

Teaching online presents new challenges and questions about safety. Remind students that classroom rules still apply. They cannot simply walk away from the computer or go to the bathroom without asking. Select activities and equipment that will not result in an injury or damage to a student's house. This limits what you can reasonably implement. What happens if a student is injured while completing a scavenger hunt? What happens if a student goes outside to gain

more space? Is the environment outside safe? Are students still being watched? Teachers need clarification beforehand about the level of exertion allowable and whether outdoor spaces are permissible. Safety is the only attribute more important than learning, and safeguards must be in place, especially for elementary students.

Wellness Instructional Strategies

This section focuses on specific instructional strategies and activities that can be used in the classroom. It is organized into selected domains of wellness, which can be linked to specific SHAPE America Outcomes (2013) and National Health Education Standards Performance Indicators (JCNHES, 2007).

Physical Wellness

It is important that any program emphasize physical wellness. The physical domain is what distinguishes wellness education from other subject areas. Carefully consider how to meaningfully incorporate physical wellness as much as possible. Begin by taking advantage of the wide variety of resources the Internet offers.

Warm-Up

Before engaging in physical activity, complete a warm-up. YouTube has a wide assortment of gamification videos with which students can follow along. Because it is fun, students hardly realize they are moving. Here are four excellent examples:

- Dance, Dance, Revolution (DDR)—Start by finding DDR videos on YouTube, either individual videos or entire playlists. (Playlists are multiple videos grouped under the same name and URL.) Save individual videos or playlists to a YouTube library. In class, have students set up four paper plates on the floor in the correct DDR pattern. Share the videos and have students follow along. Individual scores are not being calculated, but students hardly notice. Increase the play speed to make videos more challenging (1.25, 1.5, 1.75, 2) or decrease the play speed to make them easier (0.75, 0.5, 0.25).

- Guitar Hero—Find and save Guitar Hero You-Tube videos or playlists. During the videos, five colored discs glide toward students as if on the fretboard of a guitar. To represent the discs, have students place five paper plates on the floor; coloring them is optional (figure 4.4). Share the video; students attempt to step on the plates in the order prescribed or balance briefly. Select videos aligned to students' grade and motor-skill level.

- Just Dance—The goal of Just Dance is for students to mirror a dance being performed by one or more dancers. Search YouTube for playlists devoted to kids. Videos featuring the alphabet and counting are available. Share the screen, play the video, and have students try to mirror the dancers on the screen.

- OhShape VR—The goal of OhShape VR is for students to move their whole body in accordance with oncoming objects. They may be asked to dodge obstacles, poke objects, pass through walls, jump, or step around barriers. All videos are set to music and are available onYouTube.

Additional warm-up activities include the following:

- Scavenger hunts: Provide a list of items that students collect in their home within a given time limit. Points are awarded for each item and may be customized depending on the scarcity of the item. Sample objects include a family picture, drinking straw, flip-flop, baseball cap, toothbrush, helmet, and stuffed animal.

- Balance contest: Students able to hold a prescribed shape for 15 seconds get a point for each.

- Simon says: This is a classic game that translates well online. Play a non-elimination version in which students try to accrue as few mistakes as possible.

- Minute to win it: Students complete a challenge while a timer counts down seconds. For example, count the number of successful water bottle flips, cups knocked over with the overhand throw, shuttle runs between two cups, and exercises performed (lunge, squat, sit-up) while balancing an object.

For these activities, embed a demonstration of the challenge and a timer into a PowerPoint slide. If possible, embed a video from a computer file. This is more reliable than streaming a video from the Internet or YouTube.

Psychomotor Skills

Teaching psychomotor skills online is challenging. Here, more than elsewhere, a teacher needs to exhibit creativity given equipment, space, and personnel limitations.

STRIKING LESSON

For a typical F2F striking lesson, students may use a short-handled racket and tennis ball. When the lesson is online, allow students who have a racket to use it. If they don't have one, substitute a plate, book, notebook, or lid (Mellon, 2020). For the ball, substitute a foam ball, paper ball, balloon, or similarly soft, round

Place colored spots or colored paper plates in this order facing the screen

When done, stand behind the spots

FIGURE 4.4   Colored spots or paper plates for Guitar Hero.

object. Assume that students will be playing indoors; outdoor supervision may be lacking or the weather unsuitable. Assume students will not have a partner. Plan a series of progressions aligned with SHAPE outcomes S1.E24—striking with a short implement: (1) balance the ball on the racket while moving it in different pathways and directions, (2) keep it up on the forehand side, (3) keep it up on the backhand side, (4) keep it up on alternating sides, (5) air toss and hit, (6) toss and hit against a wall, (7) toss and hit over a towel line, and (8) volley against a wall. These activities are not as realistic as striking F2F but are a close approximation and will promote learning.

UNDERHAND TOSS

For a lesson on the underhand toss, have students gather three sock balls, one bath towel, and one plastic cup from the toolbox (Persia, 2020). Teach the underhand toss by having students mirror the demonstration and practice it without equipment. Set up by having students lay open a bath towel on the floor seven paces away from a plastic cup. Students attempt to hit the towel; if successful, fold the towel in half. Do this a maximum of four times. After the fourth successful toss, the towel is reset. See how many resets students can accrue. Next, play a game of cornhole; students position a cup on the "board" and earn one point for landing a sock ball on the board and three points for knocking the cup over. Play multiple rounds.

CATCHING

Catching is one of the most fundamental sport skills students learn. While welcoming students to class, display the equipment needed: two sock balls and four cups (Niedzwiecki, 2020b). Use the "On the Bank, In the River" YouTube video (level 3 or 4) as the warm-up. Teach catching using the following progressions: (1) toss and catch with two hands, (2) toss and catch with one hand, (3) toss, spin, and catch, (4) toss and catch low, (5) toss and catch high, (6) toss and catch behind the back, (7) rainbow toss (one hand to the other), (8) double rainbow toss, (9) toss, clap, and catch (vary the number of claps), (10) toss and move forward or backward then catch, (11) toss and move sideways then catch, (12) move diagonally and catch with outstretched arm, (13) toss under the leg and catch, (14) toss and catch in a plastic cup, and (15) toss and catch off the wall.

Fundamental Movement Patterns and Nonlocomotor Skills

For younger grades, include instruction related to fundamental movement patterns and nonlocomotor skills. For example, have students create an obstacle course that they navigate using different fundamental movement patterns. Have students create a river using two bath towels that are slightly different widths at both ends. Students "cross the river" using different takeoff and landing patterns. Have students do fitness activities and create various balanced shapes when the music stops. Create gymnastics challenges where students produce routines incorporating gymnastic skills, fundamental movement patterns, static balances, and dynamic balances.

Fitness Education

Fitness education is more prevalent online because of the ease by which it can be adapted to online education (Harris, 2009; Daum & Buschner, 2018; SHAPE America 2018). Many resources are available that mirror the explosion of online fitness content for adults, such as fitness classes, personal training, and activity-specific exercises such as those provided by the Peloton app. Continue to focus on SHAPE America Standard 3 by conducting the FitnessGram assessment for fourth and fifth graders. Prepare a document explaining how the tests will be modified and create a teacher demonstration video of each test. Play any required FitnessGram audio via Zoom while students complete each test. Follow the FitnessGram test conditions unless noted in the following list.

1. PACER test—Use the shorter 15-meter distance; mark the distance by placing two cups 15 meters apart. For students lacking an appropriate space, have them complete the YMCA step test or another cardiovascular activity. The step test result cannot be compared to the Healthy Fitness Zone, but it will provide a related activity.

2. Body composition—Use the BMI test because it requires no special tools and serves a cross-curricular function.

3. Muscular strength—Use the 90-degree push-up test.

4. Muscular endurance—Use the curl-up test; 9-year-old students create tape marks 3 inches (7.6 cm) apart. The distance apart is 4.5 inches (11.4 cm) for 10-year-olds.

5. Flexibility—Use the back-saver sit-and-reach test. Students should tape a ruler onto a box or stair step so that the 9-inch (23 cm) mark aligns with the edge (figure 4.5).

Students put their scores into a Google Form and answer yes or no depending on whether they achieved

Matthew Cummiskey

FIGURE 4.5   Homemade sit-and-reach box.

the Healthy Fitness Zone. Based on results, students create a personal fitness plan that includes specific SMART goals. Lay the groundwork by teaching four at-home fitness units: (1) body weight exercises, (2) free weight exercises, (3) static stretching, and (4) dynamic flexibility. Each topic is well suited to online fitness education because of the minimal equipment requirements and freedom to exercise anywhere. For free weights, substitute household items such as soup cans or water bottles. The Darebee website has a wide range of exercises from which to select, and the ACE Fitness website allows users to sort by exercises without equipment. Students can create a personal circuit that includes five dynamic flexibility exercises, five body weight exercises, five free weight exercises, and five static-stretching exercises. Provide a template with spaces to enter the exercise name along with a GIF. A GIF is an animated image that conveys motion using much smaller file sizes than a video. When students do an image search, specify the file format as GIF.

Fitness-Oriented Games

Fitness can be disguised as a game. That way, students improve their fitness levels and have fun at the same time. The following is a selection of fitness-oriented games available on the SHAPE America share drive.

- Alphabet workout (document)—Do exercises that correspond to the letters in a student's name. For example, B is for burpees. Students who finish their name restart.
- Choose it fitness (PowerPoint)—Roll a die. Students choose an exercise corresponding to rolls one through six. Teachers can roll an actual die or pause an embedded video.

- Draw it fitness (PowerPoint)—Assign an exercise to each playing card in one suit. Play a video that quickly rotates through all 13 playing cards. When a student yells, "stop," pause the video, and everyone completes the exercise corresponding to the card shown.
- Deal or no deal (PowerPoint)—A student picks one of two cards that is a hyperlink to an exercise. A student says "deal" if they want to complete the exercise pictured. If a student says "no deal," the second exercise shown must be done.
- $10 fitness (document)—Assign monetary values to different exercises (e.g., three push-ups are worth 25 cents). The goal is for students to accrue $10. Students fill in a table with the following headers: exercise name, monetary value, number of times, and total.
- AMRAP (document)—Create a circuit that includes four exercises (e.g., 10 lunges, a 15-second plank hold, 10 push-ups, and 10 burpees). The circuit runs for 10 minutes, and students repeat it for as many rounds as possible (AMRAP).
- Grocery bag fitness (PowerPoint)—Students perform a series of exercises with grocery bags by following along to videos embedded in a PowerPoint.
- Water bottle flip (document)—List a series of exercises. On go, students flip a water bottle. If they miss it, they do the exercise. If they land it, they can rest briefly until the next round.
- Coin flip (PowerPoint)—Display two exercises on a slide. Flip a coin or use an embedded coin flip video. If heads, do the exercise on the left; if tails, do the exercise on the right.
- Fee fi fo fitness (document)—Create breakout rooms of two, three, or four students. Students say, "fee fi fo" and then show zero to five fingers on one hand. Add the total number of fingers to determine the exercise. Vary the activity by changing the grouping size and number of fingers and add multiplication for older students.
- Would you rather . . . (PowerPoint)—Share two choices on one a slide such as "eat the school lunch" or "bring lunch from home." Students choose by holding up one or two fingers. The next slide reveals the exercise corresponding to each choice.

Popular YouTube fitness videos include the Get Kids Moving series, workouts based on the Avengers

and Harry Potter, workouts using balloons and towels, Tabata workouts using paper plates, and music playlists. There are many fitness apps, but most elementary students do not have smartphones, and most schools do not permit students to install apps on school-owned devices. Some functions of apps, MapMyRun for example, are available via Internet browsers (e.g., Chrome, Safari). However, this is not commonplace. The following journal articles offer additional information on mobile apps:

- Instructional Tools for Online PE: Using Mobile Technologies to Enhance Learning Fitness Apps (Goad et al., 2019)
- An Integration of Mobile Applications into Physical Education Programs (Yu et al., 2018)
- Motivating Students to Move (Martin et al., 2015)
- There's an App for That: Smartphone Use in Health and Physical Education (Cummiskey, 2011)

The SHAPE America Appropriate Instructional Practices guidelines urge teachers to extend "experiences from in-class activity lessons to community and family activities" (SHAPE America, 2009, p.18). Incorporate the SHAPE America activity calendars by performing selected activities during class and assigning students to complete five or ten outside of class (SHAPE America, 2020). As of 2021, SHAPE had created 41 activity calendars stretching back to 2016. You can mix and match activities or combine them into a bingo-board fitness activity.

Dance

Dance is well suited to being taught online and directly aligns with SHAPE outcome S1.E5. Teachers can lead dances or create their own instructional videos. The latter is recommended because teachers can better supervise and provide feedback. There are many dance videos on YouTube and specific playlists created by physical educators. Two popular options are SPARK Dances K-6 and Dance It Out! with Mr. C.

Physical Activity Tracking

To track physical activity, have students complete a physical activity log. SHAPE America provides one as part of its take-home packet resources for COVID-19 (SHAPE America, 2020); there are also many others online. Because of concerns about validity and honesty (Daum & Buschner, 2018), have a parent or guardian sign the form. Upload completed fitness logs to the LMS or use Google Docs. The advantage of Google Docs is that teachers can view the logs in real time and provide formative feedback. There are many fitness-tracking devices such as the Apple Watch, Fitbit, Garmin watch, and others, but these are impractical because of the cost. However, there are work-arounds. If students are outside walking or riding a bike, encourage them to create and measure a route using the computer browser version of MapMyWalk (Bumgardner, 2020). Another option is to use Google Maps. Right click at the starting point, select "measure distance," and then click along the map to create a route. Google Maps automatically updates the total distance. Students screenshot the route including the total distance and upload the image file to the LMS. To take a screen shot, use the snipping tool on a PC or press command-shift-4 on a Mac.

Intellectual Wellness

Intellectual wellness helps students make healthy choices for life (Brooks & Schneider, 2020). While it is important to convey knowledge, it is also important to build health-enhancing skills, whether they are related to the SHAPE America outcomes (2013) or the health education performance indicators (JCNHES, 2007). Start by asking which intellectual skills students need, and then fit the content into the skills. In many ways, teaching health-enhancing skills is similar to teaching physical skills—start with the hook, explain the steps of the skill (like critical elements), demonstrate (model) the skill, and practice it in increasingly complex, realistic environments (Brooks & Schneider, 2020). Provide feedback throughout and use formative or summative assessments or both to evaluate performances.

A way to build health-enhancing skills is through project-based learning, where students apply learning in higher-order tasks aligned with real-life scenarios. Educational technologies and online instruction are well suited to these pedagogical approaches. As an example, consider the applications of technology shown in table 4.1 in a unit on stress and anxiety for students in grades 3-5. Stress and anxiety are timely topics, considering the many changes the pandemic has wrought on F2F learning, families, and commu-

TABLE 4.1 Applications of Technologies in School Wellness Education

Topic, activity, or project	Educational technology and description
Sources of stress in students' lives	Word cloud—Students identify stressors in their lives. Use Poll Everywhere to create a word cloud and discuss the results. Adapt instruction to the lived experiences of students.
BrainPOP stress topic	BrainPOP—View animated instructional videos for kids along with quizzes and materials.
Basic information on stress	Online quiz—Create an age-appropriate online quiz using the LMS, a Zoom poll, or Google Forms.
Basic information on stress	EdPuzzle—Find and download an appropriate video from YouTube. Upload it to EdPuzzle and create embedded questions students must answer before continuing. Analyze the results.
Effects of stress on the body	WebQuest—Create a QR code WebQuest. Students scan QR codes that direct them to different websites. There they research information to answer questions on the short- and long-term effects of stress on the body.
Public service announcement	Google Doc—Students create a fictitious announcement to be read over the loudspeaker for students who are feeling stressed. Student groups collaborate on separate cloud docs that the teacher evaluates online.
Unhealthy coping strategies	Nearpod—The teacher creates a self-paced Nearpod presentation addressing unhealthy coping strategies such as overeating, displacing anger, withdrawal, and excessive media consumption. Web links, quiz questions, videos, and open-response questions are embedded in the presentation.
Stress game	Breakout rooms—Organize students into breakout rooms of four or five students per room. Play the stress game in which one student attempts to roll a 7 with two dice while another is writing 1 to 100 on paper and so on. Use the game to highlight changes in the body caused by stress.

(continued)

TABLE 4.1   *(continued)*

Topic, activity, or project	Educational technology and description
Acts of kindness	Brainstorm—Acts of kindness reduce stress levels. Use the Brainstorm function in Poll Everywhere to collect and show responses visible to everyone. Discuss selected responses.
Stress journal	Google Blogger—Each day for three days have students blog about stresses, which management techniques worked best and worst, and possible changes to make in the future.
Laughter does a body good	Google Drive and clickable image—Send students the link to a shared Google Drive folder where they upload a funny meme, image, or GIF that may or may not be related to stress. Upload the pictures to Poll Everywhere and use the clickable image function for students to select their favorite. Discuss how humor is an effective stress reliever.
Exercise is the best medicine	Webcam video (camera or QuickTime)—Students record themselves performing a series of yoga exercises and catalog how their stress levels changed before, during, and after exercise. Upload the completed video to the LMS.
Stress scenarios	Flipgrid—Students read different scenarios about elementary students experiencing stress. In Flipgrid, they (1) briefly summarize the scenario, (2) label the emotion or emotions, and (3) analyze the person's response. Students must comment on at least two other Flipgrid posts.
Body's response to stress	Kahoot!—Design a 10-question kahoot that focuses on the body's response to stress. The kahoot can be used in class or completed independently outside of class.
Music	Zoom—Play calming music as part of a visualization or meditation activity. Use the share "music or computer sound only" function in Zoom.
Skits	Screen recording—Interpersonal conflict is a major driver of stress. Students perform conflict resolution skits in breakout rooms. Assign one student to record, and each group's best recording is uploaded to the LMS. In the main room, groups volunteer to share their video or you pick.
Personality types	Jamboard—Four personality types affect stress. For the activity "Whose corner are you?" have all students create a note with their name in Jamboard. When you read off a trait or scenario, students move their note to one of the four corners labeled as a personality type or move it somewhere in between.
Coping mechanisms	Google Slides—Assign student groups a stress-coping mechanism. Groups create a five- to ten-page graphic novel (like a comic strip) focusing on that coping mechanism. Each slide is a different picture and caption in their novel. Use Kiddle or another kid-friendly search engine to find images.
Time management	Google Sheets – Managing one's time correctly is an important aspect of stress management. Create a Google Sheets template; students log how they spend their time for three consecutive days. Google sheets will automatically tally the totals.
Poster assignment	Google Drawing—Student groups create a poster about a stress-related topic using Google Drawing. Include specific requirements and a rubric. This is similar to a bulletin board project.
Gratitude and mindfulness	Online discussion and leaderboard—Students find their favorite YouTube Kids video related to gratitude and mindfulness. They post its title and URL in an LMS discussion. You pick the top five and then students vote for their overall favorite using the Poll Everywhere Leaderboard. Students watch the winning video synchronously next class.
Progressive muscle relaxation	Video editing and screen sharing—Create an edited video of progressive muscle relaxation exercises using Video Editor or iMovie. Share the video using the "portion of screen" function. Students perform the exercises synchronously while you observe students in the nonshared portion of the screen.

nities, all of which create stress for students. These applications are not meant to be included in one unit, but to showcase possibilities for teachers. They may be adapted for different topics.

Discussions are one of the most common and effective asynchronous tools. For example, students post in a discussion their experience creating healthy snacks and include a picture. Teachers should monitor and frequently engage in the discussion (Papadopoulou, 2020). This motivates students and produces higher-quality work. Contribute comments and, when possible, copy or reference the statements to which you are responding. Prompt students with questions or ask for more in-depth insights. Beforehand, post a code of conduct so conversations remain appropriate (O'Hara, n.d.).

Consider incorporating a flipped classroom format in which students learn information asynchronously first (Persky & McLaughlin, 2017). Use synchronous class time on higher-order skills, application, and problem-based learning. For example, students watch a YouTube video about bike and street safety and complete a five-question Google Form asynchronously. Then in class, students analyze different scenarios, determine whether the bike rider acted appropriately, and, if not, what adjustments are needed.

Social and Emotional Wellness

The COVID-19 pandemic affected the social, emotional, and mental well-being of children (Leeb et al., 2020). Students were confronted with numerous challenges, including changes in their routines, closed schools, social isolation from family and friends, fear of sickness, missing significant life events (birthdays, vacations), and decreased security (food, caregivers). Compared with the same period in 2019, emergency department (ED) visits for mental health increased 24 percent in 2020 for 5- to 11-year-olds. This statistic does not include school nurse and non-ED mental health visits. Therefore, it is imperative that schools address social and emotional wellness in a systematic, progressive, and concerted way to meet head-on the challenges of the pandemic and overall mental health. However, teaching about social and emotional learning (SEL) is challenging in the first place, let alone doing so online. Topics like nutrition and body systems are more cut and dried than the softer skills. The hardest part is sometimes just making a commitment to teach SEL with greater frequency and taking that first step. In time, with reflection and professional development, teachers will grow more adept.

SEL activities are available in the lesson plan chapters, with adaptations made for online delivery. The format of SEL lessons is similar to that of adventure education—the teacher presents the activity, students complete it, and then the teacher processes the experience with students to promote SEL. Focus the processing on the three *what* steps: what happened, what does it mean, and what do I do with the information in my everyday life? Beforehand, decide on the SEL learning goals, which can be aligned with any of the themes listed here:

- Accountability (admitting fault, taking blame)
- Attention to detail
- Automatic thinking
- Being a builder
- Being yourself
- Big picture and little picture
- Bullying
- Comfort and how it affects ability to perform
- Communication
- Concentration and focus, staying in the game
- Empathy
- Exclusion
- Fear and courage
- Fear of conflict
- Frustration level
- Goal setting and goal commitment
- Impulsiveness
- Individuals in crisis
- Leadership styles
- Level of perceived difficulty
- Making mistakes
- Mindfulness
- Overcommitment
- Patience
- Perseverance and fortitude
- Perspective
- Fair play and honesty
- Process and product
- Resource use
- Roles
- Rules—imposed and implied
- Seeking help and support
- Struggle
- Success, defining success
- Teasing

Cross Domain

The domains of wellness affect one another. For example, poor social and emotional wellness can affect physical wellness and vice versa. The domains should be balanced and mutually supportive. The goal is to have ideal wellness across all domains. To encourage this idea, incorporate technology-based assignments that incorporate multiple domains, such as a portfolio or wellness plan. For example, students at the Florida

Virtual School created a wellness plan that included goals, reflection questions, fitness assessments, and technology tools (Florida Virtual School, n.d.). Melanie Lynch, a SHAPE America National Teacher of the Year, created the Dimensions of Wellness Project in which students take pictures to document artifacts related to each domain. For instance, to document the physical domain, students could take pictures of being physically active outside, flossing their teeth, or doing household chores. To submit the project, students created a Google Slide presentation with pictures embedded on domain-specific slides.

Assessing Online Learning

Assessment should be an "ongoing and integral part of the learning process for all students" (SHAPE America, 2009, p.20). What is best practice face-to-face should be duplicated as much as possible online. Assessing the cognitive domain online is easier because of the wide variety of assessment platforms. However, measuring the psychomotor domain is more challenging. This section focuses on online wellness assessment and is not meant to comprehensively address overall assessment practices, instruments, and analyses.

Videos are the key to assessing the physical domain and motor skills (Mohnsen, 2012). Both teachers and students can view and critique actual performances (Casey & Jones, 2011). Videos can be paused, rewound, and played in slow motion—something not possible in real time (Laughlin et al., 2019). Consider using Coach's Eye, Hudl, or other specialized apps or programs to augment the basic functions of most media players. Unfortunately, reviewing and scoring videos can be time consuming, especially given the fact that elementary wellness educators typically have hundreds of students (Beseler & Plumb, 2019). Therefore, only assess those skills deemed critical. For example, K-2 skills might include the fundamental movement patterns, jumping and landing, balance, weight transfer, underhand throw and roll, catching with hands, and volleying. Skills for grades 3-5 might include dance, skill combinations, fitness skills (push-up, curl-up, lunge, plank), FitnessGram, overhand throw, striking, and foot control (trapping, passing, dribbling).

Younger grades are less technologically proficient. Therefore, record all student performances simultaneously in the Zoom gallery view. Set it up by having students put a paper plate on the floor to mark their standing position. Verify that all students are visible. Next, have them execute underhand rolls for 60 seconds. Use the video communication service to record the gallery view. After class, play back, analyze, and score the student performances. The tiles will be small but scoreable. An alternative is to have K-2 students record their own videos using the device camera and upload them to the LMS, typically Seesaw. This approach may require the assistance of an adult but will result in higher-quality videos, assuming students are in view. This approach is more time consuming to grade.

Students in grades 3-5 can be relied on to record videos using their device. There are two approaches. The first is identical to the approach for K-2 where students upload videos to the LMS and are scored by the teacher. A second approach is to use Flipgrid. Communicate the requirements to students, including the Flipgrid join code. An advantage of Flipgrid is that the recording and uploading functions are bundled. There is no need to record the video first, find the file, and upload it to the LMS, which can be challenging, even for adults. In Flipgrid, all videos are quickly accessible in one place. When setting up the Flipgrid, enable "topic moderation" so videos remain hidden from other students. Encourage students to record multiple videos and submit their best one (mastery approach). Set conditions to reduce grading time, such as grading only the first two attempts or the first 30 seconds of a video.

Use videos for self-assessments. First, create a demonstration video or find one on YouTube. Students view the video, record themselves executing the same skill, and analyze their technique. Show students how to play both videos simultaneously in two adjoining windows. Students analyze each critical element and indicate in a Google Form whether each critical element was correctly executed (Laughlin et al., 2019).

Zoom breakout rooms can be used for peer assessments. Put two students in a breakout room; one performs while the other analyzes. For younger students, do one cue per attempt, and use symbols such as smiley faces instead of words. Older students can submit their peer analysis as a private chat message to the teacher by answering teacher-designed poll questions in the main room or using Google Forms. Set Zoom to allow only private chats to the teacher. For younger students, have them hold up fingers corresponding to the number of cues performed correctly.

In a hybrid environment, use a flipped classroom approach to assess motor skills. Students practice independently outside of class using videos and specially designed at-home learning activities. Then when you are face-to-face, play small-sided games and measure higher-order skills, such as skill combinations, strategies, and tactics. Hybrid environments allow teachers to make better use of portable technologies such as step counters or heart rate monitors (Harris, 2009). For example, a teacher with 30 step counters could rotate them between classes weekly. As one class returns devices, they are distributed to another class.

There are several ways to assess the intellectual domain, most of which were presented earlier in the chapter. They include LMS quizzes, Zoom polls, Google Forms, Kahoots!, Poll Everywhere, and EdPuzzle. A variation on an LMS quiz is allowing students to work collaboratively in breakout rooms on a quiz but to submit their own quiz. This format encourages collaboration while still measuring knowledge. Take advantage of the analytics afforded by LMS quizzes. You can analyze questions more easily than with F2F pen-and-paper quizzes. In addition to basic statistics, examine the discrimination index, which measures a question's ability to separate high- and low-performing students. Link LMS quizzes to the gradebook so grades automatically transfer. For younger students, create picture-based questions with two answer options: thumbs-up or thumbs-down.

Social and emotional learning is best assessed using a rubric. For example, students are completing an online team-building activity focused on supporting others and the team. Develop a one- or two-row rubric addressing support that may include any of the following attributes: makes meaningful contributions, is involved, speaks positively, shows concern for others, and exhibits a supportive tone. Require students to contribute at least once during the activity. Score the rubric after class and post scores to the LMS.

Summary

Fittingly, this chapter will close emphasizing the last phase in the cycle of instruction: reflection. Expect setbacks and uncertainty—those are endemic to teaching. Make improvements based on the data collected. Ask students for anonymous feedback using Google Forms. Take advantage of the increased connectivity brought by online instruction. Share practices, lessons plans, and documents with other teachers. Avoid becoming overly focused on technology—remember the human (Albion, 2011). Balance technology with the right amount of human connection (McNamara et al., 2008). Expect it be difficult at first but approach the task with fortitude.

The goals of wellness education are well codified in the national standards and appropriate practice documents. What cannot be found in those documents is a roadmap for doing so. Face-to-face instruction has blazed a trail for many decades, while online wellness education is only beginning that journey. Therefore, be persistent, be patient, and be flexible while always orienting instruction toward lifetime wellness and physical activity. Make decisions based on a "students-first" mantra and seize the opportunity to positively affect quality of life in a whole new way.

PART II

Lesson Plans

The lesson plans provided in chapters 5 and 6 represent the application of a school wellness education approach. Students meet both health education and physical education standards in the same lesson plan. The content and activities, even though they may be different, are symbiotic, meaning they support one another and enhance overall wellness.

The lesson introduction establishes how teachers frame the content and context of the lesson. Instead of simply stating what students will do, the **WHAT** frames what students will learn, often in relation to a standard. The **WHY** succinctly explains why students are learning this information and how they will benefit. Lastly, the **HOW** adds a measure of accountability and transparency in terms of how the learning will be measured. Each wellness education lesson plan addresses the what, why, and how as part of an effective and comprehensive lesson introduction. Select lesson plans provide specific recommendations on Universal Design for Learning (UDL). Teachers are encouraged to use UDL and to import recommendations from one lesson plan to another where appropriate.

Teachers will notice the greatest difference from traditional health and physical education in the lesson plan activities. Wellness education activities mix psychomotor learning with cognitively oriented, stationary activities, such as worksheets, videos, discussions, and projects. Activities were chosen based on the following:

- Learning—The paramount goal is to promote mastery of the standards and learning objectives.
- Activity time—Students should move as much as possible. Activities selected keep wait time to a minimum and harness the innate desire of elementary students to move.

- Opportunities to learn (OTL)—An OTL is each occurrence in which a student performs a skill or interacts with the concept being taught. Examples include bumping a volleyball and practicing a conflict resolution skill. To that end, activities use small-sided games featuring teams of five or fewer, avoid relays, and refrain from elimination. Students who need practice are not excluded; they need more practice, not less.
- Creativity—Several novel activities or unique ways of combining existing activities are presented.
- Enjoyment—School wellness education should be fun. If wellness educators want students to lead a healthy and physically active lifestyle, enjoyment must be part of the equation. Developmentally appropriate learning experiences featuring differentiated instruction lead to success. When activities are age appropriate and students experience success, they are more likely to enjoy the lesson.
- Inclusivity—Several lessons feature challenge tasks that make the learning activity more difficult and simplified tasks that make the learning task easier. The goal is to align instruction with students' current level of performance in what is called the *growth zone*.
- Choice—Wherever possible, students are given a choice of equipment or activities or both to promote learning on their terms.

All lesson plans feature a form of assessment, often a formative authentic method such as a peer assessment. The assessments measure student progress and whether they have met the lesson objectives.

Teachers may use the information to better instructional practices, motivate students, and place students in appropriate instructional groupings.

Preparation and Prerequisites

When implementing lesson plans, start slowly, implement select ones, and gradually expand the focus to make your entire program wellness based. Apply the lessons beyond the gymnasium by involving the local community, school resources, and school personnel to create a holistic picture of wellness based on your school or district.

The lesson plans were created assuming teachers have access to the following equipment: laptop or tablet computer, whiteboard, dry-erase markers, copier, and a Bluetooth music player. A projector is referenced in several lessons, but alternative options are listed. The following terms are used as routines in some lessons. Periodically change groupings so students cooperate with other members of the class:

- Calling all kids—Students sit in a predetermined pattern for a teacher explanation.
- Dancing duo—Students pair up and do a brief move when they meet their partner.
- Learning teams—Students sit in predetermined groups depending on the size needed.

Chapter 5

Lesson Plans
for Grades K-2

Lesson plan topic	Grade level	Page	Resources
Calling 9-1-1, Listening, and Locomotor Skills	K-1	73	1: Phone Printouts 2: Assessment of Steps for Calling 9-1-1
Changing Families, Body Parts, Balance, Shapes, and Levels	2	77	1: Family Exit Ticket 2: Family Balance Collage
Dimensions of Wellness and Balance	1-2	80	1: Dimensions of Wellness 2: Tangram Shapes 3: Tangram Challenges 4: Calming Yoga for Kids 5: Wellness Self-Assessment
Fire Safety, Weight Transfer, Rolling, and Locomotor Skills	2	84	1: Rolling Peer Assessment
Getting Enough Sleep and Body Actions	K-2	90	1: Shape Peer Assessment 2: Sleep Log
Goals, Directions, and Pathways	K-1	94	1: Physical Activity Goal Log
Handwashing, Overhand Throw, and Locomotor Skills	2-3	98	1: Peer Assessment of Overhand Throw 2: Wash Your Hands Sign 3: How to Wash Your Hands 4: Handwashing Peer Assessment
Hazardous Household Products, Locomotor Skills, and Instep Kick	K-1	102	1: Pictures of Household Products 2: Instep Kick Self-Assessment Task Sheet 3: Take-Home Survey Worksheet
Healthy Relationships and Dribbling With Feet	1-2	106	1: A Friend 2: Dribbling and Trapping Peer Assessment
Hydration and Dribbling With Hands	K-2	110	1: Water Consumption Log Sheet 2: Dribbling Peer Assessment
Living Smoke Free, Jumping, Leaping, and Striking	K-2	113	1: Diagram of Respiratory System 2: Leaping and Jumping Assessment
Managing Troublesome Feelings, Seeking Help, and Overhand Throw	2	117	1: Emoji Task Cards 2: Overhand Throw Peer Assessment
Medicine Safety, Underhand Throw, and Space	K	123	1: Medicine Pictures 2: Underhand Throw Assessment
Peer Pressure, Mirror and Match, and Speed	1	127	1: Mirror and Match Assessment
Recycling, Underhand Toss, and Striking	K-1	130	1: To Be or Not to Be Recycled? 2: Underhand Throwing and Striking Assessment
Respiratory System and Underhand Roll	2-3	133	1: Diagram of Respiratory System
Secondhand Smoke and Locomotor Skills	K-2	136	1: Skipping Peer Assessment 2: Exit Ticket
Senses, Trust, and Dribbling	1	140	1: Senses Worksheet 2: ASL Alphabet 3: Eye Chart 4: Dribbling Assessment
Sneezing, Coughing, Cooperation, and Fundamental Movement Skills	1	144	1: Running Technique Assessment

Calling 9-1-1, Listening, and Locomotor Skills

GRADE LEVEL: K-1

INTRODUCTORY INFORMATION

SHAPE America Outcomes

- S1.E1.1 Hops, gallops, jogs, and slides using a mature pattern.
- S2.E3.1a Differentiates between fast and slow speeds.
- S2.E3.1b Differentiates between strong and light force.
- S4.E1.K Follows directions in group settings (e.g., safe behaviors, following rules, taking turns).
- S4.E6.1 Follows teacher directions for safe participation and proper use of equipment without teacher reminders.

National Health Education Performance Indicators

- 4.5.1 Demonstrate effective verbal and nonverbal communication skills to enhance health.
- 5.5.2 Analyze when assistance is needed when making a health-related decision.

Lesson Objectives

Students will be able to do the following:

- Identify when it is appropriate to call 9-1-1.
- Perform the steps for calling 9-1-1 correctly based on the phone type.
- Demonstrate correct technique for the hop, gallop, jog, and slide.
- Differentiate between speeds and forces.
- Follow directions given by the teacher.

Learning Materials and Technology

- 1 parachute
- 30 fleece balls
- 1 roll of scotch tape
- 1 cell phone
- Optional: 1 phone with a cord connected to the base
- Optional: 1 cordless phone with a base
- Resource handouts from HK*Propel*
  - Resource 1: 1 printout
  - Resource 2: 1 printout

Skill Cues

Hop

- Balance on one foot.
- The nonhopping leg is off the ground and bent at 90 degrees.
- Bend and extend (push off) the hopping leg to produce a flight phase.
- The nonhopping leg swings up and forward to produce additional force.
- Arms are bent at the elbow and swing from back to front in coordination with the hopping action.

Gallop

- Step forward with the lead foot.
- Push off the trail foot forcefully enough to achieve a flight phase.
- The trail foot catches up to the lead leg by touching the heel.
- Coordinate the arm swing forward with the motion of the legs to achieve distance and height.
- Land on the ball of the lead foot, with the trail foot behind the lead foot.

Jog

- Keep your head up and facing straight ahead.
- Push off of one foot to create a flight phase; swing the opposite arm forward.
- Strike with the foot underneath the body.
- Keep the shoulders open, relaxed, and down.
- Keep the arms close to the torso, bent at 90 degrees, and moving diagonally.

Slide

- Turn the body sideways to the direction of travel.
- Keep the feet shoulder width apart and arms extended sideways.
- Step to the side with the lead foot.
- Push off with the trail foot so it produces a flight phase and then chases the lead foot.
- Land on the trail foot and then the lead foot.

Skip

- Step forward with the lead foot and hop.
- Raise the opposite knee to waist height.
- The arm on the same side as the hopping foot swings up and forward; the other arm is back.
- Repeat the pattern by alternating the right and left foot.

LEARNING ACTIVITIES

Lesson Introduction

- **WHAT** are we learning today? Students will learn how to tell if there is a real emergency and when to call 9-1-1. They will also practice locomotor skills.
- **WHY** are we learning this? Being able to call 9-1-1 can be a lifesaving skill. If there is an emergency, students will need to listen carefully, act quickly, and dial 9-1-1 to summon help.
- **HOW** will learning be measured? The teacher will complete an assessment of the steps for correctly calling 9-1-1 (resource 2).

Activity 1: Video and Discussion (15 minutes)

Set up the parachute in one portion of the gym. Gather students in another portion of the gym for activity 1. Show students the YouTube video "When and How to Call 9-1-1." (See the lesson plan links file on HK*Propel* for a link to this video.) Stop the video periodically to highlight the purpose of 9-1-1, how to call using different types of phones, and which scenarios describe an emergency and which do not. Show students how to call using a cell phone and, if available, a corded phone and a cordless phone.

Activity 2: Warm-Up (5 minutes)

Demonstrate how to perform the hop, jog, gallop, slide, and skip. When the music starts, students begin moving around the gym. You will call out different fundamental movement skills while students are moving: hop, skip, gallop, jog, and slide. When the music stops, call out a fitness skill: jumping jacks, push-ups (provide choices such as wall push-ups, modified push-ups, and regular push-ups), lunges, or air squats.

Activity 3: Parachute Progressions (15 minutes)

Instruct students to sit alongside the parachute without touching it, one student per color. During an emergency, it is important that children listen to adults the first time and do exactly as they are told. Explain that students will practice good listening skills using the parachute.

Progress through the following sequence. Alternate a physical activity with a 9-1-1 scenario (listed later in the lesson plan). Read the scenario, and at the count of 3, students show thumbs-up against their chest if 9-1-1 should be called. If not, they show thumbs-down against their chest. If 9-1-1 should be called, pick a parachute color. Students at that color stand up, go to one of the six phone print-outs taped to the gym wall, and pretend to dial 9-1-1. When they are connected to the dispatcher, they hold their hand up to their ear and wait. Next, the teacher pretends to be the dispatcher and asks any or all of the following questions: Do you need police, fire, or ambulance? What is your emergency? What is your name? What is the location of your emergency? Students remain on the call until you ask them to hang up, at which time they return to the parachute.

1. Walk the chute—Hold the parachute waist high with one hand and walk in a clockwise direction (explain the term *clockwise*) and then walk counterclockwise (explain the term). While the students are moving, vary the fundamental movement skill (hop, jog, gallop, slide, and skip). (Sliding sideways requires students to hold the parachute with both hands. Their tummies face the parachute.) Remind students to practice excellent listening skills. Stop, and then read a 9-1-1 scenario.

2. Popcorn—Pop fleece balls up and down in the middle of the parachute. Pop them with light force, then medium force, and finally a strong force. Next, try to pop them out in the least amount of time possible. Repeat and try to beat the previous time record. Stop, and then read a 9-1-1 scenario.

3. Popcorn 2—Have one side of the parachute compete against the other side. Once all fleece balls have been knocked out, each team counts the number on their side. The team with the fewest balls wins. Stop, and then read a 9-1-1 scenario.

4. Submarine—Students make waves by rippling the parachute with a medium force. Call out a color; students at that color switch places under the raging sea. They crawl at a low level, trying not to touch the parachute. Stop, and then read a 9-1-1 scenario.

5. Mushroom—Students lift the parachute high above their heads, and when you say "down," students pull the parachute down behind them and sit on its edge. They cover the openings so as little air escapes as possible and the mushroom stays up longer. Stop, and then read a 9-1-1 scenario.

6. Propel—Use one ball and propel it as high as possible, potentially hitting the ceiling. Stop, and then read a 9-1-1 scenario.

9-1-1 Scenarios

1. You want to practice calling 9-1-1 to see what it is really like.
2. Your friend falls off their bike, hits their head, and isn't moving.
3. You're home alone with an adult and they start choking.
4. You see a tree fall over in your yard; it doesn't hurt anyone or anything.
5. You see a car accident and someone is hurt.
6. You scraped your knee falling off your scooter.
7. You notice a stranger in the bushes outside your house.

8. You were playing with matches and started a fire outside that is getting bigger.
9. You want help baking cookies.
10. You're bored.
11. Your bike is missing.

Assessment

Complete the assessment (resource 2) as students are using the phone printouts on the wall. Be sure students at all colors have an opportunity to call 9-1-1. Indicate on the assessment whether any of the steps were performed incorrectly.

Closure

Ask students what they should do if their location is unknown (answer: describe landmarks near them). Show students the various ways to activate the emergency button on different types of phones, whether the screen is locked or not. This is another option for calling 9-1-1. Remind students that calling 9-1-1 is not a game; calling a dispatcher as a joke might take time away from someone who needs the service. In addition, they and their parents or caregivers could get in trouble for misusing the system.

Changing Families, Body Parts, Balance, Shapes, and Levels

INTRODUCTORY INFORMATION

SHAPE America Outcomes

- S1.E7.2a Balances on different bases of support, combining levels and shapes.
- S1.E7.2b Balances in an inverted position with stillness and supportive base.

National Health Education Performance Indicators

- 1.2.1 Identify that healthy behaviors impact personal health.
- 2.2.1 Identify how the family influences personal health practices and behaviors.

Lesson Objectives

Students will be able to do the following:

- Perform wide, narrow, and twisted shapes on different body parts at different levels while maintaining control and balance.
- Connect shapes to make a family shape puzzle or collage while maintaining control and balance.
- Compare their family size and shape to others.
- Describe how families grow and change.
- Identify the benefits of healthy family relationships.
- Illustrate how their family helps them be healthy.

Learning Materials and Technology

- 2 gymnastic mats per learning team
- 1 hoop
- 2 gymnastic ribbons
- 1 beach ball (12 in. or 30.5 cm)
- 2 beanbags
- 1 foam trapezoid shape

- 1 tablet per learning team, with accessibility features such as text to talk enabled
- Blank puzzle pieces
- 5 or 6 markers or crayons per learning team
- Resource handouts from HK*Propel*
  - Resource 1: 1 per student
  - Resource 2: 1 per student

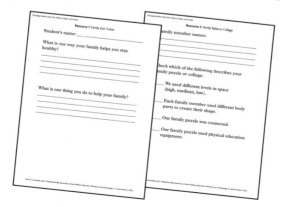

LEARNING ACTIVITIES

Lesson Introduction

- **WHAT** are we learning today? Students will create a shape puzzle (or collage) with their bodies to represent the members of a family. Students also will learn how families are the same and different from each other and how families change over time.

- **WHY** are we learning this? It is important to realize that not all families are the same and that students should appreciate each other's families. Families come in many sizes and shapes. Sometimes not all family members live together. For example, grandparents might live far away, or parents might be divorced. Sometimes families have lots of members living with them, including aunts, uncles, cousins, and grandparents. Sometimes people who are not related to each other form a family.

- **HOW** will learning be measured? Students will complete an exit ticket (resource 1) about their family. Students will also look at or have a picture described of their group family puzzle or collage and determine whether they used different levels and body parts (resource 2).

Activity 1: Making Individual Shapes With Family (10-15 minutes)

Prior to the start of this activity, place two gymnastic mats together to make a large square for each learning team. Start this activity by asking some or all of the following questions and write the student responses on a whiteboard.

- How many of you have three, four, five, or more family members?
- Does anyone have a grandma, grandpa, aunt, or uncle in your family?
- Who has someone living with you that we have not talked about?
- How do families change?
- What are fun things that you do with your family?
- What helps the members of your family get along with each other?
- What do you do to help your family?
- What do your family members do to help you stay healthy? These are possible answers: Care about you, protect and take care of you, teach you and help you learn new things, help you grow up, help when you have problems, spend time with you, help you act in healthy ways.

Next, students will get into their learning teams (e.g., five teams of six students per team). Students who sit in chairs can be assisted to the floor, or their learning team will be at a table that is accessible to those who sit in chairs.

Students are gathered in a listening and demonstration area. Demonstrate how to make three different balances on different body parts at different levels, describing each. Then verbally guide family members (learning team members) to create at least three shapes in their own personal space on their family's gymnastic mat or on the floor in an accessible area. Provide descriptive feedback such as "I see that you are on one hand and one foot and your other leg is extended into the air and you are staying balanced. Awesome job!" "Did you make a shape at a high, medium, and low level"? "Are your shapes on different body parts?"

After students have had time to create different balances, each family can demonstrate their individual shapes and balances for other families.

Activity 2: Comparing Family Puzzles and Making a Family Puzzle or Collage (10-15 minutes)

Part A

Give each student a puzzle piece for each family member living with them. Students write the name of a family member on a puzzle piece. Assign a scribe to students who need one. Use a braille labeler if needed. If students write large, they may use more than one piece per name. Next, students put their puzzle together and share it with their learning team family. Move around the gymnasium to listen and comment on family discussions.

Part B

Explain that learning team families will make a collage or group puzzle by connecting each individual's balance or shape to others in the group. Demonstrate how to connect a shape with a student or two. Options are to physically touch another family member or simply to move members closer together. You can also explain that each family member can choose their favorite balance shape from activity 1. Remind students to use different body parts, different levels, and different shapes.

Part C

Offer each learning team a piece of equipment (hoop, beach ball, gymnastic ribbons, trapezoid shape, or beanbags). Challenge students to incorporate the piece or pieces of equipment into their family puzzle.

Part D

Take a photo of each learning team family on a tablet (one for each team). Teams collectively complete an assessment of their family collage or puzzle, using resource 2. Each family must look at their picture on the tablet or have it described to them to complete the assessment form. Assessment forms should be accessible to those who cannot use a pen or pencil; those who need large print, pictures, or braille labels to read; and to those who need a reader and possibly a scribe.

Closure

Explain to students that they have learned how families are different and how they might grow and change. Ask them to do a think-pair-share activity with a classmate sitting close to them. They should talk about one difference between their families and something that is similar. Ask student partner groups to share their responses.

Universal Design for Learning

The following are additional universal design for learning considerations for all learners:

- Consider using peer buddies to move as partners with students who need more support.
- Use cones around an area if students cannot access the mats.
- When assessing using worksheets, provide means of expression such as pointing to pictures, using a communication device, answering yes or no questions, sending home worksheets to be transcribed in text to talk, using a scribe, reading out loud, and using braille when requested.
- Provide additional means to check for understanding for all by asking yes or no questions or having students say or use sign language cue words when requested.
- Use a tablet to play a video model of a variety of possible shapes on loop.
- Provide paraeducators and classroom teachers with the lesson plan or cue words for students who need to program those words (e.g., family descriptions) into their communication devices.
- Provide individual cards with pictures of a variety of body shape and balance ideas.
- Work with an American Sign Language interpreter, if there is one, for vocabulary words directly related to this lesson (e.g., the names of body movements).
- Provide some students with their directions in words, as pictures, or in braille.
- Provide alternative means to access the print assessments such as a scribe, a reader, an MP3 player asking the questions, braille, or putting stickers on the worksheet instead of using a pen.

Dimensions of Wellness and Balance

GRADE LEVEL: 1-2

INTRODUCTORY INFORMATION

SHAPE America Outcomes

- S1.E7.2a Balances on different bases of support, combining levels and shapes.
- S5.E1.2 Recognizes the value of "good health balance."
- S5.E1.1 Identifies physical activity as a component of good health.

National Health Education Performance Indicators

- 1.2.1 Identify that healthy behaviors affect personal health.
- 1.2.2 Recognize that there are multiple dimensions of health.
- 7.2.1 Demonstrate healthy practices and behaviors to maintain or improve personal health.

Lesson Objectives

Students will be able to do the following:

- Identify four of the seven dimensions of wellness.
- Describe how the dimensions are interrelated and affect one another.
- Demonstrate both static and dynamic balance.

This is a two-day lesson.

Learning Materials and Technology

- 1 pedometer per student
- 1 balance board (with 4-6 strings attached) per 4 students
- 1 fleece ball per 4 students
- 1 tennis ball per 4 students
- 1 hanger hung with paper strips labeled with the dimensions of wellness (mobile)
- 1 large printout of graphic of allergens
- 10 foam shapes
- 5 jump ropes
- 2 tall cones

- 1 tunnel
- 2 folding mats
- 10 hoops
- 7 task cards with the name of each dimension of wellness on a different card
- Resource handouts from HK*Propel*
  - Resource 1: 1 printout
  - Resource 2: 2 envelopes of cutup tangram shapes
  - Resource 3: 2 printouts
  - Resource 4: 2 printouts
  - Resource 5: 1 printout per student

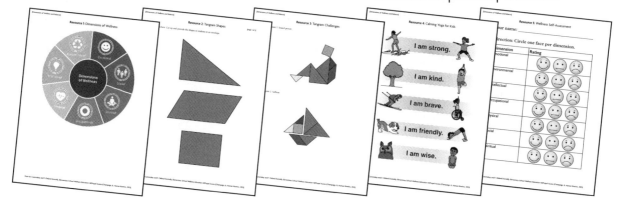

Skill Cues

Balance

- Keep arms out to the side.
- Focus eyes forward (not down).
- Keep the center of the body over the base of support.
- Bend the joints to absorb force.
- Adjust the body to maintain balance.

LEARNING ACTIVITIES

Lesson Introduction

- **WHAT** are we learning today? Students will learn about different ways to stay healthy and to keep their balance.
- **WHY** are we learning this? Wellness has different parts and is made up of more than just physical wellness. It includes taking care of emotions, friendships, the environment, and other areas of life. Maintaining each component in a balanced way leads to positive overall health. If one of the dimensions gets out of balance, it can negatively affect other components in a dominolike fashion.
- **HOW** will learning be measured? Students will complete a dimensions of wellness self-assessment (resource 5).

Activity 1: Wellness Stations (40 minutes)

Show and discuss the Dimensions of Wellness (resource 1). Convey that overall wellness is made up of different components and that the components can affect one another. For example, too many allergens, such as dust, can affect physical health, or a lack of emotional control can affect relationships with friends (social). Common allergens in the home include dust, pollen from trees and plants, cat and dog hair, tiny pieces of fabric from clothes, carpeting, stuffed animals, and cooking residues. When sunlight comes through a window, students may be able to see the allergens floating in the air. Ask whether anyone has seen that. If so, what did it look like?

To learn about the different dimensions of wellness, students will rotate through the following stations. Label each station with a task card identifying the aligned dimension of wellness. (Note that this lesson plan purposely does not discuss the financial dimension of wellness.) Demonstrate each dimension with the assistance of students, four students per station.

1. Physical Wellness

Back-to-back—Student pairs sit back-to-back on the floor. They must stand up using the other person for support. Their choices are (1) hook elbows and try to stand up, (2) use their hands to push up from the floor, or (3) perform without using their hands or arms (only their backs touching). Attempt first with two students, then three and four. Students perform back-to-back over mats on the floor.

Partner pull-up—Partners sit facing each other, with their toes touching. They reach forward, bend their knees, grasp hands, and pull in an attempt to stand up and then sit down. Attempt first with two students, then three and four. Students perform partner pull-up over mats on the floor.

2. Intellectual Wellness

Tangrams—Cut up two copies of the tangram shapes (resource 2) and place each set in a separate envelope. Students form groups of two. Each group is given one set of tangram shapes. Students attempt to use the shapes to form the image of a seated person. If they are successful, repeat the activity using the sailboat shape. All pieces will be used. When finished, put the shapes back into the envelope for the next group. The answers to both tangrams are provided on resource 3.

3. Environmental Wellness

Hike—One of the best ways to promote physical activity and protecting the environment is by hiking. Design a "hiking trail" in the gym and have students follow it. A sample map is shown. Before starting, each student puts on a pedometer and resets the step count. (Pedometer setup would have been taught in a prior lesson.) Add all or some of the following elements to the trail:

- Foam balance shapes to simulate walking on large rocks
- Two ropes in a V shape to simulate a river to leap over (children may choose to leap over a narrow or wide end)
- Ropes suspended between tall cones to crawl under or leap over to simulate brush in the woods
- A tunnel to crawl through to simulate a hollow log
- Hoops to jump in and out of to simulate jumping over muddy parts of the trail
- Jump ropes in a line to walk on to simulate balancing on a log

4. Social Wellness

Spaghetti soup—Tie the ends of a 20-foot (6 m) rope (or jump ropes) together so they won't come apart. Jumble or coil the rope on the floor in a pile (see the photo). Students surround the rope, bend over, and grab a section of rope on the opposite side with one hand. Once they grab the rope, they can't move their hand. Students stand up and return the rope to a circle formation without releasing their grip.

Matthew Cummiskey

5. Emotional Wellness

Calming yoga—The world can be a busy place. A good solution is to step back, breathe deeply, and try simple yoga poses to help relax. Students complete each pose on resource 4. If a student finishes all the poses in a sequence before you indicate that time is up, they should repeat the sequence.

6. Spiritual Wellness

Spiritual wellness is about having a sense of meaning and purpose in one's life. Show a video that highlights how athletes fought for diversity, equity, and inclusion. (See the lesson plan links file on *HKPropel* for a link to a video on Jackie Robinson.)

7. Occupational Wellness

Occupational wellness is about feeling satisfied and productive about your job or occupation. For kids in school, their job is to be a good student. Another occupation is being a dancer. Have students follow a dance video projected onto an appropriate gymnasium space or shown on a laptop. (See the lesson plan links file on HK*Propel* for a link to a sample video.)

Activity 2: Balance (20 minutes)

Discuss how the dimensions of wellness are interconnected. Use a hanger mobile to illustrate the dimensions and how they must be equally spaced for the hanger to be balanced. Students should strive to be balanced and achieve optimal health in all dimensions. If one dimension becomes unhealthy, the imbalance can spread to other dimensions. The next activity works on balance, physical wellness, and spiritual wellness.

Students will in succession balance a beanbag on their head, shoulder, elbow, knee, and foot in a stationary position. When the music starts, students walk around the gym balancing the beanbag on body parts called out by the teacher. Vary the speed (slow, medium, fast) and the fundamental movement skill depending on the age and skill level of the students. If the beanbag falls off, the student picks it up and resumes.

Continue the activity, but now if a beanbag falls off, the student must freeze and wait for another student to pick it up. If the rescuer's beanbag falls off, both students are frozen. They stay frozen until another player frees them.

When the music stops, students balance on one body part (BP), then two BPs, three BPs, four BPs, and a crazy shape. Repeat, but this time, go around and gently nudge students to see if you can get them off balance. Discuss how wide bases of support are more stable than narrow ones.

Have students play balance tag. Balance tag is a version of everybody's it tag where each student can tag any other student. If tagged or the beanbag falls off, students hold a low or high balance shape to a count of 10 and then resume the game.

Activity 3: Balance Board (20 minutes)

Students form groups of four and are given one balance board (see the photo). A balance board can be made from a 2-by-3-foot (.6-by-1 m) panel of rigid foam, a double-thick sheet of cardboard, or plywood. At multiple locations, a 5-foot (1.5 m) string is tied. Place a ball in the center of the board. For younger grades use a fleece ball; older grades can use a tennis ball. The ball represents students, and the strings represent the dimensions of wellness. When you say go, each group walks around the gym trying to keep their ball on the board. The group must communicate (social wellness) and maintain control of their emotions (emotional wellness). If the ball falls off, the group performs five jumping jacks and continues.

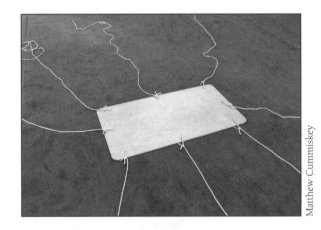

Matthew Cummiskey

Extensions

- Extra balls—Use multiple balls, up to one for each person holding a rope.
- Race—Line up all groups on one end of the gym and see who can navigate to the other end and back first. If a group's ball falls off, they must sing the entire refrain of "Row, Row, Row Your Boat" and then continue. Limit each group's speed to a minimum of a fast walk.
- Tag—Spread all groups throughout the gym. If tagged by another group or their ball falls off, all group members do a funny dance.

Closure

Students complete the dimensions of wellness self-assessment (resource 5) with a focus on physical, intellectual, emotional, and social awareness. Discuss what students perceive as their stronger areas of wellness and what areas need improvement.

Fire Safety, Weight Transfer, Rolling, and Locomotor Skills

GRADE LEVEL: 2

INTRODUCTORY INFORMATION

SHAPE America Outcomes

- S1.E8.1 Transfers weight from one body part to another.
- S1. E9.1 Rolls with either a narrow or curled body shape.
- S1.E1.1 Hops, gallops, jogs, and slides using a mature pattern.

National Health Education Performance Indicators

- 3.2.1 Identify trusted adults and professionals who can help promote health.

Lesson Objectives

Students will be able to do the following:

- Transfer weight from feet to hands while crawling at a low level.
- Perform a log roll, keeping legs tight together and arms extended straight overhead, on a mat and incline surface.
- Crawl to the top of and then back down a ladder positioned on a low to medium incline.
- Use a variety of locomotor skills to travel through an obstacle course that simulates an escape route from one's home in case of fire.
- With assistance from their caregiver, draw a fire escape route of their home.
- With assistance from their caregiver, find out if their home has ample smoke detectors and a fire extinguisher.

Learning Materials and Technology

- 10 tall cones
- 5 long ropes
- 2 trapezoid foam shapes (to move over)
- 3 foam shapes for obstacle course (to move through)
- 25 poly spots
- 10 standard cones

- 4 hoops
- 4 hoop holders
- 1 Bluetooth speaker
- 5 gymnastic mats
- Resource handout from HK*Propel*
  - Resource 1: 1 per student

Skill Cues

Log Roll

- Extend the arms overhead.
- Keep the body tight.
- Extend the legs straight like a pencil.
- Use the core to initiate the rolling action.
- Alternative movements can include rotating a wheelchair 360 degrees in a tight area; rotating the head from one side to another; extending the legs only and keeping them together;

extending the arms only to the front, side, or above the head; performing trunk twists from a sitting position; and rolling from front to back or back to front.

Gallop

- Step forward with the lead foot.
- Push off the trail foot forcefully enough to achieve a flight phase.
- The trail foot catches up to the lead leg by touching the heel.
- Coordinate the arm swing forward with the motion of the legs to achieve distance and height.
- Land on the ball of the lead foot, with the trail foot behind the lead foot.

Slide

- Turn the body sideways to the direction of travel.
- Keep the feet shoulder-width apart and arms extended sideways.
- Step to the side with the lead foot.
- Push off with the trail foot so it produces a flight phase and then chases the lead foot.
- Land on the trail foot and then the lead foot.
- Alternative movements can include rotating the body to the right or left while sitting; extending the arms only to the side at shoulder level; moving the hands or fingers in an out and in (open and shut) pattern; moving the legs in an open and shut pattern while lying on the back on a mat (like a jumping jack); moving a wheelchair in a pattern such as quarter turn to the right and push four times, then quarter turn to the left and push four times.

Skip

- Step forward with the lead foot and hop.
- Raise the opposite knee to waist height.
- The arm on the same side as the hopping foot swings up and forward; the other arm is back.
- Repeat the pattern by alternating the right and left foot.
- Alternative movements can include raising one knee at a time from a sitting position; stepping one foot at a time off a footrest or the floor from a seated position; swinging the arms only in an alternating motion from a stationary standing or sitting position; moving a wheelchair in a pattern such as two arm pushes and then one arm push or two big pushes and then swing the arm right and left.

Hop

- Balance on one foot.
- The nonhopping leg is off the ground and bent at 90 degrees.
- Bend and extend the hopping leg to produce a flight phase.
- The nonhopping leg swings up and forward to produce additional force.
- Arms are bent at the elbow and swing from back to front in coordination with the hopping action.
- Alternative movements can include bending one knee and then the other from a lying or sitting position; with arms bent at elbows, swinging the arms only forward and back; moving a wheelchair in a pattern such as push wheelchair–swing arms and repeat action.

Leap

- Run and take off from one foot forcefully to create a flight phase.
- Swing arms up and forward to aid take off.
- Extend the opposite leg forward.

- Land on the opposite foot.
- Bend the knees to absorb force.
- Alternative movements can include extending the legs from a sitting position one at a time; performing only the arm movement of a leap, with one arm in front and the other behind, with a trunk twist; move a wheelchair in a pattern such as four fast pushes, glide with one arm in front and one toward the rear; while lying on the side, imitate the way a leap would look in a frozen position, with one leg forward and one back and arms in opposition.

Jump: Two Feet to Two Feet

- Swing both arms back behind the buttocks.
- Bend the knees.
- Swing the arms forward and up.
- Push off both feet simultaneously.
- Land on both feet simultaneously and bend the knees.
- Reach arms forward.
- Alternative movements can include swinging the arms from back to front while sitting or lying on the side or from a half-kneeling position; bending both knees at the same time from sitting or lying; swinging only the arms forward and up from sitting or lying; putting both feet in the air simultaneously from sitting or lying; moving a wheelchair by giving one big wheel push and then gliding with the arms reaching forward.

LEARNING ACTIVITIES

Lesson Introduction

- **WHAT** are we learning today? Students will learn how to safely respond to an emergency. They will learn how to dial 9-1-1, how to respond to a fire in their house, and investigate how to prevent fires in their home.
- **WHY** are we learning this? It is important that students and their families understand how to prevent fires in their homes and have a plan for escaping from their homes in case of a fire.
- **HOW** will learning be measured? Student performance will be measured through a formative assessment on the completed drawing of their fire escape route from their home and their performance of the log roll or alternative movement such as a wheelchair push or half log roll (resource 1).

Flipped Classroom Activity

Children will view an age-appropriate screen recording of dialing 9-1-1. (See the lesson plan links file on *HKPropel* for a sample video.)

Activity 1: Fire Safety Stations (7-20 minutes)

Set up four stations before class begins as described the next section. Students in the stations will start on a music cue or a pretend fire alarm and stop when the music stops or on a cue from you. A Bluetooth speaker and a phone with music that simulates a fire station bell could be used. Alternative ideas include having students with sensory issues wear noise-canceling headphones and use a picture of the fire alarm and cues such as "the fire alarm is ringing, what do we do now?"

Station A: Crawling

Students at this station practice crawling at a low level to avoid the smoke that naturally rises during a fire. Children begin at a designated starting point and crawl under the ropes. Alternative movements can include stringing a rope across several cones tall enough for someone to lie on a scooter to scoot through or wheel under if using a wheelchair. Include pictures next to the roped cones that show someone crawling; allow students to scoot on their bottom or push themselves forward using their feet.

- Movement task: Crawling using hands and feet at a very low level along the ground.
- Setup: Space several tall cones or chairs through the station. Put long or short jump ropes into the slats on the cones or tie them to the chairs. The setup needs to be wide enough for one or two students to crawl under simultaneously or for a wheelchair or walker. Indicate the direction of travel with arrows on the floor. Paper smoke clouds may be hung from the ropes.

Station B: Stop, Drop, and Roll

Students practice a log roll or series of log rolls after stopping and dropping. Students previously have practiced the log roll. Alternative movements can include rotating a wheelchair 360 degrees in a tight area; rotating the head from one side to another; extending the legs only and keeping them together; extending the arms to the front, side, or above the head; performing trunk twists from a sitting position; and rolling from front to back or back to front.

- Movement task: Explains that if a student's clothes were on fire, it is important to immediately stop, drop to the ground, and roll to put out the fire. Demonstrate this two or three times. On your signal, students practice these three skills. A peer assessment (resource 1) could be conducted at this station. This assessment should be enlarged to accommodate children's writing skill level. If using a wheelchair, put on brakes, transfer to floor, and roll or crawl.
- Setup: Assign one to three students per mat and spread the mats out in the station.

Station C: Climb

Use developmental gymnastics equipment, trestle and ladder, and place a stuffed animal at the top. Children go up the ladder to rescue a person (the stuffed animal). You could also use trapezoid foam shapes and folded mats to create a gradual incline if a ladder is not available. Alternative movements can include moving the hands to virtually climb a ladder that is taped to the wall; moving hands in a climbing motion from a sitting or lying position; moving legs in a marching manner while sitting, standing stationary on floor, or lying, as if climbing a ladder; having an adult or peer buddy hold an agility ladder in front of a sitting or stationary standing student while the student uses the hands to "climb" by moving one hand after the other onto the rungs, with a stuffed animal taped to one rung.

- Movement task: The student crawls up the ladder or folded mats, rescues the stuffed animal, and crawls back down the ladder.
- Setup: Place a ladder or mats resting on a trapezoidal foam shape. The top of the mats should be two feet (.6 m) off the ground. Place at least three of these within the station. Position a stuffed animal at the top of the ladder to simulate a person to be rescued from a house window.

Station D: Fire Escape Route

Students move through an obstacle course that simulates an escape route from their house. Create an obstacle course of shapes to crawl under and poly spots to jump on, to hop on, to slide between, and to leap from one to another. Task cards to elicit a specific locomotor skill could be placed on cones to remind students what to perform. Equipment to create the escape route could include poly spots, foam shapes, solid foam shapes to crawl over, plastic arrows to mark escape route, and ropes hung on cones. A sample section of the escape route is provided here.

Alternatives for each locomotor movement required could include using an arm movement from a sitting or stationary position in a manner similar to the locomotor movement or using a movement pattern in a wheelchair, such as wheeling backward or using a certain number of pushes forward before doing a 360-degree turn.

Closure

Lead a discussion on the purpose of the lesson. Students could do a think-pair-share activity and answer the following questions:

- If your clothes catch on fire, what should you do?
- If you think there is a real emergency, what should you do?
- What happens when you call 9-1-1? What information do you need to give the person you are talking to?

Alternate ways to check for understanding include informing the classroom teacher about the lesson so that augmentative communication devices can have fire safety words programmed in; using yes or no questions; using statements such as "If you think you should do 'this,' nod your head"; displaying a poster that someone can point to instead of verbalizing; using photos and asking "Which one is the correct way to . . ."

A sample drawing of a fire safety escape route from a house is shown here. This could be sent to parents as an example or posted on the school's learning management system. Children, with their caregiver's help, would draw their own escape route and bring it to school. An alternative would be to collaborate with the classroom teacher and draw an escape route from their classroom through the school to a safe exit outside of the school.

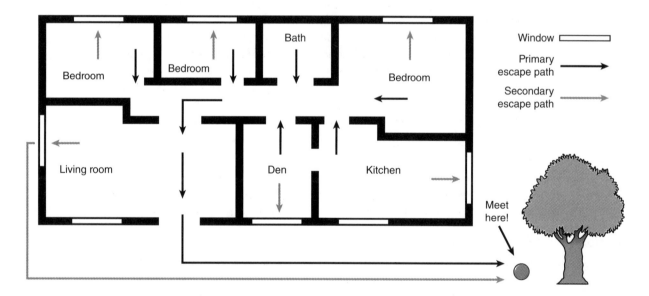

Universal Design for Learning

The following are additional universal design for learning considerations for all learners:

- Consider smaller groupings such as one-on-one for students who need less sensory information.
- Decrease the speed of movements and response to the activities by asking children to move slowly.
- Provide additional task meaningfulness by using photos of children in the class performing log roll, gallop, skip, hop, and jump. Also include photos of the alternative movements.

- When assessing children whose mobility is different from others, consider using broader language and breaking the tasks into more levels of achievement, especially at the beginning of the task.
- Consider using floor tape to make an alley that is large enough for students who use wheelchairs and other assistive devices or use a human guide.
- Provide additional means to check for understandings by asking yes or no questions, by having students say or use sign language cue words when requested, or by doing the movement for you before they are assessed.
- Use cones to help designate an area of play for students who need that extra information.
- Use a tablet to display a video model of each of the skills of hopping, jumping, galloping, log rolling, leaping, skipping, and sliding.
- Change the goal of the activity to include looking in the direction of the movement, pointing to the correct motor skill, using assistance, tolerating a particular movement, or moving arms only.
- Provide paraeducators and classroom teachers with the lesson plan or cue cards for their role with students.
- Use peer buddies for students who might need additional demonstrations or cue words.
- Provide students who do not use print or read visually with auditory cues or braille. Provide students with low vision with large bold print. Use pictures with words.

Getting Enough Sleep and Body Actions

GRADE LEVEL: K-2

INTRODUCTORY INFORMATION

SHAPE America Outcomes

- S1.E10.K Contrasts the actions of curling and stretching.
- S1.E10.1 Demonstrates twisting, curling, bending, and stretching actions.
- S1.E10.2 Differentiates among twisting, curling, bending, and stretching actions.

National Health Education Performance Indicators

- 1.2.1 Identify that healthy behaviors impact personal health.
- 6.2.1 Identify a short-term personal health goal and take action toward achieving the goal.
- 7.2.1 Demonstrate healthy practices and behaviors to maintain or improve personal health.

Lesson Objectives

Students will be able to do the following:

- Make a variety of shapes with different body parts at different levels.
- Connect shapes by performing movement transitions such as stretching to change from one shape to another.
- Explain how many hours of sleep students their age need.
- Explain the benefits of getting enough sleep.
- With the help of a caregiver, determine how many hours of sleep they get over a period of seven days.

Learning Materials and Technology

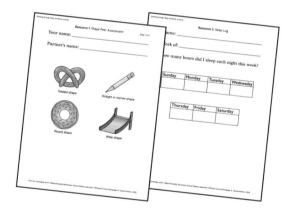

- 10 laminated pictures of different shapes (at least one set with puff paint outlining the shapes)
- 1 music player with Bluetooth
- 1 drum
- 1 laptop
- Resource handouts from HK*Propel*
  - Resource 1: 1 per student
  - Resource 2: 1 per student

LEARNING ACTIVITIES

Lesson Introduction

- **WHAT** are we learning today? Students will make up a creative dance about sleep. They will explore making different sleeping shapes with their bodies while performing them at different levels and connecting the shapes with different movements like stretching or yawning. Students will learn why it is important to get the right amount of sleep and examine how much sleep they get every night for a week. Finally, students will learn how to set a short-term goal related to getting enough sleep every night.

- **WHY** are we learning this? Getting enough sleep helps students' brains and bodies work better. It prepares them for learning every day and provides them with the energy to be physically active.
- **HOW** will learning be measured? During a peer assessment (resource 1), students will observe a partner making at least three shapes while using a stretching or yawning action to move from one shape to another. Students, with assistance of their caregivers, will complete a weeklong log (resource 2) of how much sleep they get.

Learning Activity 1: Benefits of Sleep (10 minutes)

Show a video clip on the benefits of sleep. (See the lesson plan links file on HK*Propel* for a sample video.) The video should have an auditory description and closed captioning. Students do a think-pair-share activity at the end to answer these questions on the whiteboard:

1. Why is sleep so important? (Answer: helps process information, helps children grow, reduces chances of injury, increases attention span, improves learning)
2. How does sleep help the brain? (Answer: it prepares the brain to learn new things the next day)
3. How does too little sleep make you feel? (Answer: it can make it difficult to remember things and make you feel tired)
4. What is a sleep routine? (Answer: going to bed at regular time each day, brushing your teeth before bed, reading a book before bed)
5. What shouldn't be part of a sleep routine? (Answer: keeping a TV on in your bedroom, keeping a phone or tablet near your bed, eating a heavy meal)
6. How much sleep should you get? (Answer: 9 to 12 hours for elementary students)

Learning Activity 2: Making Sleep Shapes With My Body (5 minutes)

Begin by asking the class to make a shape in their personal space that represents what they look like when they are asleep in their bed. Ask children to volunteer to show others their shape. You could also show children the shapes they make with their body when they sleep.

Show different laminated shapes and discuss the different types of shapes our body can make. These laminated shapes will be displayed using cones with a slat.

Universal Design for Learning

- Provide braille labels on the shape cards
- Use puff paint over the shapes for tactile learning
- Provide alternatives to making shapes with the full body for students who sit or stand with assistive devices (e.g., making the shape with arms only, making half a shape and a partner makes the other half)
- Make a shape with their mouth or with their hands or fingers
- Use sign language to teach other children the American Sign Language for the shape they are making
- Trace the shape if they cannot make it with their body

Learning Activity 3: Making Three Sleeping Shapes (20 minutes)

Task 1: Exploring Sleep Shapes

Guide students, who are in their personal space, through making three shapes on different body parts at different levels in space. Children respond to your prompts. Here are some sample prompts:

- Let me see you make a standing shape as if you were sleeping!
- Can you make a shape on the floor that looks like you when you are sleeping?
- Are your shapes twisted, round, long and narrow, or wide? Try to make each of your shapes very different.

Universal Design for Learning

- Use tactile modeling for students who are unfamiliar with the shapes by letting the student touch the arms or legs of a doll that is arranged in the shape
- Use two-word prompts to decrease the complexity of the prompts
- Give one direction at a time
- Repeat the directions and demonstrations

Task 2: Yawning and Stretching!

Demonstrate different ways to stretch the body as if yawning, or ask children to explore different ways to stretch their body as if they were yawning. The children practice one or two ways of "yawning" with their body. Beat 8 counts on a drum to prompt students to use 8 counts to perform each yawn.

Universal Design for Learning

- Provide a visual cue (exaggerated hitting of the drum) and priority seating for students who cannot hear the drum
- Use arm movements only for those who sit

Task 3: Putting Sleep Shapes Together With Transition of Yawning

1. Verbally guide children through creating a movement sequence: sleep shape 1 + stretching and yawning + sleep shape 2 + stretching and yawning + sleep shape 3 + stretching and yawning.

2. Practice the sequence with no counting. Count out loud while playing a drum, prompting children to perform each movement for 8 counts.

3. Now have children perform their sleep shape sequence to music. Prompt each movement by counting out loud for the children. Children in grades 1 or 2 or who have music experience can count for themselves, thus holding their sleep shape still for 8 counts and then stretching for 8 counts into the next sleep shape.

Universal Design for Learning

- Provide multiple demonstrations
- Allow peers to pair up with students who need extra support
- Provide verbal cues for students who cannot see the demonstration
- Use visual means of counting for students who cannot hear a drum
- Allow students in wheelchairs to transfer onto a mat during shapes or lock their wheels and make shapes from the chair

PEER ASSESSMENT   Have children find a fist-bump partner. One partner is the observer, and the other is the performer. Kindergarten children watch and provide verbal feedback about the assessment criteria represented by the graphic shapes on the peer assessment (resource 1). These shapes could be enlarged and laminated (each partner group could have the four shapes), and the kindergarten partner could hold up the shape that corresponds to the shape their partner made. First- and second-grade students complete a peer assessment. Assessment sheets could be on a clipboard.

Universal Design for Learning

- Provide an accessible format for worksheets for students who have difficulty reading print or who need to use communication devices to respond.

Task 4: Making Sleep Shapes and Yawning While Moving Through Space (5 minutes)

Verbally prompt students to perform each shape while stationary, but the yawning transition moves through general space for 8 counts. Students perform sleep shape 1 in place for 8 counts and then "yawn" while moving through space to a new spot for 8 counts. Students repeat this process for shapes 2 and 3.

Teaching Options

- Half of the class performs for the other half so that children learn that dance is a performance movement form and a movement form to enjoy observing.
- Children practice creating contrasting shapes with a partner. One child makes a shape with their body, and the other partner tries to create a contrasting or opposite type of shape.
- Children with a partner attempt to mirror each other's sleep shape or copy it exactly.

Closure

Bring the class together in the calling all kids area. Children sit with their partner. The teacher summarizes the lesson by saying the following:

- Show your partner your favorite sleep shape.
- Do as many jumping jacks or jumping jack arms or finger jumping jacks as the number of hours you should sleep every night.
- Tell your partner one benefit of getting enough sleep each night.

Pass out copies of the sleep log (resource 2). Ask children to get the assistance of their caregivers and complete a weeklong log of how much sleep they get. Students return the sleep log to the classroom teacher when complete. You will collect the logs later from the classroom teacher.

Universal Design for Learning

The following are additional universal design for learning considerations for all learners:

- Consider using peer buddies who have training in providing additional verbal and visual cues.
- Use a visual representation of counting during the drum activity, such as nodding your head to the beat or using a scarf attached to the drumstick to provide a visual cue.
- When assessing by using worksheets, provide means of expression such as pointing to pictures, using a communication device, using yes or no questions, sending home worksheets to be transcribed in text to talk, and using braille when requested.
- Consider using a raised representation of the shape cards. This can be done with puff paint or waxed strings. Or ask a child's vision teacher to emboss them on a special printer.
- Provide additional means to check for understandings by asking yes or no questions, or having students say or use sign language cue words when requested.
- Learn sign language for the different shapes and use the signs during the lesson.
- On a tablet, play a video model of each of the shapes and activities that will be performed. Play it on loop so student can keep looking at a demonstration.
- Change the goal of the activity to include using the mouth, hands, or fingers to make shapes; pointing to shapes; tracing the shape on the floor with a wheelchair, cane, crutch, or walker.
- Provide paraeducators and classroom teachers with the lesson plan or cue cards for their role with students.

Goals, Directions, and Pathways

INTRODUCTORY INFORMATION

SHAPE America Outcomes

- S1.E1.1 Hops, gallops, jogs, and slides using a mature pattern.
- S1.E7.1 Maintains stillness on different bases of support with different body shapes.
- S5.E1.1 Identifies physical activity as a component of good health.
- S2.E2.K Travels in three different pathways.
- S2.E2.1a Travels demonstrating low, middle, and high levels.

National Health Education Performance Indicators

- 1.2.1 Identify that healthy behaviors affect personal health.
- 6.2.1 Identify a short-term personal health goal and take action toward achieving the goal.

Lesson Objectives

Students will be able to do the following:

- Identify a short-term physical activity goal and create specific action steps toward meeting that goal before the next wellness education class.
- Travel in the correct pathway and direction.
- Create a movement sequence incorporating the required elements.

Learning Materials and Technology

- 30 poly spots
- 4 scarves
- 4 Gator balls
- 2 or 3 pinnies
- 1 music player
- Choice of equipment for movement sequence (e.g., jump ropes, hoops, fleece balls, scoops, beanbags, cones, streamers, foam cylinders, bean bags, scooters)
- Resource handout from HK*Propel*
  - Resource 1: 1 printout per student

Skill Cues

Gallop

- Step forward with the lead foot.
- Push off the trail foot forcefully enough to achieve a flight phase.
- The trail foot catches up to the lead leg by touching the heel.
- Coordinate the arm swing forward with the motion of the legs to achieve distance and height.
- Land on the ball of the lead foot, with the trail foot behind the lead foot.

Slide

- Turn the body sideways to the direction of travel.
- Keep the feet shoulder width apart and arms extended sideways.
- Step to the side with the lead foot.
- Push off with the trail foot so it produces a flight phase and then chases the lead foot.
- Land on the trail foot and then the lead foot.

Skip

- Step forward with the lead foot and hop.
- Raise the opposite knee to waist height.
- The arm on the same side as the hopping foot swings up and forward; the other arm is back.
- Repeat the pattern by alternating the right and left foot.

Hop

- Balance on one foot.
- The nonhopping leg is off the ground and bent at 90 degrees.
- Bend and extend the hopping leg to produce a flight phase.
- The nonhopping leg swings up and forward to produce additional force.
- Arms are bent at the elbow and swing from back to front in coordination with the hopping action.

Leap

- Run and take off from one foot forcefully to create a flight phase.
- Swing arms up and forward to aid take off.
- Extend the opposite leg forward.
- Land on the opposite foot.
- Bend the knees to absorb force.

Jump: Two Feet to Two Feet

- Swing both arms back behind the buttocks.
- Bend the knees.
- Swing the arms forward and up.
- Push off both feet simultaneously.
- Land on both feet simultaneously and bend the knees.
- Reach arms forward.

LEARNING ACTIVITIES

Lesson Introduction

- **WHAT** are we learning today? Students will learn how to create an age-appropriate physical activity goal and how to combine pathways, directions, and fundamental movement skills into a movement sequence.
- **WHY** are we learning this? Younger students will be introduced to the process of working toward a physical activity goal and tracking progress. Goals give people direction and help them achieve more.

- **HOW** will learning be measured? Students will use the physical activity goal log (resource 1) to identify activities they enjoy and record their physical activity over seven days. The completed resource will be returned to the teacher.

Activity 1: Physical Activity Goal Discussion (5 minutes)

Begin by asking students why they take wellness education. Guide the discussion toward the idea of promoting a healthy and physically active lifestyle that carries forward into adulthood. A major part of wellness is being physically active. Ask students to identify benefits of being physically active. Write student responses on a whiteboard. If their responses do not include the following benefits, add them.

Physical Benefits

- Makes muscles and bones stronger
- Reduces various illnesses
- Boosts energy
- Controls weight
- Helps you sleep better

Mental and Social Benefits

- Reduces stress
- Improves mood and enthusiasm
- Helps you feel better about yourself
- Lets you socialize with friends and family
- It is fun

Conclude by asking students how many minutes they should be physically active per day. If students need help, ask them if anyone has heard about the program called NFL Play 60. The goal is for students to be physically active for at least 60 minutes per day. For the remainder of the class, students will accumulate minutes of physical activity while learning various physical skills and terminology.

Activity 2: Directions and Pathways (20 minutes)

Task 1: Direction Jumble

Scatter poly spots in the general space. Ask students to identify the seven directions: forward, backward, sideways right, sideways left, up, down, diagonal. After each correct response, have all students practice the direction for 15 seconds. After practicing each direction, all students move in general space when the music starts. Each time they move over a poly spot, they change direction. When performing the up and down direction, students may either leap or hop. Demonstrate how to perform the leap and hop.

Stop the music and ask students to stand in place and put their hand over their heart. Ask them to feel how fast it is beating. Challenge students to open and close their free hand to match their heartbeat. Another option is to ask students to tap their thigh with their free hand to match their heartbeat.

Extension: Students pair up; one is the leader and the other the follower. Repeat the activity with the follower copying the movement of the leader. Switch roles after a few minutes.

Task 2: Partner Direction Tag

Students sit with a partner; one is the chaser and the other is the fleer. Each person picks a direction to move. They may only move at walking speed. If the chaser tags the fleer, they both stop and agree on a new direction to travel. The chaser gives the fleer a head start by counting to 3 and then begins the chase. Students may not move faster than walking speed.

Task 3: Pathways

Ask students to identify the three pathways: straight, curved, and zigzag. When a student provides the correct answer, ask them to demonstrate. When the music starts, students move in the general space. Each time they move over a poly spot, they change pathways.

Extension: Using the same partner as before, repeat the pathway activity, with the follower copying the movement of the leader. Switch roles after a few minutes.

Task 4: Pac-Man Tag

Students may move only on the lines of the gym. Designate two or three ghosts by having them hold pinnies. The ghosts tag the other students. If a student is tagged or falls off a line, they step to the side, perform 10 jumping jacks, and then return. Periodically, stop the music, yell "power pellet," and randomly toss out four Gator balls. The students who pick them up are able to tag the ghosts. Any ghost tagged does 10 jumping jacks. When the music resumes, ghosts again are the chasers. Change ghosts periodically.

Extension: After the last round, have a balance contest. Students stand on one foot on the line. If their other foot touches down or they hop on the planted foot, they step off the line and restart but can no longer win the event.

Activity 3: Partner Movement Sequence (10 minutes)

Students create a movement sequence with a partner that incorporates the following elements:

- 10 steps
- 3 pathways
- 2 directions
- 2 levels
- 1 piece of equipment

Both partners must be active during the sequence. When finished, ask students to share their movement sequence. They may request to perform the sequence to music.

Closure

Distribute a copy of resource 1 to students. Students fill in their name and the day of their next wellness class. Next, they circle any activities in which they enjoy participating. Students may draw pictures instead. When finished, students turn to a partner and explain what specific activities they are going to undertake to meet their goal. Students take the resource home; parents complete the bottom portion, and the student returns it to school for their next wellness class.

Handwashing, Overhand Throw, and Locomotor Skills

GRADE LEVEL: 2-3

INTRODUCTORY INFORMATION

SHAPE America Outcomes

- S1.E6.3 Performs a sequence of locomotor skills, transitioning from one skill to another smoothly and without hesitation.
- S1.E14.3 Throws overhand, demonstrating three of the five critical elements of a mature pattern, in nondynamic environments (closed skills), for distance and/or force.

National Health Education Performance Indicators

- 7.5.2 Demonstrate a variety of healthy practices and behaviors to maintain or improve personal health.
- 7.5.3 Demonstrate a variety of behaviors that avoid or reduce health risks.

Lesson Objectives

Students will be able to do the following:

- Demonstrate multiple locomotor skills with appropriate transitions between each.
- Perform the overhand throw using correct critical elements.
- Identify and perform appropriate handwashing technique.
- Identify and execute the correct series of steps when using a bathroom.

Learning Materials and Technology

- 1 medical glove per student
- 5 carpet squares
- 5 large storage tubs
- 15 red fleece balls
- 5 buckets
- 5 blue fleece balls
- 5 foam cylinders or similar item
- 5 scarves
- 5 scooters

- 5 hockey sticks
- 5 large cones (must have opening at the top)
- 15 washable markers
- Resource handouts from HK*Propel*
  - Resource 1: 1 printout per student
  - Resource 2: 1 printout per 2 students
  - Resource 3: 1 printout per 2 students
  - Resource 4: 1 printout per student

Skill Cues

Overhand Throw

- Keep side to the target.
- Put throwing arm behind the head with the elbow bent at a 90-degree angle (L shape).
- Step toward the target with the opposite foot.
- Rotate the chest and hips toward the target as the throwing arm is extended toward the target.
- Follow through across the body to the opposite hip.

INSTRUCTIONAL ACTIVITIES

Lesson Introduction

- **WHAT** are we learning today? Students will learn about handwashing and how to throw overhand using correct technique.
- **WHY** are we learning this? Nobody likes being sick, so it is important that students understand that handwashing is an easy way to stay healthy so that they don't miss school and are able to play sports and participate in other activities.
- **HOW** will learning be measured? Students will complete the overhand throw peer assessment (resource 1) and the handwashing peer assessment (resource 4).

Activity 1: General Discussion (10 minutes)

Part A

Ask students why they think handwashing is important:

- Handwashing with soap kills germs. Germs are tiny living organisms, such as viruses and bacteria, that cause illness. Teachers may choose to share pictures of germs.
- Handwashing prevents illnesses and the spread of sickness to others.

Part B

Tell students that there are six occasions when they should wash their hands. Students work with a partner nearest them to brainstorm as many occasions as possible in two minutes. When finished, students share their work. Write correct responses on a whiteboard or project them on a wall.

1. Before, during, and after preparing food
2. Before eating food
3. Before and after caring for someone who is sick
4. After blowing your nose, coughing, or sneezing
5. After using the bathroom
6. After touching garbage

Part C

Ask students what sports and activities use the overhand throw. Possible answers include baseball, football, and handball. Other sports such as volleyball and tennis use a modified overhand throw while serving. Demonstrate correct technique by throwing a fleece ball toward a hoop target taped to the wall. Use the command style and have students shadow you for two throws. Then have students perform ten imaginary throws in their self-space. Next, students get a partner and practice throwing back and forth using correct technique from a distance of 15 feet (5.4 m). After a few minutes, students throw at hoops taped to the wall. The thrower stands on a poly spot placed a minimum of 15 feet (5.4 m) from the target to elicit proper form. The poly spot may be moved farther from the wall, depending on skill level and success. One partner completes the overhand throw peer assessment (resource 1) before rotating to become the thrower.

Activity 2: Inflated Chicken Activity (5 minutes)

Students form groups of three. Explain that they will receive an inflated medical glove (the chicken). Using markers, students label one side "palm" and the other "back." Next, they shade the areas most likely to be missed during handwashing. Give students two minutes to complete the task and then review. Share resource 2 and ask students to compare their shading to the resource. Discuss.

Activity 3: Germ Crusaders (15 minutes)

Distribute resource 3 to students or project it and demonstrate how to properly wash their hands.

Tell students they will create a pretend bathroom using the materials provided. The bathroom consists of a doormat (carpet square), upside-down storage tub (sink), one red and one blue fleece ball (hot and cold faucets), a foam cylinder (soap dispenser), a scarf (paper towel) on a cone (dispenser), and a bucket (waste basket). Arrange the bathroom according to the diagram shown here.

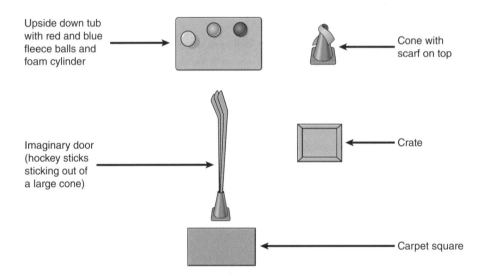

For second grade, set up one bathroom station as an example. The students' mission is to use the bathroom by following these steps:

1. Stand on the doormat (carpet square) and open the imaginary door (turn the blade of the hockey stick) using either their forearm or elbow.

2. Turn on the hot and cold faucets (1 red, 1 blue fleece ball) with the back of their hand. Pretend to wet their hands.

3. Get soap from the dispenser (foam cylinder).

4. Wash their hands using proper technique with warm water for the proper duration.

5. Dry their hands with the paper towel (scarf draped over the cone) from the dispenser (cone).

6. Use the paper towel (scarf) to turn off both faucets.

7. Pull the handle to open the imaginary bathroom door using the paper towel.

8. Drop the paper tower (scarf) into a waste basket (bucket) as they exit. Try not to touch anything else while exiting.

Organize students into groups of five and give them five to seven minutes to set up the bathroom using the equipment provided. Students enter the bathroom one at a time, wash their hands, and exit. Students not using the bathroom will complete the peer assessment (resource 4) on each group member.

Activity 4: Pass the Soap Tag (10 minutes)

This is a version of everybody's it tag. Ask for two student volunteers to act as germs and another two to act as soap dispensers. When tagged by a germ, students must perform vertical jumps until aided by a soap dispenser. Soap dispensers throw a fleece ball (the soap) to a tagged person from a distance of 15 feet (4.5 m); the soap is then thrown back." If neither person drops it, the tagged person pretends to wash their hands using correct technique while singing, "row, row, row your boat, gently down the stream, merrily, merrily, merrily, merrily, life is but a dream." This prevents students from washing their hands too quickly. Afterward, they may rejoin the game. Continually vary the locomotor skill being performed. This can be done after a stoppage or during the game. Possible locomotor skills include walking, jogging, skipping, galloping, hopping, and sliding sideways. After two minutes, rotate taggers.

Differentiations

- Challenge task 1: Ask students how viruses and bacteria are handled differently by the medical community. (Answer: Antibiotics are effective against bacteria; vaccines are effective against viruses.)
- Challenge task 2: Some bathrooms use air dryers and not paper towels. In the bathroom activity, take away the paper towels and see how students respond.
- Simplified task: Provide a handout with the steps and allow students to perform germ crusaders with a partner.

Closure

Handwashing is important in preventing the spread of germs and preventing sickness. Ask each student to remain seated and get a partner. One partner shows and tells the steps to handwashing. Next, the other partner identifies on what six occasions hands should be washed. Each time, the nonspeaking partner fills in any missing information.

Hazardous Household Products, Locomotor Skills, and Instep Kick

GRADE LEVEL: K-1

INTRODUCTORY INFORMATION

SHAPE America Outcomes

- S1.E1.K Performs locomotor skills (hopping, galloping, running, sliding, skipping) throughout general space with body control.
- S1.E21.K Kicks a stationary ball from a stationary position, approaches with a three-step walking approach or uses a continuous running approach to kick a stationary ball using emerging elementary or mature stage characteristics.

National Health Education Performance Indicators

- 1.2.4 List ways to prevent common childhood injuries.
- 7.2.2 Demonstrate behaviors that avoid or reduce health risks.

Lesson Objectives

Students will be able to do the following:

- Explain why household products are harmful if ingested or inhaled.
- Identify poisons as safety hazards in the home.
- Apply safety rules for being safe around poisons.
- Review various locomotor skills as they travel through general space with control.
- Perform the instep kick from a stationary position, three-step approach or running approach; ball is stationary using emerging elementary or mature stage characteristics.

Learning Materials and Technology

- 1 laptop computer
- 20-30 cones
- 4 red hoops
- 4 green hoops
- 1 soccer ball or playground ball per student
- 25-30 poly spots or plastic footprints
- 60 cones to create kicking zones
- 40-50 beanbags

- Resource 1: 1 displayed on a large poster board and 10 copies of each picture to place under cones for activity 1
- Resource handouts from HK*Propel*
  - Resource 1: 1 printout
  - Resource 2: 1 per student
  - Resource 3: 1 per student

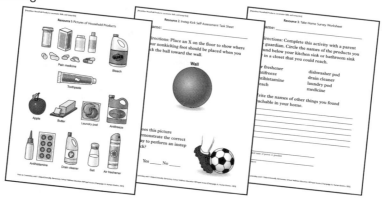

Skill Cues

Instep Kick (Shoelaces)

- Focus eyes on the ball.
- Take a two- or three-step approach, with the last step on the nonkicking foot.
- Position the nonkicking foot beside and slightly behind the ball.
- The leg action is from the knee on down. Contact the ball with the shoelaces. Contact the middle of the ball for a low kick (trunk leans forward); contact lower on the ball for a lofted kick (trunk leans backward; body weight is forward over ball).
- Extend the leg toward the target at a low level.

LEARNING ACTIVITIES

Lesson Introduction

- **WHAT** are we learning today? Students will learn about products in their homes that can be dangerous if they are ingested or inhaled.
- **WHY** are we learning this? More than 900,000 children drink or eat deadly poisonous household products every year.
- **HOW** will learning be measured? Students will complete a self-assessment task sheet on how to perform an instep kick (resource 2). Students also will take a worksheet home (resource 3) and, with their parents' or caregivers' assistance, see if there are hazardous products in their homes that are easy to get to and should be stored in a safer place.

Activity 1: Warm-Up (5 minutes)

Position 20 to 30 cones throughout the general space (inside or outside). Using cutouts of resource 1, place a hazardous product or a safe product under each cone. Additional examples may be added. Place a green hoop labeled "safe" and a red hoop labeled "hazardous" on the middle of each sideline (four red, four green). Call out a locomotor skill and start the music. When the music starts, students perform a designated locomotor skill to find the household products placed under the cones. After finding the products, students place them in either a red hoop or a green hoop. Manage movement by stopping the music and announcing a different locomotor skill. After you stop the activity, assign learning teams to the hoops on the sideline to discuss whether the products were placed in the proper hoop.

Activity 2: Indoor Stationary Kicking Review (15 minutes)

Position students in an observation area and demonstrate a stationary instep kick toward the wall a minimum of three times, with and without verbalizing the skill cues. Children can shadow the kicking-leg action and foot action as they stand in their personal space. Dismiss students into their pairs to kick a stationary ball toward the wall.

- Task: Students use a short to moderate (one- to two-step) approach to kick a ball with their instep (shoelaces) between two cones placed against the wall (two students per set of cones).
- Setup: Position cones approximately 5 to 10 feet (1.5-3 m) from the wall. Pairs of students kick toward the wall. One partner is the performer and the other is the retriever. Balls can be slightly deflated and kept inside bins or hoops in the middle of the gymnasium. For stationary kicking, place six- to eight-inch (15-20 cm) playground balls on half cones.

While students are kicking, move around and observe their performance and provide descriptive and prescriptive feedback.

- Knowledge of performance descriptive: "You contacted the ball with your shoelaces. That's awesome!"
- Knowledge of performance prescriptive: "Be sure to point your nonkicking foot toward your target."
- Knowledge of results: "What do you think made the ball go high off of the floor?"

Activity 3: Outdoor Kicking to Zones (15 minutes)

- Practice task: Kick the ball to distances that require an approach and full windup. The approach is optional; some children may need to start with the nonkicking foot beside and slightly behind the ball. You can put a rubber footprint or poly spot there. Other students may take a three-step walking approach, and others may take a running approach.
- Setup: This activity is best conducted outside. Zones can be created using tall cones for children to kick into (see the figure that follows). Divide students equally into the zones with their partners. Place six- to eight-inch (15-20 cm) playground balls on the ground along a kicking line. Designate four or five zones with approximately four to five feet (1.5 m) between each zone to maximize practice time for all children. The distance each zone is from the kicking line can vary based on the skill level of the children. Provide starting and stopping cues for retrieving playground balls, or organize children into partner groups. One partner serves as a retriever and stands at the far end of the zone. On your signal, the retriever gets the playground ball their partner kicked and rolls it back to them.
- Hazardous product review: Place the products from the warm-up in each of the colored A, B, and C zones under poly spots or beanbags. Once a ball lands or is kicked into the zone, the retriever gets the ball and picks up one product. The retriever takes it back to their partner and they decide whether it is a safe or hazardous product. Once again, red hoops are for hazardous products and green hoops are for safe products. The yellow kicking zone provides an example of where to place the hoops.

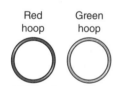

Red hoop Green hoop

Area 1	Area 2	Area 3	Area 4	Area 5
Kicking line				
15 feet Zone A1	Zone A2	Zone A3	Zone A4	Zone A5
20 feet Zone B1	Zone B2	Zone B3	Zone B4	Zone B5
25 feet Zone C1	Zone C2	Zone C3	Zone C4	Zone C5

Activity 4: Kicking a Rolling Ball (10 minutes)

- Practice task: Kick a rolling ball from a stance to different distances.

- Setup: Organize students into groups of three. One child is the roller (positioned about 10 feet [3 m] from the kicker), one is the kicker, and the third is the retriever. Students kick toward one of the four corners of the gymnasium. This task can be done using five or six kicking stations. If conducting this activity outdoors, all children can practice the same skill progression, with kickers in an inner circle, rollers 10 feet (3 m) from the middle circle, and retrievers on the outer circle. See the diagram. Use commands to indicate when rollers should pitch and when retrievers should return the ball to the rollers.

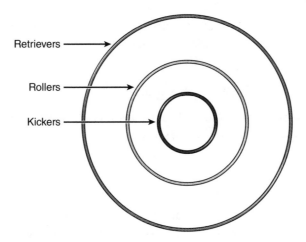

Closure

Gather students in the calling all kids area and give them a self-assessment task sheet on the instep kick (resource 2). When students are finished, discuss the correct answers on the self-assessment. Lastly, distribute and explain the take-home survey (resource 3). Students will complete the survey with their caregiver and return it in the next class.

Healthy Relationships and Dribbling With Feet

GRADE LEVEL: 1-2

INTRODUCTORY INFORMATION

SHAPE America Outcomes

- S1.E18.1 Taps or dribbles a ball using the inside of the foot while walking in general space.
- S1.E18.2 Dribbles with the feet in general space with control of ball and body.
- S2.E2.1b Travels demonstrating a variety of relationships with objects (e.g., over, under, around, through).

National Health Education Performance Indicators

- 2.5.3 Identify how peers can influence healthy and unhealthy behaviors.
- 7.5.1 Identify responsible personal health behaviors.

Lesson Objectives

Students will be able to do the following:

- Identify characteristics of a healthy relationship and friendship.
- Correctly perform soccer dribbling with the inside of the foot while moving through general space.
- Travel demonstrating different relationships with objects.

Learning Materials and Technology

- 1 soccer ball per student
- 10 hoops
- 20 hoop holders
- 30 poly spots
- 6 empty cardboard shoe boxes
- 10 jump ropes
- 1 tape dispenser
- Resource handouts from HK*Propel*
  - Resource 1: 1 printout per two students
  - Resource 2: 1 printout per student

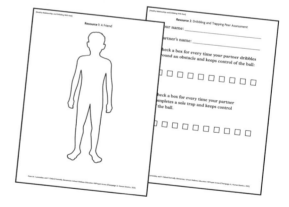

Skill Cues

Soccer Dribble

- Tap the ball forward gently with the inside and outside of the foot.
- Keep the ball close to your body, no more than an arm's length in front of you.
- Keep the head up.
- Travel at a slow to medium speed.
- Hold the arms out for balance, with the elbows bent.

LEARNING ACTIVITIES

Lesson Introduction

- **WHAT** are we learning today? Students will learn the characteristics of healthy relationships with other people, such as friends, teachers, coaches, and family members. Student will explore spatial relationships in general space while dribbling a soccer ball.

- **WHY** are we learning this? Being able to get along with others is an important lifelong skill. It doesn't happen by accident; it must be practiced. Being able to dribble a soccer ball effectively helps a team keep possession and move the ball around the field to score.

- **HOW** will learning be measured? Students will list traits a good friend would and would not exhibit (resource 1) and will complete the dribbling and trapping peer assessment (resource 2).

Activity 1: Quotes and Being a Friend (15 minutes)

A relationship is a connection that occurs between two people or two objects. When friends play together, they are working on developing good relationships by sharing toys, making decisions about what to play, and following the rules. Students navigating an obstacle course are working on relationships as well, but with objects. Over, under, and near are examples of relationships with objects. Students will learn about both types of relationships in this lesson.

Organize students in groups of three and read the following quotes. Students discuss what the quote means and share with the class when asked.

- "Life is a team sport." Many aspects of life, whether it be in school, in your neighborhood, or at the playground, depend on students getting along with others. Just as a successful team works well together, so too should people. Show a video of a team sport or a photo of K-2 children in a small-sided game.

- "If you want a friend, be a friend." Decide how to treat a friend by considering "Would I like this being done to me?" If the answer is yes, go ahead with your action. If not, what would a better action be?

- "A friend is not a shadow who is present only when the sun shines." A friend sticks with someone, helps through hard times, and is always honest.

Distribute a copy of resource 1 to each group. Provide them with a bin of crayons or pencils. Instruct students to write the traits of a good friend inside the figure. After an appropriate amount of time, ask students to write the traits a friend should not exhibit outside of the figure.

Activity 2: Relationship Jungle (15 minutes)

Task A

Ask for a student volunteer and give them a hoop. The student demonstrates the following relationships with their hoop: in front of, alongside, behind, around, through, over, under, and on top of. Next, have students get a partner and demonstrate each relationship except on top of. For example, one student could stand in front of their partner to demonstrate that relationship.

Task B

Demonstrate the correct technique for soccer dribbling and stopping the ball with the sole of the foot. Students practice dribbling to music throughout general space. When the music stops, students follow this series of progressions. Repeat each step multiple times:

1. Perform a sole trap to stop the soccer ball.
2. Perform a sole trap and then a pull-back.
3. Perform a sole trap and then use the sole of the foot to dribble right followed by normal dribbling.

4. Perform a sole trap and then use the sole of the foot to dribble left followed by normal dribbling.

Task C

Students assist you in scattering equipment on the floor: poly spots (lily pads), tunnels, boxes (rocks), jump ropes (vines), and hoops standing in hoop holders. Students practice soccer dribbling with different parts of their foot (inside, outside) at different speeds and directions. When the music stops, students stop dribbling, find a piece of equipment, and demonstrate a relationship called out by the teacher with that object.

- Extension 1: Incorporate the soccer ball into a relationship.
- Extension2: Create a relationship using a partner and both soccer balls.

Task D

On go, students get a partner, one printout of resource 2, and a pencil. One partner completes the peer assessment on the side of the gymnasium while the other dribbles in general space. After 3-5 minutes, switch.

Differentiations

- Challenge task—Dribble with the instep (laces area), or alternate feet with each contact.

Activity 3: Gallery Walk and Discussion (10 minutes)

Students return to their three-person groups. Each group tapes their "friend" (resource 1) to the gym wall 10 feet (3 m) apart. Next, students perform a gallery walk and circulate freely from one "friend" to another, reading the work of their classmates. After the gallery walk, students sit in front of their "friend," nominate a spokesperson, and share two attributes from their "friend." Write their responses on the whiteboard. Discuss the benefits of being able to form positive interpersonal relationships and the importance of the whole class treating one another with kindness and respect.

Ask students what they should do in these situations:

- You see someone alone.
- Someone asks to join a game.
- Someone is not sure where to sit at lunch or on the playground.
- Someone falls down on the playground.

Ask students what they should do in these situations:

- Someone keeps bothering you.
- Someone grabs something from you.
- Someone tells you they won't be your friend anymore.
- Others won't let you join in.
- Someone won't take turns.

Activity 4: Spider Web (10 minutes)

Form circles of six to eight students. Give each group a ball of string or yarn. The first student says the name of someone in the circle; says something positive about them; and holds on to the end of the yarn and passes, tosses, or rolls the ball to that person so that the ball unrolls. That person holds on to the string, says the name of another student and something positive about them, and passes the ball to them. Continue until everyone is holding a portion of the string. Ask students why the spider web represents friendship or a group of friends. (Answer: What affects one person affects everyone.)

Ask if students have heard the phrase, "Sticks and stones may break my bones, but words will never hurt me." Ask if the phrase is true. (Answer: Not at all.) Discuss that words can be just as hurtful as a physical injury and are harder to see. Remind students to be careful, because words have weight.

Students stand up and try to walk with their spider web around the gym, keeping the threads taut. Students should practice communication and problem-solving skills.

Closure

Ask students to get a partner and explain one way to be a better friend to others in the school and then to switch. Ask whether anyone would like to share their idea. Also ask students to touch the part of their foot used for dribbling a soccer ball.

Hydration and Dribbling With Hands

GRADE LEVEL: K-2

INTRODUCTORY INFORMATION

SHAPE America Outcomes

- S1.E17.K Dribbles a ball with one hand, attempting the second contact.
- S1.E17.1 Dribbles continuously in self-space using the preferred hand.
- S1.E17.b Dribbles using the preferred hand while walking in general space.

National Health Education Performance Indicators

- 1.2.1 Identify that healthy behaviors impact personal health.

Lesson Objectives

Students will be able to do the following:

- Perform dribbling with two hands, one hand, and alternating hands while stationary and on the move and using correct form.
- Explain the benefits of drinking five cups of water each day.
- Identify why sugary drinks are not a substitute beverage for water.
- Identify of the signs of dehydration.

Learning Materials and Technology

- 1 ball per student
- 35-30 hoops
- 2 poly spots per rope pathway
- 25 jump ropes to make pathways
- 8 tall cones
- 1 movement task card per four stations
- Resource handouts from HKPropel
  - Resource 1: 1 printout per student
  - Resource 2: 1 printout per student

Skill Cues

Dribbling With Hands

- Use the finger pads to push the ball down.
- Keep the ball in front of and slightly to the side of the body (to the right if dribbling with the right hand; to the left if dribbling with the left hand).
- Keep the elbow of the dribbling arm flexed.
- Keep the wrist firm.
- Dribble the ball waist high.
- Keep the chest and head up.

LEARNING ACTIVITIES

Lesson Introduction

- **WHAT** are we learning today? Students will learn how to dribble a ball with two hands, one hand, and alternating hands while stationary and on the move. They will also learn the importance of drinking enough water and how to recognize symptoms of dehydration.
- **WHY** are we learning this? We all need to provide our body with the nutrients it needs. Water contains no calories or sugar. It good for the body by keeping joints, bones, and teeth healthy. It helps the blood circulate and can help kids maintain a healthy weight into adulthood.
- **HOW** will learning be measured? Learning will be measured though a water consumption log (resource 1) and a dribbling peer assessment (resource 2).

Classroom Management and Setup

Before this lesson, arrange for students' caregivers to send them to school with a water bottle labeled with the students' names. Messages could be posted on the school website or learning management system. Students place their water bottles in their learning team's hoop (a different color for each team). While students sit in the middle of the gymnasium, explain and demonstrate each station. After completing each station, children go to their learning team and get a drink of water. Verbally direct this aspect of the lesson. After students have completed two stations, bring all students to the middle of the gymnasium and explain what dehydration is. You could begin by asking children, "Has anyone really been thirsty and did not have water? What were you doing when you got so thirsty? Oh, playing on a playground . . . yes!" List the following symptoms of dehydration:

- You have dry lips or a sticky mouth.
- You haven't urinated or don't urinate very much when you go to the bathroom.
- You are sleepy and grumpy.
- You have red (flushed) skin.

Place playground or junior-sized basketballs in a hoop at each station (a quarter of the gymnasium for each station) so students do not have to carry their ball from one station to the next.

Here is content you'll need for discussion with the students. All living things need water to survive. Along with milk, plain water is the best drink choice for children. Being well hydrated makes you feel better and helps you to remember things! And it's economical; tap water is much less expensive than sport drinks, sodas, and juice.

Tell the students that children their age need five cups of water a day, and show them how much five cups of water is in the water bottles. Explain that they can also get water from vegetables and fruit, such as lettuce and watermelon.

Tell the students they also will be reviewing dribbling a ball. Ask them who remembers some of skill cues for how to dribble a ball. (Answer: tummy high; use finger pads; keep ball away from your feet). Next, demonstrate a two-handed dribble, a 1-handed dribble, and an alternating hand dribble. Explain to students that they can perform whichever dribble they choose.

Station 1: Dribbling Along Pathways (7 minutes)

Place poly spots or jump ropes in curvy and zigzag pathways throughout the station area. Tall cones mark the rectangular movement space. The task card should read, "dribbling along pathways." Each student gets a ball from the hoop. Two students go to one pathway. After completing a pathway, students change to a different one. Students place balls back in the hoop when you stop the station activity.

Station 2: Dribbling While Following a Partner (5 minutes)

Each student gets a ball from the hoop. One partner is the leader and one is the follower. The leader dribbles through general space while the partner follows. Partner groups decide when to change leaders. Students can also change speeds. Students place the balls back in the hoop when you stop the activity.

Station 3: Dribbling While Changing Speeds (5 minutes)

Each student gets a ball from the hoop. A Bluetooth player is at this station, with music that changes speeds. Direct one student to start the music. Students dribble the ball any direction at a speed prompted by the music. Students place the balls back in the hoop when they rotate.

Station 4: Dribbling in and out of Hoops (5 minutes)

Ten to fifteen hoops are placed on the floor throughout the rectangular station area. Each student gets a ball from a hoop. The task card states, "Dribble your ball in and out of each hoop. Then move to a new hoop and dribble in and out of that hoop. See how many hoops you can go to!" Student pairs complete the peer assessment at this station (resource 2).

Closure

Children are gathered in the calling all kids area. Collect the peer assessments from station 4 and review the results with the students. Students find a partner and discuss the skill cues for proper dribbling form. Distribute the water consumption log sheets (or upload it to the learning management system). Explain how to complete the log sheet.

Living Smoke Free, Jumping, Leaping, and Striking

INTRODUCTORY INFORMATION

SHAPE America Outcomes

- S1.E3.K Performs jumping and landing actions with balance.
- S1.E3.1 Demonstrates two of the five critical elements for jumping and landing in a horizontal plane using two-foot take-offs and landings.
- S1.E24.K Strikes a lightweight object with a paddle or short-handled racket.
- S2.E2.K Travels in three different pathways.

National Health Education Performance Indicators

- 1.2.1 Identify that healthy behaviors affect personal health.
- 2.2.1 Identify how the family influences personal health practices and behaviors.
- 4.2.3 Demonstrate ways to respond when in an unwanted, threatening, or dangerous situation.

Lesson Objectives

Students will be able to do the following:

- Identify the function of the lungs, basic structures of the respiratory system, and how smoking damages the lungs.
- Jump and land using two feet.
- Strike a balloon with an open hand and be able to control its direction of flight.

This is a two-day lesson.

Learning Materials and Technology

- 1 jump rope per 3 students
- 3 sets of 10 balloons, each a different color
- 1 drinking straw per student
- 10 poly spots
- 10 cones
- 10 hula hoops
- 10 jump ropes
- Resource handouts from HK*Propel*
  - Resource 1: 1 printout
  - Resource 2: 1 printout

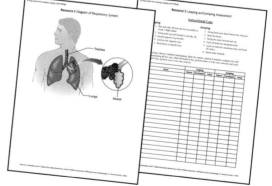

Skill Cues

Leap

- Run and take off from one foot forcefully to create a flight phase.
- Swing arms up and forward to aid take off.

- Extend the opposite leg forward.
- Land on the opposite foot.
- Bend the knees to absorb force.

Jump

- Swing both arms back behind the buttocks.
- Bend the knees.
- Swing the arms forward and up.
- Push off both feet simultaneously.
- Land on both feet simultaneously and bend the knees.
- Reach arms forward.

Striking With an Open Hand

- Turn the shoulders so the nondominant shoulder points to the target.
- Bring the striking arm back.
- Contact with an open hand and the arm fully extended.
- Adjust the hand and arm action to create the desired trajectory.

LEARNING ACTIVITIES

Lesson Introduction

- **WHAT** are we learning today? Students will learn how to correctly leap and jump and how the lungs work.
- **WHY** are we learning this? The leap and jump can be used in many games and sports. It's important to keep the lungs healthy so students can continue to leap and jump without getting tired and winded.
- **HOW** will learning be measured? Learning will be measured through the leaping and jumping assessment (resource 2).

Activity 1: Respiratory System Discussion (10 minutes)

Ask students whether they know what the respiratory system and lungs do for the body. The main function of the respiratory system is to get air (oxygen) into the blood so the body can use it. Have students put their hand in front of their mouth and breathe in and out so they can feel the air moving. Show students a printout of resource 1 or project it onto the wall. Name the major parts of the respiratory system and their function:

- Lungs: You have two lungs, and they are the major organ of the respiratory system.
- Trachea: It is also called your windpipe, and it gets air from the mouth down into the lungs. It has hair, called cilia, on the inside. Ask students to feel their windpipe in the front of their neck.
- Alveoli: Air passes into the blood through these small, thin sacks that are like inflated balloons.

Show the respiratory system BrainPOP video. (See the lesson plan links file on *HKPropel* for a link to this video.)

Explain that smoking and vaping can damage the lungs, the trachea, and the alveoli. Partially inflate a balloon and explain that it is soft and spongy like the alveoli in the lungs. Put the balloon on a chair and ask a student to try to pop it by sitting on it. It will pop but will take some bouncing. Next, overinflate a balloon nearly to the point of breaking. This is what smoking does to the alveoli. It stiffens and enlarges them. Ask a different student to sit on the overinflated balloon. It should be easier to pop. Inhaling smoke also can make it harder to breathe and exercise. Elementary students are too young to smoke and purchase cigarettes, but they may be exposed to adults smoking. It is important that they avoid smoke whenever possible and communicate their discomfort in being exposed to secondhand smoke.

Ask students what they should do if an adult in a room begins to smoke. Write their responses on the whiteboard and add any of the following options that may have been missed. If they know the adult well, ask them to stop. Other options include telling a parent and moving to another room.

The best way to have healthy lungs is to exercise and avoid smoking. Explain to the students that they will practice jumping, leaping, and striking to strengthen their respiratory system.

Activity 2: Jump the Snake (10 minutes)

Demonstrate to students the correct technique for jumping. Students stand up and practice the technique in the general space. After students sit down in groups of three, explain the activity: Two students hold opposite ends of a jump rope and wiggle it back and forth on the ground. The third uses correct technique to jump over the rope without touching it. If students are successful, they can add challenge by wiggling it back and forth over a larger distance. Change jumpers after two to three minutes per student.

Complete the jumping and leaping assessment (resource 2) for activities 2 and 3.

Activity 3: Raging River (15 minutes)

Demonstrate to students the correct technique for leaping. Place equipment such as hoops, poly spots, cones, and shapes randomly throughout the general space. Place five sets of two jump ropes on the floor. The jump ropes should be closer together at one end than at the other (see the figure). When the music starts, students leap over any object except the jump ropes. Encourage students to start with the easier objects and progress to harder ones (e.g., start with poly spots and progress to shapes, hoops, cones). Stop the music and explain that the jump ropes will be included next. Students should leap over distances that are challenging. Define challenging as a distance that is not too easy nor too hard. Start on the narrower end and progressively leap greater distances. When the music stops, students continue to walk. Ask them to place their hand over their mouth to feel the air being inhaled and exhaled.

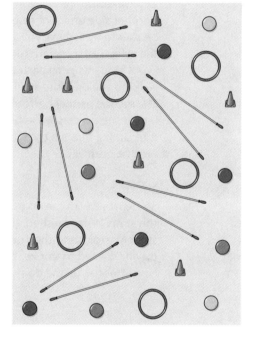

Activity 4: Balloon Volley Challenge (25 minutes)

Cigarette smoke contains a lot of harmful ingredients, including a drug (nicotine), the same fumes as car exhaust (carbon monoxide), poison (cyanide), a fertilizer ingredient (ammonia), and a dead-body preservative (formaldehyde). These harmful ingredients contribute to cancer. Cigarettes also contain tar, a sticky, black substance like oil.

Show one or both of the following YouTube videos (see the lesson plan links file on HK*Propel* for links to these videos):

- "How Smoking Just 1 Cigarette Affects Your Lungs"
- "How Smoking 30 Packs of Cigarettes Wrecks Your Lungs"

Show or display resource 1 again. Explain that the trachea is lined with small hairs called cilia that filter out dust and other debris so that they don't end up in the lungs. When a person smokes, the cilia get weighed down with tar and cannot function as well.

- Partner volleying: Students play a game that mimics the effects of tar on the cilia. Start by demonstrating how to strike a balloon with an open hand. Next, students in pairs practice hitting back and forth using correct technique. Lastly, groups of three hit two balloons in a clockwise direction.

- Balloon volley challenge: Students stay in their groups of three, and each group has two different colored balloons. The object is for each group to travel from one end of the gym and back while keeping both balloons in the air. A player cannot strike the same color balloon two times in a row. Once a player strikes a balloon, they must strike the other balloon before returning to the first. If a balloon hits the floor, the group must return to the starting line and begin again.
- Extension: The students represent normally functioning cilia in the trachea. However, with smoking, the cilia become weighed down with tar. Play the volley challenge again, but this time students can use only one arm. Play the volley challenge a third time, but students cannot use either arm. This is analogous to cilia not working. Typically, a smoker will need to cough repeatedly to expel debris.

Differentiations

- Challenge task: Play the game with three different colored balloons.
- Simplified task: Play the game with one balloon instead of two.

Activity 5: Lung Relay (15 minutes)

Another side effect of smoking is that it can narrow the airways leading to the lungs. This can also be caused by asthma, which makes breathing more difficult. Students will play a game that mimics the effects of a constricted airway.

All students get a partner and sit along the long sideline of the gym. On go, one partner speed walks to the opposite sideline, does five jumping jacks and five lunges, and then speed walks back. The second partner performs the same actions upon return of partner one. For round two, students repeat the process while breathing through a drinking straw. They compare the difficulty of each. If breathing through the straw becomes too difficult for a student, they can remove the straw and breathe normally.

Closure

Students sit with their partner from activity 5, and one partner explains how to correctly perform the jump. When finished, the other partner explains how to correctly perform the leap. Next, one student explains to their partner how they would respond if an adult in the room where they were playing started to smoke. When finished, the other partner explains the negative effects smoking cigarettes has on the body.

Managing Troublesome Feelings, Seeking Help, and Overhand Throw

GRADE LEVEL: 2

INTRODUCTORY INFORMATION

SHAPE America Outcomes

- S1.E14.2 Throws overhand demonstrating two of the five critical elements of a mature pattern.
- S1.E1.2 Skips using a mature pattern.

National Health Education Performance Indicators

- 1.2.1 Identify that healthy behaviors impact personal health.
- 7.2.2 Demonstrate behaviors that avoid or reduce health risks.

Lesson Objectives

Students will be able to do the following:

- Move through general space, stopping and starting while changing directions and speeds.
- Perform the overhand throw during practice tasks using correct form.
- Identify how their feelings about themselves may affect personal health.
- Know where and when to seek help for worrisome thoughts, feelings, or actions about themselves or their friends.

Learning Materials and Technology

- 6 tall cones (different colors)
- 40 yarn balls
- 40 beanbags
- 2 crates
- 6 hoops
- 12 hoop holders
- 5 targets that can be taped to the wall (e.g., hoops, cartoon characters, seasonal decorations)
- 12 bowling pins

- 10 cardboard boxes or 10 sets of large foam shapes
- 30 poly spots (different colors)
- 6 rope segments to hang hoops from a basketball hoop
- 10 floor arrows
- Resource handouts from HK*Propel*
  - Resource 1: 1 printout
  - Resource 2: 1 printout per two students

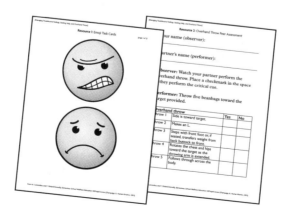

Skill Cues

Overhand Throw

- Keep side to the target.
- Put throwing arm behind the head with the elbow bent at a 90-degree angle (L shape).
- Step toward the target with the opposite foot.
- Rotate the chest and hips toward the target as the throwing arm is extended toward the target.
- Follow through across the body to the opposite hip.

Skip

- Step forward with the lead foot and hop.
- Raise the opposite knee to waist height.
- The arm on the same side as the hopping foot swings up and forward; the other arm is back.
- Repeat the pattern by alternating the right and left foot.

LEARNING ACTIVITIES

Activity 1: Expressing Feelings

Set up six or more colored cones (red, blue, yellow, green) to create an "emotions lane." The lane should be at least 36 inches (91 cm) wide to accommodate children who use assistive mobility devices. Tape an emoji face (resource 1) and the associated emotion vocabulary word, including a braille label, to the first cone in each lane. Read the word on each set of cones and ask students to skip or perform an alternative movement (e.g., lifting one bent knee at a time or moving arms, hands, or head in a swinging motion) in and out of the lane of cones. The movement should be based on the emotion they have felt at school. At the last cone, students skip or perform an alternative movement

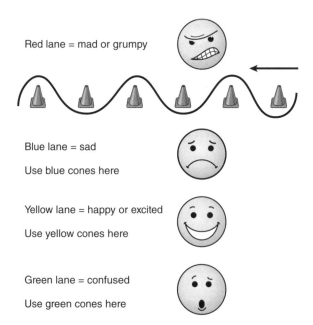

Red lane = mad or grumpy

Blue lane = sad

Use blue cones here

Yellow lane = happy or excited

Use yellow cones here

Green lane = confused

Use green cones here

such as knee raises or the arm, hand, or head swinging back to the beginning of the lane (slightly raised arrows are placed on the floor to guide students). After three to five minutes, bring students to a calling all kids area to conduct the lesson introduction. Show the "Emotions" video (see the lesson plan links file on *HKPropel* for a link to this video). The video should include open or closed captioning with descriptive wording of what is being shown on the screen.

Lesson Introduction

- **WHAT** are we learning today? Students will learn about different feelings and do activities to help them express their feelings through movement.
- **WHY** are we learning this? It is normal to have feelings, and it's important for students to know how to recognize their feelings and act on them appropriately.
- **HOW** will learning be measured? Students will complete the overhand throw peer assessment (resource 2).

Activity 2: Overhand Throw Stations

While students are in the calling all kids area, demonstrate the overhand throw while giving a play-by-play verbal account. Use a yarn ball and then a beanbag. The students verbally, through sign language, or acting it out state the four skill cues, "side to target," "make an L," and "step and throw" as you verbally state them out loud.

Students stand up, sit tall, or lie on a mat in their personal space and shadow the overhand throw while you state the verbal skill cues. Students do this a minimum of three times while you observe and provide feedback.

Demonstrate the overhand throw at each station while the children observe. Dismiss the children by their learning team (a group of students similar to forming squads) to an assigned station. Rotate students after five to seven minutes of practice at each station.

Station 1: Sad Station

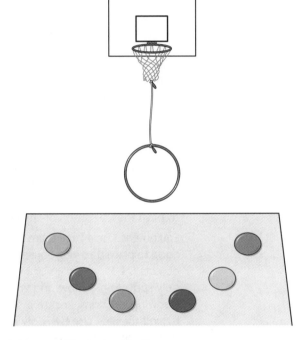

- Description: Students stand, wheel, kneel, or lie on colored poly spots and try to throw through the hoop. If everyone cooperates, the spots can be moved. Demonstrates the overhand throw three times. Children say the cues during a fourth demonstration. Be sure children are sitting on the throwing side of the teacher (e.g., on the right side if the teacher is right-handed).

- Equipment: Use 1 hoop, 1 rope, 6 poly spots, 10 beanbags and yarn balls placed in 1 or 2 crates behind the poly spots so the students can retrieve the throwing objects as needed. A large sad emoji task card is placed on a tall cone at this station. For universal design for learning considerations, add a wheelchair bowling ramp and small table the height of 1 hoop.

- Setup: Suspend the hoop from a basketball hoop using a jump rope. Place the six poly spots in a semicircle around the basket 10 yards (9 m) from the basketball hoop. Vary the distance slightly to account for high- and low-performing students.

- Teacher directions: After students practice the overhand throw at this station for five to seven minutes, ask students to get together in a group and discuss when and why they have recently felt sad. One student can volunteer to report to the class if they feel comfortable doing so.

Station 2: Excited Station

- Description: At this station partners assess each other's throwing performance as they throw from different distances to a hoop. Demonstrate and explain that children will throw from different distances. Ask a student to watch you for the purpose of explaining how to use the peer assessment. At least one set of assessments needs to be braille and at least one set needs additional pictures. Students who have difficulty writing can respond by pointing or putting a sticker on the correct response.

- Equipment: Use hoops and hoop holders, poly spots, and yarn balls or beanbags, a large excited emoji task card with a braille label placed on a tall cone, peer observation forms, and clipboards with attached pencils at this station. Provide an alternative method for recording for students who cannot use a pencil and form or cannot read print. Place a plastic bin for completed peer assessments and a sound device behind the hoop.

- Setup: Set up four to six hoops (six substations) with a hoop holder along the wall so that one student practices at one station. Place poly spots different distances from the wall. Use different colors for each distance: 10 feet (3 m), 15 feet (4.5 m), and 20 feet (6 m). Students throw toward the wall. The hoops with the yarn balls should be behind the poly spots. Students who sit or cannot use their hands will have a peer buddy pick up the balls for them. Students who cannot throw can use a bowling ramp or a table in front of them to push the ball off of, or they can drop the ball onto a hoop that is placed on the floor as a grasp and release task.

- Teacher directions: Explain that each person may take 3 to 5 practice throws and then their partner administers the peer assessment. After practicing the overhand throw for five to seven minutes, ask students to get together in a group and discuss when and why they have recently felt excited. One student can volunteer to report to the class if they feel comfortable doing so.

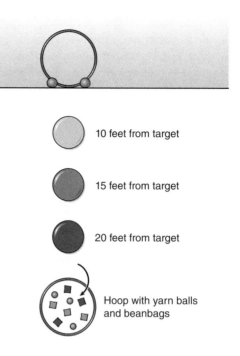

10 feet from target

15 feet from target

20 feet from target

Hoop with yarn balls and beanbags

Station 3: Grumpy Station

- Description: Demonstrate standing on one of three poly spots to throw at the bowling pins on top of a foam shape or cardboard box. Students need to reset the bowling pins after throwing at their substation. Students who sit or cannot use their hands will have a peer buddy pick up pins for them. Students who cannot throw can use a bowling ramp or a table in front of them to push the ball off of, or they can drop the ball onto the pins as a grasp and release activity.

- Equipment: Use 4 large foam shapes or large cardboard boxes, 30 plastic bowling pins, a bin or hoop to place throwing objects in, throwing objects (24-30 yarn balls or beanbags), and poly spots (red, yellow, and green) to mark throwing locations. Locate a sound device behind the pins. Use two poly spots on top of each other to make it easier to sense their location. Use a bathmat to act as big poly spot for wheelchair users or students who need a larger base of support, and use a stable chair for students who need to sit.

- Setup: Place three bowling pins on each foam shape or cardboard box. Place three poly spots in a line in front of the pins 10 feet (3 m), 15 feet (4.5 m), and 20 feet (6 m) from the target.

- Teacher directions: After students practice the overhand throw for five to seven minutes, ask students to get together in a group and discuss when and why they have recently felt grumpy. One student can volunteer to report to the class if they feel comfortable doing so.

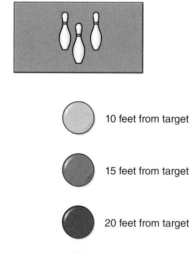

10 feet from target

15 feet from target

20 feet from target

Bin with throwing objects inside

Station 4: Confused Station

- Description: Demonstrate standing on a poly spot and throwing toward a target on the wall.
- Equipment: Use throwing objects (25-30 yarn balls or beanbags), 4 or 5 large targets, and 6 to 8 poly spots. Locate a sound device behind the pins. Use two poly spots on top of each other to make it easier to sense their location. Use a bathmat to act as big poly spot for wheelchair users or students who need a larger base of support, and use a stable chair for students who need to sit.
- Setup: Tape the targets to the wall at varying heights and place the poly spots approximately 10 feet (3 m) from the wall in a line parallel to the wall. Place a bin containing the throwing objects behind the line of poly spots.
- Teacher directions: After students practice the overhand throw for five to seven minutes, ask students to get together in a group and discuss when and why they have recently felt confused. One student can volunteer to report to the class if they feel comfortable doing so.

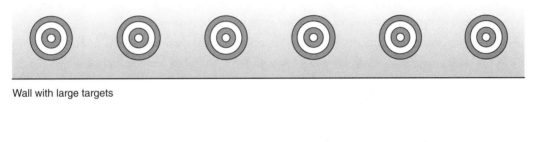

Wall with large targets

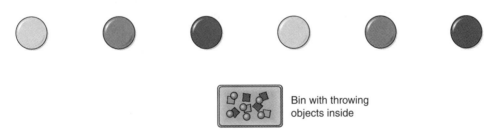

Bin with throwing objects inside

Closure

Bring the children together in the calling all kids area. Students will get together with their partners. One partner is the "clay" and the other is a "molder." The molder shapes the clay into the correct position for the beginning of the throw and then the correct follow-through or ending position for the overhand throw. Partners share one of the feelings from the lesson that they felt earlier in the day or at home.

Ask for volunteers to share something about their feelings and remind children that they can always contact the school guidance counselor, their teacher, a good friend, or a relative to talk about their feelings.

Universal Design for Learning

The following are additional universal design for learning considerations for all learners:

- Consider using peer buddies to support students who cannot reach the floor to pick up the throwing objects.
- Use auditory devices behind targets such as an MP3 player with music, loud metronome or metronome app on a phone, phone alarm app, or a commercially made device from the American Printing House for the Blind.

- When using assessment worksheets, provide means of expression such as pointing to pictures, using a communication device, answering yes or no questions, sending home worksheets to be transcribed in text to talk, using a scribe, reading out loud, and using braille when requested.
- Consider raising the poly spots by using two, one on top of the other, or a larger and thicker spot such as a rubber bathmat.
- Provide additional means to check for understandings by asking yes or no questions, having students say or use sign language cue words when requested, or asking students to perform the movement for you before beginning.
- Learn sign language for the cues of the overhand throw and the emotions.
- On a tablet, play a video model of the overhand throw cues and what is to be done at each station.
- Change the goal of the activity to include pushing a ball off of the lap, pushing a ball off a wheelchair bowling ramp, dropping a ball out of the hand onto a target, or pushing a ball across a table toward the target.
- Provide paraeducators and classroom teachers with the lesson plan or cue words for students who need to program the words into their communication device.
- Use peer buddies for students who might need additional demonstrations or cue words.
- Work with an American Sign Language interpreter, if available, on vocabulary words directly related to this lesson.
- Provide directions in words, picture, or braille.
- Use rubber footprints on the floor as additional cues for foot placement.
- Because it is difficult to throw while using assistive devices, provide a chair for students who use canes or crutches so they can throw while sitting.
- Preteach the lesson to students who need extra support.

<table>
<tr><td></td><td>Medicine Safety, Underhand Throw,
and Space</td><td></td></tr>
</table>

Medicine Safety, Underhand Throw, and Space

GRADE LEVEL: K

INTRODUCTORY INFORMATION

SHAPE America Outcomes

- S1.E13.K Throws underhand with opposite foot forward.
- S2.E1.Ka Differentiates between movement in personal (self-space) and general space.

National Health Education Performance Indicators

- 1.2.1 Identify that healthy behaviors affect personal health.
- 1.2.4 List ways to prevent common childhood injuries.
- 2.2.1 Identify how the family influences personal health practices and behaviors.
- 4.2.3 Demonstrate ways to respond when in an unwanted, threatening, or dangerous situation.
- 7.2.2 Demonstrate behaviors that avoid or reduce health risks.

Lesson Objectives

Students will be able to do the following:

- Define the word *medicine*.
- Identify safe and unsafe responses to scenarios involving medicines.
- Maintain personal space and general space during activities.
- Demonstrate the underhand throw using correct form from a distance of 10 to 15 feet (3-4.5 m) toward a stationary target.

Learning Materials and Technology

- 40 small cones
- 2 folding mats
- 50 fleece balls
- 1 "safe" sign
- 1 "unsafe" sign
- 1 hoop per student
- 1 half pool noodle per student
- Resource handouts from HK*Propel*
  - Resource 1: 1 printout
  - Resource 2: 1 printout

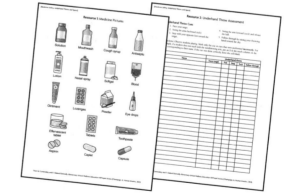

Skill Cues

Underhand Throw

- Face your target.
- Swing the arms backward (tick).
- Step with your opposite foot toward the target.
- Swing the arm forward (tock) and release the ball
- Follow through by raising your throwing hand toward the sky.

LEARNING ACTIVITIES

Lesson Introduction

- **WHAT** are we learning today? Students will learn about medicine safety, the underhand throw, and personal space.

- **WHY** are we learning this? Kindergarten students get more than their share of bumps and bruises. Safety takes practice. This lesson addresses two potential sources of injury: running into each other (collisions) during physical activity and finding unsafe medications. Students will also learn the underhand throw, which is used in many sporting activities.

- **HOW** will learning be measured? Student learning will be measured during activity 1 and through the underhand throw assessment (resource 2).

Activity 1: Discussion and Whose Side Are You On? (10 minutes)

Ask students if any of them can name a medicine. It will probably be something a trusted adult gave them. Ask students what the word *medicine* means. A medicine is something taken into the body that changes how the body works. Explain that medicines taken as directed help people feel better. However, medicines taken the wrong way can hurt people.

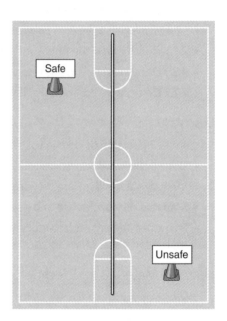

To play the game, divide the gym in half using a long rope placed on the floor. Position two large cones with signs stating "safe" and "unsafe" on opposite sides of the rope. At the start, all students stand on the rope. Read a safe or unsafe scenario from the list that follows. If the situation is safe, students move to that side; if it is unsafe they move to the other side. After reading each scenario, use a countdown of "3-2-1-go" so everyone moves at the same time. Ask students not to foreshadow their move so that others can decide for themselves. Read the scenarios in a random order. Follow up with individual students or address challenging scenarios using an awareness discussion. You may choose to incorporate fundamental movement skills while students move.

Unsafe Scenarios

- You find pills on the floor and put them in your mouth.
- You have a tummy ache at your friend's house, so you ask your friend for medicine.
- You start to feel weird after taking a medicine (side effect).
- You have a headache at home and your parents are sleeping so you get some medicine.
- You have taken medicine, but it doesn't seem to be working so you get more.
- You take a puff on an e-cigarette left on the couch by an adult.
- You take a vitamin pill offered by a friend because it tastes good.
- You repeatedly sniff something under the bathroom sink because you like how it smells.

Safe Scenarios

- You ask your grandparent for Tylenol.
- You ask to see the doctor because you feel sick.
- You don't touch medicine bottles sitting on the counter.

- You stay away from medicine in the bathroom cabinet or closet.
- You ask to leave the room when someone is smoking.
- You refuse to try a treat given to you by a stranger.

Activity 2: Space Invaders (15 minutes)

Another way to be safe is to move throughout the gymnasium without bumping into other people. That's called *collision avoidance*. It's a skill used on the playground, in the grocery store, at an amusement park, and especially in crowded places. Students will practice collision avoidance and recognizing personal space and general space. Instruct each student to get a hoop and sit quietly in general space without touching it. Define and demonstrate personal space. Explain to the students that their personal space is the area they can reach with any body part while they are in the same spot. If they are using equipment, such as a racket or bat, their personal space includes the area they can reach with the equipment. During the activities, each student holds a hoop around their waist to visually represent their personal space.

Crisscross

Split the class in two; half sits on one side of the gym and the remainder sits on the other. When the music begins, students walk back and forth across the gym as many times as possible without bumping into another hoop or person. Periodically stop the music and check for adequate personal space; point out both excellent spacing and potentially problematic spacing. Ask students what strategies they used to avoid collisions.

Extension: Students hold the hoop with one hand and half a pool noodle in the other. Extend the noodle outside the area of the hoop. Repeat the activity. Discuss how personal space expands when someone is using equipment. This is especially true with objects such as hockey sticks.

Shrinking Gym

Delineate the general space by placing cones in a rectangular shape, preferably along existing lines. Students move throughout the general space using different fundamental movement skills. Increase and decrease the speed, and then discuss how speed affects safety and personal space. As the music plays, gradually decreases the general space by moving the boundary cones closer together. Discuss afterward how the size of the general space affects safety.

Space Invaders Tag

Designate 3 to 5 students as taggers or use hoop colors to distinguish taggers. The taggers attempt to touch their hoop to the hoop of other students. If tagged, students drop their hoop, do five vertical jumps, and rejoin the activity. This activity can be done with hoops held around the waist or with hoops on the ground. If playing with hoops on the ground, students shuffle the hoop with their feet.

Activity 3: Returning Unsafe Medicines (15 minutes)

Project the pictures of medicine (resource 1) onto a whiteboard to illustrate that medicines come in all shapes and sizes. Explain the three rules all kids should follow. First, never put found medicines in your mouth. Second, give found medicines to an adult. Third, only take medicines when given by a trusted adult. Students turn to another student and repeat the three rules.

Explain to students that they will pretend to return unsafe medicines to the bottle. Create a medicine bottle by standing up two folding mats. Ask for two student volunteers to stand inside the mats. Form a poly spot circle around the folding mats 15 feet (4.5 m) away from the "bottle." Scatter fleece balls (medicines) on the floor outside the poly spot circle. On go, students use correct underhand throwing technique to return the medicines to the bottle. Demonstrate how to perform an underhand throw. The students inside the bottle act as gremlins (playful troublemakers) and throw the medicines back over the top of the mats. Rotate students through this role.

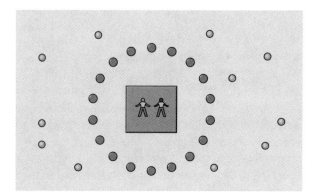

Extension: Students throw with the nondominant hand, or they underhand throw the medicine to another student, who throws it inside.

During activity 3, complete the underhand throw assessment (resource 2).

Closure

Ask students what are the three rules of medicine. Accept responses one at a time. Next, all students stand up and pretend to underhand throw an object to you. They continue until you tell them to stop. Point out students who are doing it well and provide corrective feedback to students who need it.

Peer Pressure, Mirror and Match, and Speed

GRADE LEVEL: 1

INTRODUCTORY INFORMATION

SHAPE America Outcomes

- S2.E2.1b Travels demonstrating a variety of relationships with objects (e.g., over, under, around, through).
- S2.E3.1a Differentiates between fast and slow speeds.
- S3.E2.1 Engages actively in physical education class.

National Health Education Performance Indicators

- 2.2.1 Identify how the family influences personal health practices and behaviors.
- 4.2.1 Demonstrate healthy ways to express needs, wants, and feelings.

Lesson Objectives

Students will be able to do the following:

- Mirror and match the movements of another student.
- Describe the terms *mirror* and *match* and explain how speed affects performance.
- Define peer pressure and identify how it can affect health.

Learning Materials and Technology

- 1 scarf per student
- 1 streamer per student
- 1 pool noodle per student
- 1 hoop per student
- 40 poly spots
- Simon says video (created by teacher)
- Resource handout from HK*Propel*
  - Resource 1: 1 printout

LEARNING ACTIVITIES

Lesson Introduction

- **WHAT** are we learning today? Students will learn about how pressure from other students (peer pressure) can affect health. Students will also learn how to mirror and match other students while changing speeds.
- **WHY** are we learning this? Peer pressure is a factor in everyone's life. Sometimes it's OK to "go with the flow," but at other times students will need to do their own thing. Knowing what to do can affect health.
- **HOW** will learning be measured? Learning will be measured through a mirror and match assessment (resource 1).

Activity 1: Look Up, Look Down (10 minutes)

Students form two circles 10 yards (9 m) apart. In each circle, students face the center and stand elbow-length apart. When you say, "Look down," all students looks down at their toes. When you say, "Look up," they look at the face of someone else in their circle and hold that stare until the next "look down" command; they should not look at one person and then change their glance. If two students are looking at each other, they both let out an emphatic scream, jog to the other circle, and join that circle. If a student's eyes don't meet another's, they remain in the circle. Continue saying look up and look down every 5 to 8 seconds. Toward the end of the game, students whose eyes meet step to the side and cheer on the remaining students until only one is left. This student bows while the others applaud.

Ask students how often their eyes met those of a classmate when they looked up (Answer: not very often). In school, how often do they think other students are watching them carefully (Answer: not very often either). Explain that sometimes it may feel like others are watching us, especially if we're concerned about our clothes or our hair that day. Most of us keep busy thinking about our own lives. So don't worry about other's perceptions; be yourself.

Activity 2: Mirror—Match—Speed (15 minutes)

Lead a mirroring activity by using upper-body movements only. Mirroring is like looking into a mirror. For example, as the teacher raises their left arm, students raise their right arm. Students spread out in general space facing the teacher. Have students mirror your upper-body movements for two minutes. Next, students find a partner; one partner is the leader and the other partner mirrors the leader. Leaders should start with slow movements of the upper-body only. Extend the mirroring task by prompting students to use lower-body movements, change levels, and vary the speed of movements. Switch the leader after 3 to 5 minutes.

Repeat the previous activity but now use matching. Matching involves moving the same body part as the leader. For example, as the teacher raises their left arm, students also raise their left arm. This is challenging because the teacher is facing the students. Next, each pair of students gets two scarves, streamers, or pool noodles (positioned along the side of the gym). Both partners must have the same object and use them when matching their partner's movements. After 3 to 5 minutes, switch the leader and the follower. Teachers may add direction changes, pathway changes, and level changes.

Takeaway message: Explain that in life there are times when you want to match (copy) what your friends might be doing, but at other times it's better to mirror, or do the opposite. Ask students for an example.

- Match examples: taking turns on the slide, working hard on schoolwork, sharing crayons
- Mirror examples: using putdowns, taking toys, cutting in line

Peer pressure can be positive or negative. When your classmates or friends are doing the right thing, it's a good idea to match (positive peer pressure), but when they are doing the wrong thing (negative peer pressure), you should mirror, or do the opposite.

Activity 3: Rock, Paper, Scissors (10 minutes)

Create two lines in the middle of the gym about five feet (1.5 m) apart using poly spots. Divide students into two teams. Each team stands on a separate line and faces the other team. Teach students how to play rock, paper, scissors. Most students will already know the rules: rock smashes scissors, scissors cuts paper, and paper covers rock. To prepare, each team forms a secret huddle and decides in 20 seconds or less their primary symbol (rock, scissor, or paper) and a backup symbol. To complete the activity, teams line up facing one another. On the count of 3, each team shows their primary symbol. The winning team chases the other team back to the safe line. Anyone tagged before reaching the safe line joins the winning team. If both teams flash the same primary symbol, the backup symbol is used. Continue for a certain amount of time or until one side is eliminated (this rarely happens).

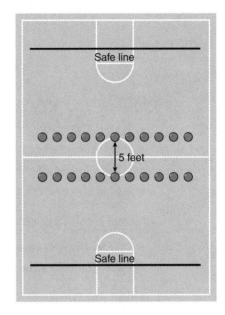

Takeaway message: Quite often in this game, individual students or even entire teams will run the wrong way. For example, the winning team runs back, thinking that it lost. This is usually driven by students watching what others are doing instead of interpreting for themselves the symbols being shown. This can come from not being able to interpret the sign fast enough or just following what others do. Remind students to make decisions for themselves whenever possible and do what they feel is best. They may make the wrong call, but it is their own.

Activity 4: Simon Says (5-10 minutes)

Before class, record a video of yourself leading a Simon says game. The speed and difficulty should be suitable for first grade. In round one, students match the actions on the screen. In round two, students mirror the actions. While students are following the video, complete the mirror and match assessment (resource 1). Students start each round in a hoop. If they make a mistake, they step outside the hoop but continue the activity. The last person inside a hoop wins.

Extra-Time Activity: Noodle Tag

Designate 3 to 5 students as taggers and give a pool noodle to each student. Play tag. Students tagged create a balanced, frozen shape. To become unfrozen, another student must mirror the shape and hold it for a count of 5. Afterward, the frozen student is free. Taggers may not tag helpers. During the activity, vary the speed and locomotor pattern. Change taggers periodically.

Closure

Students sit with a partner. The teacher recites the statement, "Be yourself; everyone else is taken." Partner 1 explains to their partner what they believe the statement means. Next, the teacher recites, "We are the company that we keep." This time, partner 2 explains to their partner what they believe the statement means. Discuss after each.

Recycling, Underhand Toss, and Striking

GRADE LEVEL: K-1

INTRODUCTORY INFORMATION

SHAPE America Outcomes

- S1.E13.K Throws underhand with opposite foot forward.
- S1.E13.1 Throws underhand, demonstrating two of the five critical elements of a mature pattern.
- S1.E24.K Strikes a lightweight object with a paddle or short-handled racket.
- S1.E24.1 Strikes a ball with a short-handled implement, sending it upwards.

National Health Education Performance Indicators

- 1.2.1 Identify how healthy behaviors affect personal health.
- 2.2.1 Identify how the family influences personal health practices and behaviors.

Lesson Objectives

Students will be able to do the following:

- Identify how recycling affects wellness.
- Determine whether items are recyclable or not.
- Describe how family practices influence recycling.
- Demonstrate two of five critical elements of a correct underhand throw.
- Strike an object with a short-handled paddle, demonstrating two of the five critical elements.

Learning Materials and Technology

- 1 poly spot or flying disc labeled "heads" or "tails" on each side
- 1-3 laundry bins or large ball carts on wheels
- 2 gator balls or similar soft balls per student
- 1 racket or paddle per student
- Resource handouts from HK*Propel*
  - Resource 1: 1 printout
  - Resource 2: 1 printout

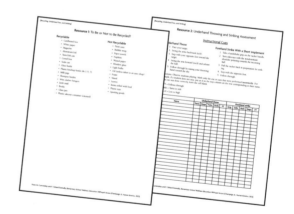

Skill Cues

Underhand Throw

- Face your target.
- Swing the arms backward (tick).
- Step with your opposite foot toward the target.
- Swing the arm forward (tock) and release the ball.
- Follow through by raising your throwing hand toward the sky.

Forehand Strike

- Take a handshake grip on the racket handle.
- Turn sideways with the nondominant shoulder pointing towards the incoming ball.
- Pull the racket back in preparation for striking.
- Step with the opposite foot.
- Follow through.

Backhand Strike

- Turn sideways with the dominant shoulder pointing towards the incoming ball.
- Pull the racket back in preparation for striking.
- Step with the same-side foot.
- Following through.

LEARNING ACTIVITIES

Lesson Introduction

- **WHAT** are we learning today? Students will learn about the importance of recycling, what items may be recycled, how to correctly perform the underhand toss, and how to strike an object with a short-handled implement.
- **WHY** are we learning this? Recycling has many benefits for the environment, the nation, and its people. It's important to take care of the Earth because it is our only home. The underhand toss and striking are essential skills incorporated into more advanced sports such as softball, tennis, and badminton.
- **HOW** will learning be measured? Learning will be measured using a teacher-administered underhand throwing and striking assessment (resource 2).

Activity 1: Heads and Tails Tag (5 minutes)

Students decide whether they are heads (place both hands on head) or tails (place both hands on low back). To start the activity, flip a poly spot or flying disc that has one side identified as "heads" and the other as "tails." If the flip is heads, the heads chase the tails. When a student is tagged, they join the other team by moving their hands. The game continues until all students are either heads or tails. Students must keep their hands in the correct location even when running; they cannot change their call sign. Play multiple rounds and invite different students to be the flipper, or select the last person tagged.

Activity 2: Recycling Discussion (10 minutes)

Ask students why we should recycle. Guide student responses toward the following benefits and fill in any missed. Write student responses on the whiteboard.

- Reduces the amount of waste going to landfills (dump) or being burned.
- Uses natural resources (trees, minerals, materials) more slowly.
- Uses more resources already in the United States (don't have to import so much from other countries).
- Saves energy by not having to make items from scratch.
- Reduces pollution to our air, water, and ground.

Read the list of items in resource 1 one at a time. If the item can be recycled, students place a thumbs-up against their chest. If the item cannot be recycled, students place a thumbs-down against their chest. Discuss reasons why some items can be recycled and others cannot.

Activity 3: Recycling Truck (10 minutes)

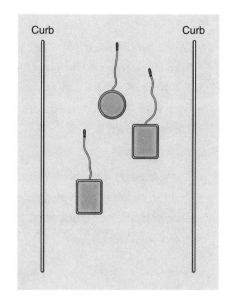

Demonstrate the underhand throw while students copy you, and if desired, practice the underhand throw back and forth with a partner. Next, demonstrate how to hit a moving target. Pretend large storage bins or carts are recycling trucks. Students are positioned on either side of the gym behind a line called the "curb." The "trucks" are pushed or pulled through the middle, while students use an underhand throw to toss their recyclable items (balls or other soft objects) into the moving cart. If multiple large carts are available, students volunteer as drivers. The cart may be pushed directly with two hands or pulled by an affixed rope. When the truck reaches the end of the gym, it turns around and heads back. One truck moves slowly, another faster, and the third changes speed and direction. When students have exhausted their supply of recyclable items to throw, the round is over. To clean up, students look both ways before entering the street to retrieved missed recyclables. No student may enter the street while the trucks are moving. Have as many soft balls and throwable items available as possible so students get multiple opportunities to practice per round. Complete the underhand throw assessment (resource 2) during the activity.

Differentiations

- Challenge task: Aim for the faster-moving truck, and take one step back from the throwing line (curb).
- Simplified task: Aim for the slower-moving truck.

Activity 4: The Pollutians (15 minutes)

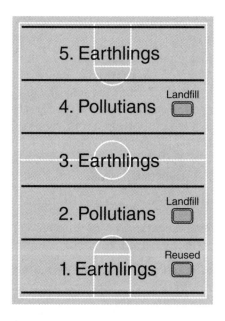

Divide the gym into five zones lengthwise. In zones 1, 3, and 5 are Earthlings; in zones 2 and 4 are Pollutians. Pollutians are fictitious characters who pollute and use up the Earth's precious resources. The balls represent recyclables. All recyclables start out in zone 1. On go, the Earthlings use the forehand striking pattern and a paddle or racket to strike recyclables along the floor to their teammates in zones 3 and 5. Teammates must absorb the force of the moving ball to control it in their zone. If the recyclable is intercepted by a Pollutian or moves out of an Earthling zone, it is gleefully put in a bin labelled "landfill" by a Pollutian. After a recyclable item makes its way to zone 5, it is processed and turned into a new product. It is then hit back to zone 3 and eventually to zone 1, where it is put in a bin labelled "reused." The goal is to have more items in the reused bin than the landfill bin. Play multiple rounds and rotate students after each round. Complete the striking assessment (resource 2) during the activity.

Alternative: Instead of a racket, have students strike the ball with an open hand.

Closure

Students work in pairs to identify as many items that can be recycled as possible. Ask students to raise their hand if their family recycles at home. Ask how students can contribute to recycling even if it is not done at home. (Answer: Recycle at school and in the community. Encourage their parents to buy recycled products or start recycling at home.)

Respiratory System and Underhand Roll

GRADE LEVEL: 2-3

INTRODUCTORY INFORMATION

SHAPE America Outcomes

- S1.E13.3 Throws (rolls) underhand to a partner or target with reasonable accuracy.
- S2.E5.3a Applies simple strategies and tactics in chasing activities.

National Health Education Performance Indicators

- 1.5.1 Describe the relationship between healthy behaviors and personal health.
- 2.5.2 Identify the influence of culture on health practices and behaviors.
- 5.5.3 List healthy options to health-related issues or problems.

Lesson Objectives

Students will be able to do the following:

- Demonstrate correct underhand roll technique.
- Describe the major functions of the respiratory system and its parts.
- Identify ways to keep the respiratory system strong and maintain its health.

This is a two-day lesson.

Learning Materials and Technology

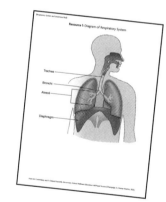

- 50 fleece balls
- 1 hoop for every 2 students
- 6 cardboard boxes or milk crates
- 50-100 balloons (can be different sizes and shapes)
- 5-10 hand pumps
- 1 straw per student
- 1 ping pong ball for every 2 students
- Resource handout from HK*Propel*
  - Resource 1: 1 printout

Skill Cues

Underhand Roll

- Face your target.
- Step with your opposite foot toward the target while lowering the body toward the ground.
- Swing the arm backward (tick).
- Swing the arm forward (tock).
- Release the ball on the ground while following through toward the target.

Underhand Throw

- Face your target.
- Swing the arms backward (tick).
- Step with your opposite foot toward the target.

- Swing the arm forward (tock) and release the ball
- Follow through by raising your throwing hand toward the sky.

LEARNING ACTIVITIES

Lesson Introduction

- **WHAT** are we learning today? Students will learn about the lungs and how to keep them healthy. At the same time, students will practice and refine their underhand rolls and underhand throws.
- **WHY** are we learning this? The lungs and respiratory system are what the body uses to breathe. The underhand throw and roll are important skills used in softball, bowling, and other activities.
- **HOW** will learning be measured? Learning will be measured by evaluating multiple performances of the underhand roll and throw according to the cues.

Activity 1: Discussion (10 minutes)

Ask students to identify functions of the respiratory systems. Answers may include moving air in and out of the lungs, getting oxygen into the body, and removing carbon dioxide from the body.

Show students a printout of resource 1 or display it digitally using a projector or smartboard. Explain the different structures:

- Trachea: The trachea is known as the windpipe and allows air to flow from the mouth down into the lungs. It is lined with cartilage rings so it stays open. Invite students to gently touch the front of their neck to see if they can feel the rings.
- Bronchi: The bronchi are similar to the trachea except they allow air to flow into the right and left lung.
- Alveoli: Show students a blown-up balloon. Explain that the lungs are filled with millions of tiny sacs called alveoli. The walls are so thin that oxygen can pass into the blood, and carbon dioxide (a waste) can pass into the lungs to be exhaled. The thin nature of the alveoli aids gas exchange but also means they can be damaged easily.
- Diaphragm: This is a muscle. When you breathe in, it contracts and moves down. When you breathe out, it relaxes and moves up. Ask students to give it a try by taking a deep, deep breath. Can they feel the diaphragm moving down?

Students get a partner. One partner breathes normally while the other partner counts the number of breaths for 30 seconds. Ask students how to find their breathing rate. The answer is to multiply their count by two. Switch roles. The normal rate for a child 6 to 12 years old is 18 to 30 breaths per minute.

Differentiations

- Challenge task: Ask students what someone's breathing rate would be if they took 10 breathes in 15 seconds (answer: 40) and 6 breathes in 10 seconds (answer: 36).

Activity 2: Catch and Release (10 minutes)

Students get a partner and one uninflated balloon. On go, students inflate the balloon using one of the hand pumps. After inflation, remove the balloon from the pump and pinch the end to prevent air from escaping. Do not tie the balloon. The partners find an open space, and one student throws the balloon up into the air while the other tries to catch it before it hits the ground. Reinflate the balloon and switch roles. When returning to the filling station, students can choose a different balloon. Tell students not to blow up the balloon with their mouth. If they forget, discard the balloon.

A few minutes into the activity, yell, "freeze." Students sit without touching the equipment. Ask students, "Can anyone explain what makes the balloon travel?" (Answer: The air inside the balloon is packed together much more tightly than the air outside the balloon. So, when the pinch is released, the air moves quickly out, and the balloon flies.) Next ask, "How does this same idea apply to the lungs?" (Answer: When the diaphragm relaxes and moves up, the air in the lungs gets compressed more tightly than the air outside, so the air moves out.) Allow students to return to the activity.

Extensions

- Inflate two balloons. Partners throws their balloon up simultaneously and each balloon must be caught by the other partner.
- Students spin one time before catching or must catch with only their nondominant hand.

Activity 3: Clean Room (15 minutes)

One of the biggest threats to the respiratory system is contaminants that come from pollution, allergens like dust and pollen, and smoking. It is important to avoid breathing in contaminants.

Demonstrate the underhand roll. Students get a partner and practice rolling back and forth for three minutes. During that time, students must provide two examples of positive or constructive feedback related to the cues.

Scatter two teams on opposite sides of a dividing line. Spread contaminants (fleece balls) out on the floor on both sides. Two-thirds of the way back on each side, place three boxes or crates lying on their side. These represent alveoli. On go, teams use proper underhand roll technique to move contaminants to the other side. Contaminants may not be removed from the alveoli; students may not guard the alveoli. Play for a few minutes and stop; count the number of contaminants on each side. Teams get one point for each item, plus three for each item in the alveoli. See which side has the fewest contaminants.

Extension: If a contaminant hits someone in the feet, they must perform five jumping jacks before returning.

Activity 4: Wind Power (10 minutes)

Students get a partner and sit on opposite sides of two gym floor lines, approximately two to three feet (0.6-1 m) apart. If no such lines are available, use two jump ropes. In the middle, place a ping pong ball. On go, students blow through a straw, attempting to push the ping pong ball over their partner's line. After each score, reset the ball in the middle. Play for two minutes and rotate to a new partner.

Extension: Place two side-lying shoe boxes on the ground five feet apart with their tops removed. The boxes represent hockey goals. Students score by blowing the ping pong ball into the box.

Closure

Ask students a series of questions:

1. Did or does anyone feel tightness in and around the bottom of their ribs? This is the area where the diaphragm can be found.
2. How successful were you in the wind power game? Those who have a stronger respiratory system can produce more "wind."
3. One of the best ways to keep the lungs healthy is not to smoke or vape. How are those habits portrayed on TV and the Internet?
4. How can you keep your respiratory system healthy? Answers may include the following:
   - Get plenty of cardiovascular exercise.
   - Avoid triggers like allergens or secondhand smoke.
   - Avoid exposure to people with colds and flu.
   - Eat a well-balanced diet.

Secondhand Smoke and Locomotor Skills

GRADE LEVEL: K-2

INTRODUCTORY INFORMATION

SHAPE America Outcomes

- S1.1.K Performs locomotor skills (hopping, galloping, running, sliding, skipping, wheeling, scooting) while maintaining balance.

National Health Education Performance Indicators

- 1.2.1 Identify those healthy behaviors that impact personal health.
- 8.2.1 Make requests to promote personal health.

Lesson Objectives

Students will be able to do the following:

- Travel along different pathways in general space using a variety of locomotor skills at different speeds and rhythms.
- Identify what secondhand smoke is and where it comes from.
- Identify illnesses that can result from exposure to secondhand smoke (ear infection, cough, lung infections such as pneumonia).
- If their parents, caregivers, or relatives smoke, advocate to do so only outside or near an open window when indoors.

Learning Materials and Technology

- 2 rolls of floor tape (used to make pathways on the gymnasium floor; jump ropes can also be used as a substitute; add floor tape over jump ropes for students who need more tactile information)
- 1 Bluetooth player
- Resource handouts from HK*Propel*
  - Resource 1: 1 printout per student
  - Resource 2: 1 printout per student

Skill Cues

Run

- Keep your head up and facing straight ahead.
- Push off of one foot to create a flight phase; swing the opposite arm forward.
- Strike with the foot underneath the body.
- Keep the shoulders open, relaxed, and down.
- Keep the arms close to the torso, bent at 90 degrees, and moving diagonally.

Gallop

- Step forward with the lead foot.
- Push off the trail foot forcefully enough to achieve a flight phase.

- The trail foot catches up to the lead leg by touching the heel.
- Coordinate the arm swing forward with the motion of the legs to achieve distance and height.
- Land on the ball of the lead foot, with the trail foot behind the lead foot.

Slide

- Turn the body sideways to the direction of travel.
- Keep the feet shoulder width apart and arms extended sideways.
- Step to the side with the lead foot.
- Push off with the trail foot so it produces a flight phase and then chases the lead foot.
- Land on the trail foot and then the lead foot.

Hop

- Balance on one foot.
- The nonhopping leg is off the ground and bent at 90 degrees.
- Bend and extend the hopping leg to produce a flight phase.
- The nonhopping leg swings up and forward to produce additional force.
- Arms are bent at the elbow and swing from back to front in coordination with the hopping action.

Skip

- Step forward with the lead foot and hop.
- Raise the opposite knee to waist height.
- The arm on the same side as the hopping foot swings up and forward; the other arm is back.
- Repeat the pattern by alternating the right and left foot.

LEARNING ACTIVITIES

Lesson Introduction

- **WHAT** are we learning today? Students will practice different ways to travel along different pathways (e.g., straight, zigzag, curvy, diagonal). Students will also learn about secondhand smoke.
- **WHY** are we learning this? Being around secondhand smoke can cause a variety of illnesses, so it's important to for students to understand why they should avoid this and ways to ask others not to smoke near them.
- **HOW** will learning be measured? During a peer assessment (resource 1), students will observe a partner skipping (or using an alternative motion such as using arms, hands, or head in a swinging or swaying motion, or lifting knees one at a time if sitting). Students will complete an exit ticket (resource 2) about how to get away from secondhand smoke.

Activity 1: Moving Along Different Pathways (7 minutes)

As students walk or wheel along pathways in the gym, they will think about ways to stay away from secondhand smoke to keep it from getting into their lungs. They could ask anyone smoking in their house to go outside to smoke, or they could go outside and take a walk.

Create a minimum of 15 pathways on the floor using floor tape, jump ropes, or floor tape over jump ropes. With all children in the calling all kids area, demonstrate walking and moving along the different pathways. Instruct children to move from one pathway to another. Dismiss the children by learning teams to choose a pathway to walk or move along. No more than two students should be on the same pathway. Play music as children move along the pathways.

Activity 2: Moving on Different Body Parts to Travel Along Pathways (7 minutes)

Show students a different way to move along one of the pathways (e.g., on hands and feet, wheeling backward, or moving backward). Next state, "I would like to see you be creative and try different ways of traveling on different parts of your body along different pathways." Remind students to remain in control of their body. Use the same dismissal and managerial directions from activity 1.

Activity 3: Using Different Locomotor Skills to Travel Along Varied Pathways (7 minutes)

With all children in the calling all kids area, demonstrate galloping, skipping, sliding, and hopping along the different pathways. Remind students to think about taking a walk outside to get away from secondhand smoke. During the activity, you can verbally prompt students to change from one locomotor skill to another. Alternative movements can include moving the head, shoulders, arms, or hands in the way the upper body moves during the locomotor skill; using a scarf to imitate the rhythm or flow of the locomotor skill; pushing oneself on a scooter or in a wheelchair in different patterns such as two pushes forward and then spin.

Activity 4: Peer Assessment of Skipping and Role Playing (7 minutes)

When the children are in the calling all kids area with their partner, hand out the peer assessment (resource 1). You will be the performer, and the children will observe you and practice completing the assessment before they fill out the assessment with their partners.

After the children assess each other's skipping or alternative movement pattern along one of the pathways, prompt students to practice talking to their parents or caregivers about not smoking inside their house.

Possible prompts include "I know you like to smoke, but I would appreciate it if you would only smoke outside so the smoke doesn't get into my lungs. Then I won't get sick, I will have fewer ear infections, and won't cough." Provide students who need them with scripts to read or point to pictures or use the American Sign Language version of this paragraph.

Closure

Bring the students together and distribute the exit ticket about secondhand smoke (resource 2). Review the directions for completing the ticket and ask students if they have any questions.

Additionally, students can analyze your skipping form. The students watch you skip and assess whether you swing your arms and lift your knees tummy high. You can also demonstrate an alternative movement for students who sit or are unable to skip. Students do a thumbs up if you perform the skip correctly.

Universal Design for Learning

The following are additional universal design for learning considerations for all learners:

- Consider using peer buddies to move as a partner with students who need more support.
- Use auditory devices at the end of each pathway.
- When using the assessments, provide means of expression such as pointing to pictures, using a communication device, answering yes or no questions, sending home worksheets to be transcribed in text to talk, using a scribe, reading out loud, and using braille when requested.
- Consider using a raised representation of the pathways such as a rope under two-inch-wide (5 cm) floor tape or cones with jump ropes strung from one to another.
- Provide additional means to check for understanding by asking yes or no questions or having students say or use sign language cue words when requested.
- On tablet, play a video model of the skip cues and how to follow each pathway.

- Change the goal of the activity to include an alternative movement such as using the arms, hands, or head in a swinging or swaying motion or lifting the knees one at a time while sitting.
- Provide paraeducators and classroom teachers with the lesson plan or cue words for students who need to program those words into their communication devices.
- Provide cards with the pathways drawn on them and outlined with puff paint so they can be felt and include braille descriptions.
- Work with the American Sign Language interpreter, if there is one, on vocabulary words related to this lesson, such as descriptions of the pathways.
- Provide students with their directions in words, pictures, or braille.
- Use rubber footprints on the floor as additional cues for foot placement during the skip.
- Preteach the skip or the pathways to students who need extra support to be able to successfully participate in the lesson.
- Provide alternative means to access the print assessments, such as a scribe, reader, MP3 player asking the questions, braille, or putting stickers on the correct answer.

Senses, Trust, and Dribbling

GRADE LEVEL: 1

INTRODUCTORY INFORMATION

SHAPE America Outcomes

- S1.E17.1 Dribbles continuously in self-space using the preferred hand.
- S4.E4.1 Works independently with others in a variety of class environments (e.g., small and large groups).

National Health Education Performance Indicators

- 1.2.4 List ways to prevent common childhood injuries.
- 3.2.2 Identify ways to locate school and community health helpers.
- 7.2.2 Demonstrate behaviors that avoid or reduce health risks.

Lesson Objectives

Students will be able to do the following:

- Identify the five senses.
- Exhibit behaviors that build trust during the minefield activity.
- Dribble a basketball, demonstrating four of five critical elements.
- Identify school personnel whom students can approach with health concerns and questions.

Learning Materials and Technology

- 20 cones
- 40 poly spots
- 1 large sheet or tarp
- PE objects to place under the sheet or tarp (e.g., fleece ball, scoop, hockey stick, cone, beanbag, foam cylinder, balloon, deck ring, hockey puck, bowling pin, football, foam lollipop paddle)
- 1 basketball per student
- 2 laptops

- 6 plastic containers of cotton balls dipped in substances with different smells
- 2 tape dispensers
- 1 100-foot (30 m) rope or 10 jump ropes
- 1 tennis ball
- Resource handouts from HK*Propel*
  - Resource 1: 1 printout per student
  - Resource 2: 2 printouts and 50 cutouts of each letter
  - Resource 3: 1 printout
  - Resource 4: 1 printout

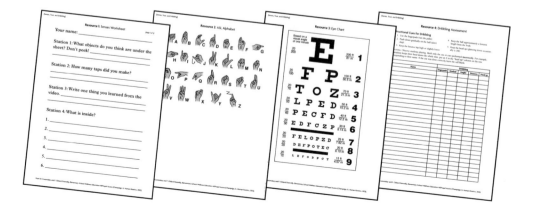

Skill Cues

Basketball Dribble

- Use the fingertips (not the palm).
- Push down gradually on the ball (don't slap).
- Keep the bounce hip high or slightly lower.
- Keep the ball approximately a forearm's length from the body.
- Keep the head up (glancing down occasionally is OK).

LEARNING ACTIVITIES

Lesson Introduction

- **WHAT** are we learning today? Students will learn about the five senses, how to dribble a basketball effectively, and behaviors that build trust.
- **WHY** are we learning this? The senses are how people take in information, and it's important to take care of them. They are often taken for granted until there is a problem. Trust allows people to feel safe and accomplish more; it's important to learn to trust others and also be worthy of their trust (trustworthy).
- **HOW** will learning be measured? Learning will be measured using a senses worksheet (resource 1) and an assessment of basketball dribbling (resource 4).

Activity 1: Dribble Warm-Up (10 minutes)

Demonstrate proper basketball dribbling technique. Scatter 10 "gates" formed by two cones three feet (1 m) apart in general space and randomly scatter 10 poly spots. When the music starts, students find a self-space and begin stationary dribbling. Provide feedback on dribbling technique. Students use their dominant hand first, then nondominant, and finally back and forth. Next, students dribble around in general space. When instructed, they pass through as many gates as possible before the music stops, keeping track of the total. Next, demonstrate for students a simplified crossover dribble. When the music starts, students continue earning points passing through gates but also earn points by doing a crossover dribble at a poly spot. Remind students to be mindful of other dribblers because they may converge at the gates or poly spots.

Activity 2: Sense Stations (30 minutes)

Students will rotate between stations. Each station highlights a different sense. Explain and demonstrate the stations; allow approximately three to four minutes per station. At stations 1 through 5 and 8, students will write information on resource 1.

Touch

- Station 1: Touch and guess—Put PE equipment or other objects under an opaque sheet or tarp. Students may crawl on top of the sheet and feel the objects, but they may not peek under or "accidentally" move the sheet. Possible objects include a fleece ball, scoop, hockey stick, cone, beanbag, foam cylinder, partially inflated balloon, deck ring, hockey puck, bowling pin, football, and foam lollipop paddle. Students may work together. Students write down their guesses on the worksheet (resource 1).
- Station 2: Dribble tap—Students dribble in general space while trying to control their basketball. At the same time, they try to tap the ball of other students. Students record the number of successful taps on the worksheet.

Smell

- Station 3: Students watch the "Smell" video on the BrainPop website and answer the question on the worksheet. (See the lesson plan links file on HK*Propel* for a link to this video.)
- Station 4: Punch holes in the lids of opaque plastic containers. Label each container with a number. Put different scented objects in each container, such as cotton balls with vinegar; cotton balls with orange juice; cotton balls with vanilla extract, cloves, cinnamon, or garlic; cotton balls with pickle juice, and so on. On the worksheet, students write down what they believe each container contains. Students may not pick up the containers.

Hearing

- Station 5: Use a noise meter to identify quiet, moderate, and harmful noise levels. Set up a computer in a "quiet" corner of the gym and activate an online loudness meter. (See the lesson plan links file on HK*Propel* for a link to a loudness meter.) Tell students that noise over 70 dB (decibels) for a prolonged time can cause hearing loss and that noise over 120 dB can cause immediate hearing damage. At the station place PE equipment such as a basketball, fleece ball, bowling pin, and other items that make noise. Students make sounds and see how loud they are on the noise meter. Generate sounds with PE equipment and without equipment (e.g., talking, stomping, clapping.) On the worksheet, students write what caused a low sound (0-30 dB), a medium sound (31-60 dB), and a loud sound (60-100 dB). Caution students to not go over 100 dB.
- Station 6: Provide two printouts of the ASL language alphabet (resource 2) and 50 cutouts of each letter. Students tape letters to spell their first name. Next, they practice finger spelling their name with one hand and then finger spelling their name to a classmate in their group.
- Station 7: Minefield—Outline a 20-by-20-foot (6-by-6-m) square using a rope or jump ropes. Scatter objects (mines) inside the space (e.g., poly spots, cones, beanbags). Students get a partner and each partner stands on opposite sides of the square. One partner is sighted (the guide), and the other closes their eyes (blind). The guide uses spoken words to help their blind partner navigate the minefield by walking from one side to the other. If the blind student hits a mine, they start over. Students switch roles after a successful trip. Multiple students can go at once.

Sight

- Station 8:
  - Task 1—Demonstrate to students how to determine their dominant eye. Pick out a distant object and point your index finger at it. Close your left eye; if your finger is still pointed at the object, then your right eye is dominant. Close your right eye; if your finger is still pointed at the object, then your left eye is dominant. Students circle *left* or *right* on their worksheet.
  - Task 2—Post an eye chart on the wall (see resource 3). Put a poly spot on the floor an appropriate distance away. For resource 3, the distance is 20 feet. Have students write on their worksheet the letters for the lowest line they could read. If a student wears glasses, have them leave their glasses on.
- Station 9: Wall Ball—This game coordinates input from three senses: sight, touch, and hearing. There are many versions of this game, so teachers may adapt these directions as needed. To play, find a flat wall. Place poly spots or cones 10 feet (3 m) from the wall. Begin the game by throwing a tennis ball or similar ball at the wall. A player retrieving the ball must allow it to bounce. Once the ball is caught, it may be thrown back at the wall. In some versions of the game, the ball is hit with an open hand. If the ball is fumbled, that student must run and touch the ball as quickly as possible. Other students grab the fumbled ball and throw it at the wall, attempting to strike the wall before the running student touches it. If the ball beats the running student, the thrower earns one point. If not, play continues. There is no elimination. The person who scored serves the next ball.

Closure

Ask students what objects were under the sheet or tarp in station 1. Students turn to another student and identify the five senses. Then they finger spell their name in sign language. It's OK if they need to look at their worksheet. Finally, ask students who in the school can be considered a health helper (wellness educator, school psychologist, school counselor, cafeteria staff, custodian). Discuss their roles in promoting wellness and what types of issues students may address with them.

Sneezing, Coughing, Cooperation, and Fundamental Movement Skills

GRADE LEVEL: 1

INTRODUCTORY INFORMATION

SHAPE America Outcomes

- S1.E1.1 Hops, gallops, jogs, and slides using a mature pattern.
- S1.E4.2 Demonstrates four of the five critical elements for jumping and landing in a vertical plane.
- S4.E4.1 Works independently with others in a variety of class environments (e.g., small and large groups).

National Health Education Performance Indicators

- 1.2.3 Describe ways to prevent communicable diseases.
- 8.2.2 Encourage peers to make positive health choices.

Lesson Objectives

Students will be able to do the following:

- Describe how to reduce germ transmission when sneezing or coughing.
- Hop, gallop, jog, and slide using a mature pattern.
- Demonstrate four of five critical elements for jumping and landing in a vertical plane.
- Contribute meaningfully toward established team goals.

Note: This lesson plan can be modified to focus on sport skills such as dribbling (soccer, basketball) if desired instead of fundamental movement patterns.

This is a two-day lesson.

Learning Materials and Technology

- 1 gallon jug of hand sanitizer
- 1 poly spot per student
- 3 scarves per student
- 1 index card per student
- 1 pencil per student
- 1 spray bottle with a mist feature
- 1 large tarp or sheet
- 1 towel
- Resource handout from HKPropel
  - Resource 1: 1 printout

Skill Cues

Hop

- Balance on one foot.
- The nonhopping leg is off the ground and bent at 90 degrees.
- Bend and extend the hopping leg to produce a flight phase.

- The nonhopping leg swings up and forward to produce additional force.
- Arms are bent at the elbow and swing from back to front in coordination with the hopping action.

Gallop

- Step forward with the lead foot.
- Push off the trail foot forcefully enough to achieve a flight phase.
- The trail foot catches up to the lead leg by touching the heel.
- Coordinate the arm swing forward with the motion of the legs to achieve distance and height.
- Land on the ball of the lead foot, with the trail foot behind the lead foot.

Jog or Run

- Keep your head up and facing straight ahead.
- Push off of one foot to create a flight phase; swing the opposite arm forward.
- Strike with the foot underneath the body.
- Keep the shoulders open, relaxed, and down.
- Keep the arms close to the torso, bent at 90 degrees, and moving diagonally.

Slide

- Turn the body sideways to the direction of travel.
- Keep the feet shoulder width apart and arms extended sideways.
- Step to the side with the lead foot.
- Push off with the trail foot so it produces a flight phase and then chases the lead foot.
- Land on the trail foot and then the lead foot.

Jump and Land in the Vertical Plane

- Swing both arms back behind buttocks.
- Bend the knees.
- Swing the arms forward and up.
- Push off both feet simultaneously.
- Land on both feet simultaneously and bend the knees.

Working With Others

- Contribute your best effort.
- Stay focused.
- Provide encouraging comments to others.

LEARNING ACTIVITIES

Lesson Introduction

- **WHAT** are we learning today? Students will learn how to reduce the spread of germs when sneezing and coughing, how to perform a variety of fundamental movements skills, and how to cooperate with others.
- **WHY** are we learning this? The best way to avoid illness is to not get sick in the first place. That means preventing the spread of germs. Fundamental movement skills are built into more complex skills, like defending space and scoring, that will be taught in later years.
- **HOW** will learning be measured? The teacher will complete an assessment of running technique (resource 1).

Activity 1: Scrambled Eggs (5 minutes)

While music is playing, students scatter into general space and perform locomotor skills as directed. When the music stops, call out commands for students: hard boiled = a tucked position on the floor; soft boiled = on the belly oozing slowly around; scrambled = moving in many directions; over easy = turning from one side to the other; fried = on the back using legs to spin in a circle. After each round, students ooze over to a partner, sit back-to-back, and stand up, if possible, without using their hands.

Activity 2: Discussion (5 minutes)

Ask students to name the smallest animal they can think of. Explain that germs are even smaller, so small they can't be seen. Germs can get inside the body and cause kids to feel sick. The two most common germs are bacteria and viruses. For example, the COVID-19 illness is caused by a virus. The best way to fight illness is to not get sick in the first place. Bacteria and viruses can be spread through the air, especially when people sneeze and cough. As an example, take a spray bottle, put it on the mist setting, and spray into the air over a large sheet or tarp spread out on the floor. A squirt is like a sneeze of cough, and each water droplet could contain viruses or bacteria. Ask students what they should do if they feel a sneeze or cough coming on. There are four choices:

1. Hands: Instruct students *not* to sneeze into their hands, because they will pass the germs on to whatever they touch next.

2. Tissue: Sneezing or coughing into a tissue is a great option if one is available and students can get to it quickly enough. If students are sick, they should put tissue boxes in places they use most (e.g., school desk, bedroom at home). Remind students to throw the tissue away after using it.

3. Elbow: If a tissue is not available, the CDC (an organizations of scientists and doctors who develops guidelines to help us stay healthy) recommends turning your head and sneezing into your elbow.

4. Sleeve or upper arm: This method is called the "vampire method." Turn your head and sneeze into your upper arm. It is similar to the elbow, but easier for some people to reach.

Students practice methods 3 and 4. Remind them to never sneeze or cough directly into the air or their hands and to always wash their hands after sneezing or coughing, even if they sneeze or cough into their elbow or upper arm.

Check the floor to make sure it's dry before moving to activity 3. Wipe up wetness with a towel if necessary.

Activity 3: Zoom and Mooz (25 minutes)

All students stand in a large circle and face the center, about an extended-elbow distance apart. Begin the activity by saying, "achoo" and pretending to sneeze into your left elbow. The student on that side quickly turns and pretends to sneeze into their left elbow as well. The "achoo" zooms all the way around the circle. Do another round, but beforehand, ask students how quickly the zoom can go from start to finish. Settle on a goal time. This activity requires students to work together toward a common goal. Ask students what working well with others would look like in this activity. Focus the discussion on the skill cues identified earlier.

Perform the activity a third time and see if students can break their previous time. After the third attempt, ask students for specific examples of how they worked well together in the activity. Next ask them for specific examples of when and where in the school day they can employ these skills.

Extensions

- Repeat the activity, but this time students must jump and land in the vertical plane before passing on the Zoom. Have students pretend sneeze into their sleeve or upper arm to practice something different.

- Mooz: Send a sneeze, "achoo," left and then immediately send a cough, "ahem," to the right. Students continue to use the correct technique to reduce the spread of germs. See what happens when the sneeze and the cough intersect.

Activity 4: Germ Pass (25 minutes)

Round 1

Give each student an index card and ask them to write the numbers 1 through 5 down the card (not across on one line). Instruct all students to travel around the room demonstrating a fundamental movement pattern (FMP). On the stop command, they pair up with the closest student and write their own name on their partner's card. On go, students demonstrate a different FMP, find a different partner on the stop command, and repeat. This continues five times so that each student has five different names on their card. Students sit as a cluster of grapes. Pick one student randomly using a spinner or the attendance book. Explain that this person had the common cold before class. Call that person student A. Instruct the other students to look at their card; anyone with student A on their card also has the cold. Whoever has student A in the first slot is called student B. Instruct the other students to look at their card; anyone with student B in the second slot or below also has a cold. Continue the pattern for the remaining three lines. See how many students have the cold. It will be eye opening.

Round 2

Repeat the activity, but now after rounds 2 and 4, students wash their hands using the hand sanitizer before resuming activity. This will stop new infections for that round only. It will not cure those who already have the cold. Compare the difference in total infections. Instead of doing fundamental movement patterns between each round, have students use correct running technique. Demonstrate correct running technique. Complete the running assessment (resource 1) during round 2.

Activity 5: Tissues Galore (15 minutes)

When students are sick, they will use a lot of tissues, and that's OK. Germs go in the trash with the tissues and not into the air or onto someone's hands. To simulate using a lot of tissues, have students get a scarf. They throw it up and catch it for 30 seconds, trying to keep it from hitting the floor and getting "dirty." They add a second scarf, and try and keep both up simultaneously. Students may not clump two scarves together or grab both in the same hand. Students may get a third or even fourth scarf if desired. Repeat this with a partner. Students should face one another about four feet (1.2 m) apart.

Sometimes when students feel a sneeze or cough coming on, the hardest part is getting to a tissue quickly. To practice, partners will stand on separate poly spots about 10 feet (3 m) apart. Both students simultaneously throw a scarf straight up and then run to the other spot trying to catch their partner's scarf. If successful on two consecutive simultaneous throws, one poly spot may be moved a step back. If a scarf is dropped, one poly spot is moved one step closer. See which groups can cover the greatest distance to get their tissues.

Closure

Part of the lesson focused on being able to work well with others. Have students turn to a partner and explain in their own words why working well together is important. Invite students to share some of their responses after the partner work. Finally, on the count of 3, have all of them show how to sneeze into their elbow and then how to sneeze into their sleeve or upper arm. If there is time, do multiple running demonstrations. Include an error in some of the demonstrations, and ask students if they can spot the error.

Chapter 6

Lesson Plans for Grades 3-5

Lesson plan topic	Grade level	Page	Resources
Asthma and Fielding Game Skills	5	151	1: Batter Up Peer Assessment 2: Asthma Worksheet
Brushing Teeth and Hockey Pass and Receive	3	155	1: Healthy Tooth and Decayed Tooth 2: Tooth-Brushing Peer Assessment
Cardiovascular System and Movement Skills	3-4	158	1: Heart Parts Worksheet 2: Fundamental Movement Skills 3: Healthy and Unhealthy Heart Habits
Conflict Resolution and Manipulative Skills	4-5	162	1: Scenarios 2: T Chart 3: Conflict Resolution Strategies Wheel 4: Self-Check Card for Creating a Game
Decision-Making and Assertiveness	4-5	165	1: Frogger Rubric
Digestive System and Underhand Throw	4-5	168	1: Anatomy of Digestive System 2: Course Setup 3: Digestive System Worksheets
Endocrine System, Hygiene, and Striking in Golf	4-5	171	1: Diagram of Endocrine System 2: Mini Golf Score Card
Flossing Teeth and Basketball Dribbling	3	174	1: Flossing Peer Assessment
Food Labels and Soccer Dribbling	3-4	179	1: Understanding the Nutrition Facts Label 2: Food Label Worksheet
Healthy Eating and Striking	3	182	1: Food Log 2: Forehand Striking Peer Assessment
Immune System, Open Space, and Person-to-Person Defense	3-4	186	1: Assessment of Moving to Open Space and Person-to-Person Defense
Inclusion and Batting	4-5	190	1: Batting Assessment
Muscular System and Fitness	5	194	1: Muscle Diagram Worksheet 2: Feel the Burn Activity
Peer Pressure	4-5	197	1: Communication Assessment
Physical Activity Pyramid, Goal Setting, and Yard Games	3-5	200	1: Physical Activity Log 2: Backhand Disc Throw Assessment 3: Children's Physical Activity Pyramid
Skeletal System and Fitness	4-5	205	1: Skeletal System Worksheet 2: Bone Pictures 3: Exercise Pictures
Stress, Coordination, and Heart Rate	3-4	207	1: Pulse Chart
Valid Health Information and Body Weight Fitness	5	210	1: Evaluating Valid Health Information on a Website 2: Body Weight Exercise Assessment

Asthma and Fielding Game Skills

GRADE LEVEL: 5

INTRODUCTORY INFORMATION

SHAPE America Outcomes

- S1.E15.5b Throws with reasonable accuracy in dynamic, small-sided practice tasks.
- S1.E16.5c Catches with reasonable accuracy in dynamic, small-sided practice tasks.
- S1.E25.5a Strikes a pitched ball with a bat using a mature pattern.
- S1.E25.5b Combines striking with a long implement (e.g., bat, hockey stick) with receiving and traveling skills in a small-sided game.

National Health Education Performance Indicators

- 1.5.5 Describe when it is important to seek health care.
- 3.5.2 Locate resources from home, school, and community that provide valid health information.

Lesson Objectives

Students will be able to do the following:

- Strike a ball off a tee using correct form.
- Catch an oncoming ball within small-sided practice tasks using correct form.
- Throw to a stationary base player within small-sided practice tasks using correct form.
- Access sources of accurate information about asthma and how to treat asthma.
- Identify physiological mechanisms related to the chronic disease of asthma.
- Identify when to seek medical care for the treatment of asthma.

Prerequisite Skills

Students have already practiced batting off a tee, fielding, and the overhand throw to a stationary target.

Learning Materials and Technology

- 1 clipboard with pencil on a string per 4 students
- 3 poly spots or bases per 4 students
- 1 Wiffle softball per 4 students
- 1 bat per 4 students
- 1 batting tee per 4 students
- 1 modified softball per 4 students (as needed)
- 1 tablet per 4 students
- Resource handouts from HK*Propel*
  - Resource 1: 1 printout per 2 students
  - Resource 2: 1 printout per student

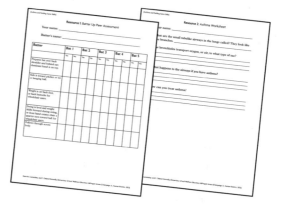

Skill Cues

Striking With a Bat

- The dominant hand is on the top of the grip.
- Prepare the bat over the back shoulder, behind ear; the front elbow is level with the shoulder.
- The side is toward the pitcher or tee; weight is on the back foot or on the back buttocks for wheelchair users; the eyes are on the ball or face is toward the beeping ball.
- The swing is level, and the weight shifts forward during the swing.
- The arms follow through across the body.

Catching

- Anticipate the ball position and move to get in front of the oncoming ball.
- Keep the eyes on the ball or face toward the beeping ball.
- Reach out for the ball with the hands or arms.
- Keep the thumbs together when catching the ball above the head.
- Keep the pinkies together when catching a ball below the waist.
- Catch with the hands only.
- Give with the body.
- Pull the ball into the body.

Overhand Throw

- Keep side to the target.
- Put throwing arm behind the head with the elbow bent at a 90-degree angle (L shape).
- Step toward the target with the opposite foot.
- Rotate the chest and hips toward the target as the throwing arm is extended toward the target.
- Follow through across the body to the opposite hip.

Open Skills

- Player fields grounders and throws the ball ahead of the runner.
- Fielding player moves toward the ball, stays low, scoops up the ball, and immediately throws to first base.
- First base player moves into position with the foot on the bag, makes a big target with the hands, and receives the throw from the fielding player.

LEARNING ACTIVITIES

Lesson Introduction

- **WHAT** are we learning today? Students will review how to strike, field a ball, and throw a ball within several practice tasks related to softball and baseball. In addition, they will examine chronic diseases, including symptoms and preventive measures. They will also learn about asthma, which is a lung problem that can make it hard to breathe.
- **WHY** are we learning this? Striking with a bat, running to a base, fielding a ball, and throwing to a base or teammate are important aspects of softball and baseball. Breathing is important when running a race or charging down the soccer field. The body needs the oxygen it gets from breathing to work properly. And the body needs even more oxygen when exercising.
- **HOW** will learning be measured? Learning will be measured through a batting technique peer assessment (resource 1).

Activity 1: Batting and Fielding Practice With Assessment (15-20 minutes)

This activity uses a home base, first base, second base, a Wiffle softball that can be hit off a tee or hit from a soft toss or pitch, and an appropriately sized bat. (A modified softball, available for purchase at various online retailers, can be used, too.) Bases should be 30 feet apart or modified to accommodate students' abilities. Poly spots can be used instead of bases.

While students are gathered in the calling all kids area, diagram on the whiteboard or poster how to play a 2v2 baseball game with the focus on trying to strike a ball (either off a tee, from a soft toss, or pitched) into the outfield. In addition, explain how the fielders should try to get the runner out at the base. For students who need additional visual information, pictures and diagrams will be described out loud. Provide a tactile board of the field. It can be made from the back of a clipboard, with waxed strings, pipe cleaners, or string taped or glued to the board.

- *Offense player 1:* This player strikes the ball and attempts to run to first base.
- *Peer assessor:* This player fills out the peer assessment (resource 1).
- *Defensive player 1:* This player is positioned in the outfield and attempts to field the ball.
- *Defensive player 2:* This player is positioned behind first base and attempts to catch the thrown ball and tag the runner out.
- *Offensive tactic:* Hit the ball to an open space to get on base.
- *Defensive tactic:* Field the ball and throw to base ahead of the runner to get the forced out.

Explain the *lead up* to the 2v2 game. Four students will demonstrate while others observe. Each player in the group of four gets five practice attempts at batting at their chosen level of difficulty. One student can be the pitcher or throw a soft toss based on the batter's choice. The fielder fields the ball, and the task repeats.

During this activity, one student per group is the peer assessor and uses the assessment tool to collect evidence about the batter's performance (resource 1). Students who need access other than visual reading will be provided a picture assessment or one that is recorded onto an MP3 player or tablet with accessibility features turned on, including text to talk, open captioning, and descriptive video features. The peer assessor should be changed when a new batter is up.

Activity 2: 2v2 Infield Game (15-20 minutes)

This activity takes place outside and integrates a 2v2 infield game with health content about asthma, heart disease, and diabetes. An offensive player pitches or offers a soft toss to the batter. The batter could also strike the ball off a tee. The offensive player bats the ball to the outfield and runs to first base, attempting to beat the throw. The defense fields the ball and tries to get a force-out at first base. A run is scored when a runner is safe at first base. Switch after three outs or three runs, whichever comes first. Demonstrate the rotation of the four players. Modifications include an auditory device behind first base, arrows on the ground or a line of poly spots leading to first base to provide visual information, or a guide runner. The group including a student in a wheelchair will play positioned on a blacktop surface.

When the batter reaches first base (successfully or tagged out), all four players run to home base. At home base is a tablet playing a video about asthma (see the lesson plan link file on HK*Propel* for a link). Descriptive video and open captioning should be available. Students watch the video and then complete the worksheets located on a clipboard (resource 2). Only one question is answered per batter. The worksheet is kept on the clipboard, and the teacher will check each group's answers during the lesson closure. A student is selected to read the worksheet aloud. Photos can be included for students who need them. The worksheet could be sent to students who need access electronically for text-to-talk options or provided as a Google Form loaded on a tablet.

Players rotate positions before the next round. The rotation could be listed on a task card taped to a cone or in a cone slot. Include braille and picture representations on the task cards.

Rotation

- Pitcher becomes batter.
- Batter becomes center fielder.
- Fielder becomes first base player.
- First base player becomes pitcher.

Extension

- After a team of four completes its worksheet, each player takes a drinking straw out of a plastic container. Each student practices carefully running to first base breathing through the straw to simulate what it is like to experience asthma symptoms.

Closure

Students sit in their groups of four. The teacher reviews the answers for the worksheet (resource 2). Students then complete a think-pair-share activity on how to strike a ball with a bat. One student is the clay, and the other student is the artist. The artist molds the clay into the correct preparation stance while verbally guiding their clay through the batting motions (i.e., execution and follow-through). Students share experiences about how their breathing was restricted when breathing through a straw while running to first base.

Universal Design for Learning

The following are additional universal design for learning considerations for all learners:

- Consider using smaller groupings such as one-on-one for students who need less sensory information.
- Decrease the speed of play by substituting other means of locomotion to the bases.
- Provide additional task meaningfulness by using photos of children in the class performing the tasks on the task cards and assessments.
- When assessing children whose mobility is different from others, add variety to the rubric such as performing the skill (batting form or catching form) without the ball.
- Consider using baseline chalk to make a path from home to first base, with first base as a large circle to encompass a wheelchair or walker.
- Provide additional means to check for understanding by asking yes or no questions, having students say or sign cue words when requested, or performing the movement for you before they are assessed.
- Use cones to help designate an area of play for students who need that extra information.
- On a tablet, play a video model on loop of the skills of throwing, batting, and catching.
- For students with higher needs for support and modifications, change the goal of the activity to include skills such as looking at the pitcher, pointing to the base, raising a hand when the correct answer is given, striking with an open hand, moving arms as if running, and so on.
- Provide paraeducators with the lesson plan or cue cards for their role with students.
- Use peer buddies for students who need additional demonstrations.

Brushing Teeth and Hockey Pass and Receive

INTRODUCTORY INFORMATION

SHAPE America Outcomes

- S1.E17.3 Dribbles and travels in general space at slow to moderate jogging speed, with control of ball and body.
- S1.E25.3 Strikes a ball with a long-handled implement (e.g., hockey stick, bat, golf club), sending it forward, while using proper grip for the implement.

National Health Education Performance Indicators

- 1.5.1 Describe the relationship between healthy behaviors and personal health.
- 2.5.1 Describe how the family influences personal health practices and behaviors.
- 7.5.2 Demonstrate a variety of healthy practices and behaviors to maintain or improve personal health.

Lesson Objectives

Students will be able to do the following:

- Describe correct tooth-brushing technique and demonstrate it on a model.
- Demonstrate correct hockey dribbling and passing technique.

Learning Materials and Technology

- 1 hockey stick per student
- 30 hockey balls (fleece balls or tennis balls may be used)
- 20 poly spots
- Resource handouts from HK*Propel*
  - Resource 1: 1 printout per 2 students
  - Resource 2: 1 printout per 2 students

Skill Cues

Hockey Dribble

- Hold the stick with the nondominant hand near the top and the dominant hand about a foot (30 cm) below.
- Push the ball along using the blade of the stick or move the stick from side to side, tapping the object.
- Use both sides of the stick.
- Keep the eyes up as much as possible except to locate the ball or other players.
- Keep the object slightly in front of the body (not too close and not too far).

Hockey Push Pass

- Hold the stick with the nondominant hand near the top and the dominant hand about a foot (30 cm) below.
- Turn sideways by pointing the dominant shoulder toward the target.
- Start with the blade of the stick resting against the back of the ball and quickly accelerate it.
- Stop the stick no higher than the knee.

Receive a Hockey Pass

- Keep the blade of the stick on the ground.
- Adjust the stick to meet the incoming path of the ball.
- Give with the ball or tap it slightly so it stays close to the receiving player.

LEARNING ACTIVITIES

Lesson Introduction

- **WHAT** are we learning today? Students will learn how to execute selected floor hockey skills and properly brush their teeth.
- **WHY** are we learning this? Dribbling and receiving are fundamental skills needed to play hockey properly, to maintain possession, and to score. For most students, their first permanent (adult) teeth have already emerged. They will continue to emerge as students grow older and won't be replaced. There are no do-overs for these teeth, so students must learn to take care of them. That process starts in childhood.
- **HOW** will learning be measured? Students will complete a peer tooth-brushing assessment (resource 2).

Activity 1: Geography of the Teeth (5 minutes)

Ask students to identify the role the teeth play in the body. (Answer: to break down food into smaller pieces.) This action aids swallowing and digestion. The bad news is that humans get just two sets of teeth (unlike sharks, who can continuously regenerate teeth). Therefore, it is important to take care of the teeth we have.

Quiz students on fun facts:

- How hard are teeth? (Answer: The enamel of a tooth is the hardest substance in the human body.)
- How many teeth does an adult have? (Answer: 32 if the wisdom teeth are present, 28 if not.)
- How often should students brush their teeth? (Answer: Two or three times per day.)

Ask if anyone can describe how and why the teeth are differently shaped.

- Incisors are in the front of the mouth and used for cutting into food.
- Canines are pointy and located on corners of the mouth and used for tearing and piercing.
- Molars are located toward the back of the mouth, are more flat, and are used for grinding.

Partner activity: Distribute one copy of resource 1 to each pair. Have one partner open their mouth, and the other partner counts the number of lower-jaw teeth and draws them in their approximate location on resource 1.

Activity 2: Demonstration (10 minutes)

Explain that tooth brushing removes plaque, the sticky substance that forms around teeth. Plaque produces acid; acid can lead to tooth decay, which can form a hole in the tooth called a cavity. If a tooth gets a cavity, a dentist needs to drill out the decayed part and fill it so that the cavity doesn't get bigger. The teacher positions 14 cones on the gym floor in the shape of the lower-jaw teeth and demonstrates how to brush the teeth (cones) using a hockey stick as a toothbrush.

- Pretend to place a pea-sized dab of toothpaste on the "brush" (hockey stick).
- Flat surface: Brush across the top of the chewing surfaces.
- Inside and outside surfaces: Angle the brush 45 degrees and move it back and forth using short (toothwide) strokes. Do not brush too hard. The "bristles" (bottom of hockey stick) should face the teeth and be flat against the tooth surface.
- Front teeth (incisors): Angle the brush vertically and use short up-and-down strokes.

In groups of two, students set up cones in the shape of lower-jaw teeth at designated points in the gym. Create a center line using poly spots. The incisors should face the center line of the gym. Students use a hockey stick as a pretend toothbrush and brush the teeth using the appropriate technique. After one practice round, students complete the peer assessment (resource 2) by watching their partner brush the teeth. Switch roles and continue. Leave the cones in position for activity 3.

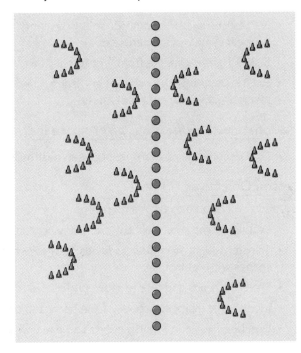

Activity 3: Dental Defenders (15 minutes)

Demonstrate the proper technique for executing a push pass and receiving a pass in hockey. Students practice both skills from approximately 20 feet (6 m) on the dominant and nondominant sides. Instruct students to be mindful not to topple any of the teeth.

Students on the same side of the center line are on the same team. The objective of the game is to pass tartar (fleece balls) toward the other team's teeth using a push pass. Any tooth or teeth that topple must stay down. Students should defend their own teeth while trying to knock down cones on the opposite side. Count the number of toppled cones on each side. Repeat the game if time allows.

Closure

The day before the lesson, soak a raw egg in cola and a chicken bone in vinegar overnight. The egg will discolor from the cola just as teeth discolor from repeated exposures without brushing. Demonstrate how the bone will become flexible. Vinegar contains acids that are similar to the acids plaque produces that weaken teeth.

Students describe to a partner the technique for the push pass. However, they must include at least one error. Their partner's job is to identify the error. Switch, but this time the partner receives a pass. Again, the partner should identify the error.

Cardiovascular System and Movement Skills

INTRODUCTORY INFORMATION

SHAPE America Outcomes

- S1.E1.4 Uses various locomotor skills in a variety of small-sided practice tasks, dance, and educational gymnastics experiences.
- S1.E8.3 Transfers weight from feet to hands with momentary weight support.
- S3.E3.3 Describes the concept of fitness (cardiovascular health) and provides examples of physical activity to enhance fitness.

National Health Education Performance Indicators

- 1.5.1 Describe the relationship between healthy behaviors and personal health.

Lesson Objectives

Students will be able to do the following:

- Leap and jump over low obstacles using correct form.
- Transfer weight from feet to hands to feet (wheeling action) to move over foam trapezoid shapes with control.
- Travel on hands and feet to move under obstacles with control.
- Identify the major structures of the heart and describe the blood flow pathways.
- Describe five heart-healthy habits and five unhealthy habits.

Learning Materials and Technology

- 50 dome cones
- 30 hoops
- 4 tunnels
- 10 scooters
- 50 poly spots
- 30 pool noodles
- 8 foam trapezoid shapes (2 per learning team)
- 4 ropes and cones with slits (4 cones per group; 2 ropes per group)

- 100 pool noodle slices
- Other suitable equipment students can use to build a heart
- Resource handouts from *HKPropel*
  - Resource 1: 1 printout per student
  - Resource 2: number of printouts depends on how used
  - Resource 3: 1 printout

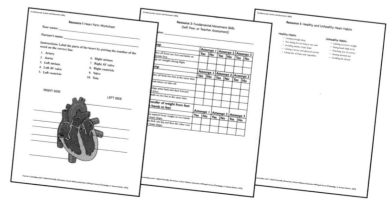

Skill Cues

Run

- Keep your head up and facing straight ahead.
- Push off of one foot to create a flight phase; swing the opposite arm forward.
- Strike with the foot underneath the body.
- Keep the shoulders open, relaxed, and down.
- Keep the arms close to the torso, bent at 90 degrees, and moving diagonally.

Leap

- Run and take off from one foot forcefully to create a flight phase.
- Swing arms up and forward to aid take off.
- Extend the opposite leg forward.
- Land on the opposite foot.
- Bend the knees to absorb force.

Jump: Two Feet to Two Feet

- Swing both arms back behind the buttocks.
- Bend the knees.
- Swing the arms forward and up.
- Push off both feet simultaneously.
- Land on both feet simultaneously and bend the knees.
- Reach arms forward.

Transfer Weight From Feet to Hands to Feet

- Place both hands simultaneously on the foam shape.
- Position the head down and between the elbows.
- Push off one foot at a time to lift buttocks into the air.
- "Hurdle" or wheel one leg over the foam shape at a time.
- Land on one foot at a time.

LEARNING ACTIVITIES

Lesson Introduction

- **WHAT** are we learning today? Students will practice the fundamental movement skills of running, leaping, jumping, and transferring weight from hands to feet within an obstacle course designed to simulate the heart and the pathway of blood through the heart.
- **WHY** are we learning this? Locomotor skills are important in a variety of activities that build cardiovascular fitness. To develop cardiovascular health, it helps to understand how blood flows through the heart.
- **HOW** will learning be measured? Students will complete the heart parts worksheet (resource 1). In addition, students' performance will be measured through a formative assessment of their fundamental movement skills (resource 2).

Activity 1: Teacher Discussion and Worksheet (10 minutes)

Students get a partner, a pencil, and one copy of resource 1, and then sit quietly in front of the teacher. Explain that the heart is about as big as a fist and is responsible for pumping blood through the body. Next, partners put both their names on resource 1 and label as many parts of the heart as possible using the word bank. Clarify that when looking at a diagram of the heart, the structures on the left are actually on the right and vice versa. After five to eight minutes, ask, "What is number 1?" and so on until all blanks have been correctly filled.

Differentiations

- Challenge task: Students explain the function of each heart part.
- Simplified task: Students point to the heart term; students draw a line from a heart term to its part.

Activity 2: Obstacle Course (15-20 minutes)

Students keep the worksheet, separate into four learning teams, and build an obstacle course representation of the heart using PE equipment. The structures should closely approximate the handout. Once the obstacle course is completed, each learning group presents their "heart" to the rest of the class and identifies each heart part. Afterward, the learning teams move through the heart on a scooter according to the blood flow pathway in the following manner:

- Move on their seat or belly and go forward, backward, or sideways.
- Move through the heart using the fundamental movement skill (leap, jump, transfer weight from hand to feet) you prescribe. Demonstrate these first.
- Move through in the least amount of time to simulate exercising at high intensity.

Fourth grade: Have students include the pulmonary artery, lungs, and pulmonary vein in their obstacle course.

Optional Assessment

Students may be assessed in one of three ways (using resource 2):

1. Self-assessment: Set up a computer and webcam to record each obstacle course. After students have completed the obstacle course using the prescribed fundamental movement skills, play the video back multiple times. Students observe themselves and complete the self-assessment.
2. Peer assessment: Conduct this similarly to the self-assessment, but with a peer. Switch roles after each fundamental movement skill is completed.
3. Teacher administered: Observe the class moving through the obstacle courses and indicate on the form which students performed a critical element incorrectly.

Activity 3: On the Line (5 minutes)

Students stand on a line. Randomly call out one of the habits listed in resource 3. If students think the habit is healthy, on the count of three, they step forward from the line. If they believe it is unhealthy, they step back. Discuss the correct answer each time, and have students return to the line.

Optional Activity: Oxygen Relay (5 minutes)

Students return to their partner from activity 1. Partner 1 stands next to hoop 1, which is filled with 15 pool noodle slices. Partner 2 stands next to hoop 2 position 10 yards away, which is empty. The noodle slices represent oxygen. Partner 1 represents oxygen transport from the outside air into the lungs. Partner 2 represents the pumping action of the heart. On go, partner 1 removes one pool noodle slice from hoop 1 and places it in hoop 2. Partner 2 then moves the pool noodle slice to hoop 3, which represents the exercising muscles. See how many oxygen molecules can be moved in one minute. Repeat and switch the starting end. Afterward, tell students that the relay represented the cardiovascular system. See if they can guess what each person or part represented. Ask why cardiovascular fitness depends on both systems working optimally.

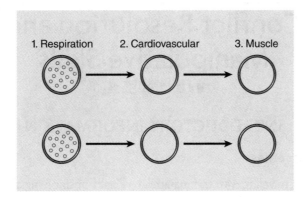

Closure

Review the objectives of the class. In partners, students take turns listing the heart parts and explaining their function. Then each partner lists one heart-healthy habit and one unhealthy habit.

Conflict Resolution and Manipulative Skills

GRADE LEVEL: 4-5

INTRODUCTORY INFORMATION

SHAPE America Outcomes

- S1.E26.4 Combines traveling with the manipulative skills of dribbling, throwing, and striking in teacher and/or student designed small-sided practice task environments.

National Health Education Performance Indicators

- 4.5.3 Demonstrate non-violent strategies to manage or resolve conflict.

Lesson Objectives

Students will be able to do the following:

- Work collaboratively to create their own game.
- Identify the eight conflict resolution strategies and apply them to scenarios.
- Identify examples of conflicts in their lives.

Learning Materials and Technology

- 3 pencils
- 1 die
- 8 scarves
- 8 poles or wands
- 8 hoops
- 8 ropes
- 8 balls
- 8 scooters
- 8 cones

- 1 blank sheet of paper per 2 students
- Resource handouts from HK*Propel*
  - Resource 1: 1 printout cut into a separate strip per scenario
  - Resource 2: 1 printout per 2 students
  - Resource 3: 1 printout per 2 students
  - Resource 4: 1 printout per 2 students

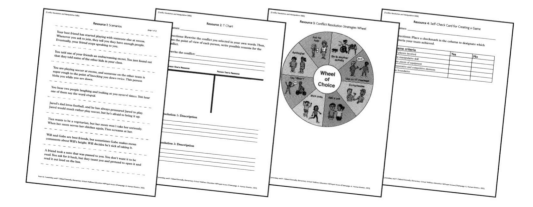

LEARNING ACTIVITIES

Lesson Introduction

- **WHAT** are we learning today? Students will learn how to settle (resolve) problems (conflicts) with other students and will learn various manipulative skills.

- **WHY** are we learning this? Conflict comes to everyone's life, usually because people disagree about something. Being able to solve problems helps people get along better, be happier, and achieve more. Plus, learning this skill in elementary school will help students solve problems throughout their life.

- **HOW** will learning be measured? Student performance will be measured using the self-check card (resource 4)

Activity 1: General Discussion (5 minutes)

Ask students what the word *conflict* means and gather the various opinions. *Conflict* is a disagreement about something. Students work with a partner and brainstorm a list of conflicts that they have experienced or can think of, and they write the list on a blank sheet of paper. Students put their names at the top. When finished, students share their list while you write responses on the whiteboard.

Next, tell students that on each strip of paper (resource 1) is an example of a conflict. Place all the strips inside an inverted cone held by the teacher. Each pair of students picks one strip of paper from the cone. The pair uses the T chart in resource 2 to identify possible underlying reasons for the conflict. The purpose of this task is for students to explore another person's perspective and motivations in the conflict. Pick one of the conflicts listed on the whiteboard and verbally discuss an example T chart before beginning.

Activity 2: Wheel (10 minutes)

Pass out the conflict resolution strategies wheel (resource 3), giving one copy to each partner group, or projecting it on the gym wall. Discuss each of the strategies and give an example. Assign each pair two of the conflict resolution strategies. On resource 2, students write out two resolutions to the conflict assigned to them. When finished, ask volunteers to share their conflict and one resolution.

Activity 3: Create a Game (20 minutes)

This activity focuses on responsible decision-making and relationship management. Explain that the small groups (i.e., learning teams or squads) will work together to create a new game. The game includes the following criteria:

- All players must be involved.
- The game must use one of the following manipulative skills: underhand throw, overhand throw, passing with hands, catching, dribbling with the hands or feet, passing with the hands or feet, kicking, volleying, striking (with a long or short implement).
- The game must use at least four pieces of equipment.
- The game must have cooperative and competitive elements.
- The game must have a designated playing area (boundaries).

Write the game criteria on a whiteboard or project it on the wall. Students have 10 minutes to create their game. Encourage the members of each team to use positive communication (super job; awesome idea; let's keep trying; you are doing great) within each group. When the group is finished, students complete a self-check task card (resource 4). Each team then presents their game.

Debrief: Ask the following questions:

- Did conflicts develop in your groups?
- How did you resolve the conflicts?
- What actions of the group were positive and helped move the group toward success?

Differentiations

- Challenge task: Ask students to define empathy and how it can apply to the activity and everyday life.
- Simplified task: Provide students with one or more steps to resolve the conflict, or shape their response with leading questions.

Closure

Ask students why there is still conflict even though there are so many conflict resolution strategies. Explain that conflict occurs when someone fails to take responsibility for their actions, fails to use conflict resolution strategies, or fails to see a conflict from someone else's perspective. Students turn to a classmate, and the pairs identify as many of the eight conflict resolution strategies as they can.

Decision-Making and Assertiveness

GRADE LEVEL: 4-5

INTRODUCTORY INFORMATION

SHAPE America Outcomes

- S4.E1.5 Engages in physical activity with responsible interpersonal behavior (e.g., peer to peer, student to teacher, student to referee).
- S4.E2.5a Participates with responsible personal behavior in a variety of physical activity contexts, environments, and facilities.
- S4.E2.5b Exhibits respect for self with appropriate behavior while engaging in physical activity.

National Health Education Performance Indicators

- 4.5.1 Demonstrate effective verbal and non-verbal communication skills to enhance health.
- 2.5.3 Identify how peers can influence healthy and unhealthy behaviors.

Lesson Objectives

Students will be able to do the following:

- Demonstrate effective decision-making skills.
- Demonstrate assertiveness when called for in the activity.

Learning Materials and Technology

- 2 ropes approximately 50 feet (15 m) long (may substitute other materials to create a round boundary)
- 40 poly spots
- 15 fleece balls or some other soft, throwable object
- 3 cones
- Resource handout from HK*Propel*
  - Resource 1: 1 printout per student

Skill Cues

Group Decision-Making

- Involve and solicit opinions from others.
- Maintain a civil and productive tone throughout.
- Manage disagreements.
- Carefully consider the options.
- Choose the best option based on the discussion.

Assertive Communication

- Exhibit a self-confident demeanor.
- Believe your opinion matters and deserves to be heard.
- Be resilient but respectful when your opinions are challenged.
- Give your honest opinion.

LEARNING ACTIVITIES

Lesson Introduction

- **WHAT** are we learning today? The class will learn about effective group decision-making and how to speak in an assertive voice.

- **WHY** are we learning this? Families, friends, jobs, and sports all rely on group decision-making and cohesion. A group that can harness the strengths of its members and avoid conflict is more likely to be successful. At the same time, it is important for group members to stand up for their opinions, but not so forcefully that it hurts the group.

- **HOW** will learning be measured? Students will complete a rubric (resource 1).

Activity 1: Rock, Paper, Scissor Warm-Up (5 minutes)

Position three cones on the floor in a line with approximately 20 yards (18 m) between each one (distance can be changed). The spots represent the Olympic medals of gold, silver, and bronze. Pairs of students line up along an imaginary line extending through the cones. When the music starts, each pair plays rock, paper, scissors; the winner goes to the gold medal, and the student who lost goes to bronze. Once arriving at a new position, students play rock, paper, scissors with someone else. If a student wins at gold, they stay there. The student who wins moves up a medal, and the student who loses moves down. Students who win at gold stay there. Students who lose at bronze stay there. The result is students running back and forth between the medals. Stop periodically to see who is in the gold-medal position. An alternative to rock, paper, scissor is odd or even.

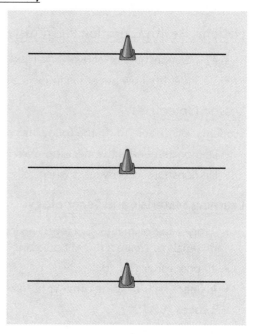

Activity 2: Heads, Shoulders, Knees, and Toes (10 minutes)

Students find a partner and get a fleece ball (or other throwable object) positioned on sidelines in hoops. All partners line up on opposite sides of a long line on the gym facing one another. Place a fleece ball on the floor between them. Students touch body parts as you name them. The options are head, shoulders, waist, knees, toes, or ball. When you yell out, "ball," both students attempt to grab the object first. Do this three times and then shift students in one line down a position. Return the ball to the line after each attempt. Play the game until each student has three or four different partners.

Processing

- How many people won their matches? How many people lost a match or two?

- How did it make you feel to lose or win?

- We all win sometimes and lose sometimes. What is important when each of these occur? (Answers: After winning, be graceful. After losing, admit the defeat, look to make changes if necessary, keep going.)

Activity 3: Frogger (25 minutes)

Use climbing ropes to form two circular "ponds" roughly 10 yards (9 m) in diameter. Each student is a "frog" and stands on the outside of the pond holding a poly spot (lily pad). Frogs enjoy sunning themselves on dry land but jump onto lily pads if threatened. The activity starts with all frogs on dry land. On your signal, the students toss their lily pad into the pond and then walk onto the lily pads without touching the rope or the water (gym floor). If a frog makes a mistake, everyone must start over on dry land. Once all frogs are on a lily pad, they count to five and return to dry land without touching the water or rope. Explain to students that because of climate change, the lily pads are dying, so after each round there is one less lily pad. The group picks which lily pad to eliminate. This pattern continues as the frogs share fewer and fewer lily pads. See how few lily pads the frogs need in order to escape the threat. For safety, no one may sit on another frog's back.

Processing

Discuss the first two themes; the remaining themes are optional.

- Decision-making: How did the group determine which lily pad to remove? Was a consensus built, and if not, did the group vote? How else could the decision have been made?
- Assertiveness: Did anyone have an idea they didn't voice? What are situations in life where assertiveness is called for?
- Leadership: Often in this activity, one person will take charge. What led to this? Was it something this individual did, or did the group somehow assign this role? Why?
- Occasionally in this activity, a bully will emerge. What actions does a bully exhibit? How should participants respond if bullied? If you are a bully, how can this be corrected?
- This is an activity of inches. Students want to use as few lily pads as possible, but this is difficult. To do so, sometimes corners are cut. An example would be someone's foot is in the water who doesn't own up to it. Why would this be the case? What peer pressures emerge in group situations that lead people to cut corners? What are some examples of peer pressures that exist in school?

Closure

Pass out a copy of resource 1 to each student. Ask students to circle the cell that best describes the group's performance. Define words that may be challenging for students. When finished, have students get a partner and share the reasons for their selections. Collect the rubrics, scan through them, and discuss any patterns that emerge.

Digestive System and Underhand Throw

GRADE LEVEL: 4-5

INTRODUCTORY INFORMATION

SHAPE America Outcomes

- S1.E10.4 Moves into and out of balances on apparatus with curling, twisting, and stretching actions.
- S1.E13.5b Throws underhand to a large target with accuracy.
- S3.E6.5 Analyzes the impact of food choices relative to physical activity, youth sports, and personal health.

National Health Education Performance Indicators

- 1.5.1 Describe the relationship between healthy behaviors and personal health.
- 1.5.4 Describe ways to prevent common childhood injuries and health problems.

Lesson Objectives

Students will be able to do the following:

- Maintain their balance while traveling over a narrow beam.
- Demonstrate correct underhand throwing technique with reasonable accuracy.
- Explain the structure and function of major digestive organs.
- Describe behaviors that promote digestive system health and what conditions may result from poor digestive system maintenance.

Learning Materials and Technology

- 30 beanbags
- 2 tunnels
- 2 balance beams (or 2 two-by-fours)
- 30 yarn balls
- 30 cones
- 4 balance boards
- 2 mini trampolines

- 1 folding mat
- 20 jump ropes
- 2 stopwatches or timing devices
- Resource handouts from HK*Propel*
  - Resource 1: 1 printout
  - Resource 2: 8 printouts
  - Resource 3: 1 printout per student

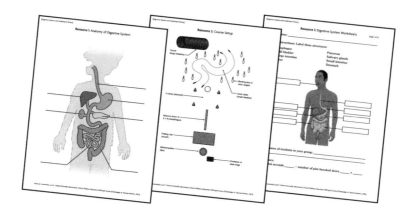

Skill Cues

Underhand Throw

- Face your target.
- Swing the arms backward (tick).
- Step with your opposite foot toward the target.
- Swing the arm forward (tock) and release the ball
- Follow through by raising your throwing hand toward the sky.

LEARNING ACTIVITIES

Lesson Introduction

- **WHAT** are we learning today? Students will learn about the digestive system and its role in breaking down foods into the raw materials that the body uses to build itself and stay healthy. Students will also learn the underhand throw.
- **WHY** are we learning this? Students may have heard the statement "You are what you eat." This means that all body systems (e.g., nervous, cardiovascular, immune) rely on the foods ingested (eaten) to stay strong and healthy.
- **HOW** will learning be measured? Students will successfully complete the digestive system worksheet (resource 3).

Activity 1: Structure Identification (5 minutes)

Display resource 1 on a whiteboard. Ask students what structures they can identify along with their function. Each time they are successful, write the name of that structure. Fill in missing information and correct erroneous information. Continue until all structures have been identified.

Activity 2: Digestive System Challenge Course (30 minutes)

Setup

Explain to students that they will create two mock digestive systems using PE equipment (see resource 2). Divide the class in half and then assign small groups to create these sections: (1) face and mouth, (2) esophagus and stomach, (3) small intestine, and (4) large intestine. Other students will set up the bowling pins. Provide handouts of resource 2 or project it on the wall. Explain what each structure is. Encourage students to work collaboratively, not rush, take their turn, and share.

Description

After each digestive system is set up, explain that the goal of the activity is to move food items (beanbags) through the digestive system in the least amount of time while transferring as much of it as possible into the blood. The activity is performed in groups of two.

- Ingesting food: Put 20 beanbags (food items) per course in a container. The teacher may call the food items a healthy food like carrots or grapes. In pairs, students "ingest" the food by throwing beanbags one at a time onto a minitrampoline, trying to land them on the nearby folding mat (the mouth). Any food items that land and stay on the folding mat are successfully ingested.
- Esophagus: Pick up only the food items that land on the folding mat and walk them across a balance beam, a maximum of two items per trip. Any food item that is dropped must stay on the floor. If a student falls off the balance beam, they must drop all food items onto the floor; they may not be picked up.

- Stomach: Cone off an area to represent the stomach. The stomach continues to break down food items by propelling them forward and backward. To represent this, students in pairs must simultaneously underhand toss two food items between them. Any food items caught are put in a hoop, while any that are dropped are tossed outside the cones.

- Small intestine: Lay down jump ropes to represent a curved, coiled tube. The primary function of the small intestine is to allow diffusion of nutrients into the blood. Set up targets (bowling pins or another appropriate item) at various distances outside the small intestine area. Students move through the small intestine and underhand toss food items at the targets. This represents moving a food item from the small intestines into the blood. Food items can only be tossed once. Knocking down a pin represents a nutrient that is successfully transported from the small intestine into the blood. Demonstrate and remind students to use correct underhand throwing technique.

- Large intestine: Students must crawl through a tunnel that represents the large intestine. The primary function of the large intestine is to reabsorb water so that it is not lost in the feces.

Rotation

While one group is in the digestive system, the "on-deck" group is responsible for resetting the station, and the group that just finished operates the timer. Other students waiting their turn complete both sides of resource 3.

Scoring

When a group finishes, record the time it took to pass through the digestive system. Subtract one second for each bowling pin successfully knocked down. Record the group's score on resource 3 using the equation. Collect the worksheets at the end of class.

Differentiations

- Challenge task: Students must use the nondominant hand when throwing all food items.

- Simplified task: Allow students to throw food items twice at the trampoline (mouth). Allow students to pick up every other food item that drops to the floor.

Closure

Students turn to another student and explain how food items pass through the digestive system from start to finish, including the role of each structure. Ask students how food choices affect health. Use specific examples of healthy and unhealthy foods.

Endocrine System, Hygiene, and Striking in Golf

GRADE LEVEL: 4-5

INTRODUCTORY INFORMATION

SHAPE America Outcomes

- S1.E25.4 Strikes an object with a long-handled implement (e.g., hockey stick, golf club, bat, tennis racket, badminton racket), while demonstrating three of the five critical elements of a mature pattern for the implement (grip, stance, body orientation, swing plane, and follow-through).

- S2.E3.5b Applies the concepts of direction and force to strike an object with a long-handled implement.

National Health Education Performance Indicators

- 7.5.2 Demonstrate a variety of healthy practices and behaviors to maintain or improve personal health.

Lesson Objectives

Students will be able to do the following:

- Demonstrate correct golf putting technique.
- Describe the endocrine system.
- Identify four endocrine system glands and one basic function of each.
- Identify three strategies to promote good hygiene.

Learning Materials and Technology

- 1 golf putter for every student (see the USGA's first tee program)
- 1 ball for every student (fleece balls, foam balls, or another type of ball that will roll effectively but not injure students)
- 20 poly spots
- Any equipment in the equipment closet students could realistically use to construct a mini golf hole
- 1 popper for every student
- Resource handouts from HK*Propel*
  - Resource 1: 1 printout
  - Resource 2: 1 printout per 3 students

Skill Cues

Golf Putting

- The target line points to the hole, and the foot line (toe-to-toe) points to the nondominant side of the target. The lines should be parallel.
- Position the ball slightly forward in the stance.
- The head is over the ball.

- Putt with a smooth stroke, using the shoulders (not the elbow or wrist).
- The follow-through is greater or equal to the backswing.

LEARNING ACTIVITIES

Lesson Introduction

- **WHAT** are we learning today? Students will learn about the endocrine system, hygiene, and putting in golf.
- **WHY** are we learning this? Students' bodies are about to begin changing dramatically as they enter into puberty. This class will inform them of some of the changes that are coming. Golf is an activity that can be enjoyed throughout a student's lifetime, and now there are many options for youth golf, including the First Tee program.
- **HOW** will learning be measured? Students will learn how to accurately keep score using a score card (resource 2).

Activity 1: Introduction to the Endocrine System (10 minutes)

The endocrine system is made up of several glands. Glands are collections of cells that produce chemical messengers called hormones. Endocrine hormones move through the body via the bloodstream and cause changes in other parts of the body. Ask whether anyone can name an endocrine gland or any gland in the body?

Watch two videos on the BrainPOP website (see the lesson plan links file on HK*Propel* for links to these videos):

- Endocrine System
- Puberty

Show students the diagram of the major glands of the endocrine system (resource 1) by projecting it, passing out copies for each student, or passing around one copy. Describe the role of each endocrine gland and point to where the gland is located in the body. Depending on the maturity of students, you may omit the reproductive glands.

Major Glands

- Pituitary: Master gland that controls other glands and tissues.
- Thyroid: Determines how fast the body's cell's burn energy.
- Parathyroid: Keeps calcium in the blood at a certain level.
- Adrenal: Regulates the effects of stress (burst of strength and speed).
- Pineal: Influences the sleep cycle.
- Pancreas: Regulates blood sugar.
- Thymus: Produces T cells that help fight infection.
- Ovaries and testes: At maturity, they enable reproduction.

Activity 2: Popper Tag (5 minutes)

To create poppers, take a pool noodle with a hollow center and cut it in half lengthwise. Then take each half and cut it into pieces one inch (2.5 cm) wide. Squeeze both ends with the fingers and it will pop away. The objective is for students to pop their poppers so that they contact another student. If struck, students do five jumping jacks and resume the game. If a student catches another student's popper, that student performs the jumping jacks or other exercise you designate.

Activity 3: Demonstration and Partner Putting (10 minutes)

Demonstrate how to correctly perform a golf putting stroke, while students shadow your demonstration. Students get a partner, stand approximately 10 feet (3 m) apart, and form Vs with their feet. The point of the V is at the heels. Students take turns executing a golf putt, aiming at the center of their partner's feet. If students are successful in contacting their partner's feet twice in a row, they may take one step back. Two successive misses equals one step forward.

Activity 4: Mini Golf Course (15 minutes)

Students form groups of three. Each group uses the equipment available to create a mini golf hole. The hole must include a poly spot at the start from which the ball is struck (the tee). The cup is a poly spot. Only a portion of the ball must roll over the cup for a student to "hole out." Liken each hole to the endocrine system. The tee is the gland, the ball is the hormone, the greenway is the bloodstream, and the second poly spot is the target of the hormone. Give students five minutes to create a hole and then begin play. Students play their own hole first, after which they may make adjustments. Establish a rotational pattern between holes. Students record the number of strokes per hole on resource 2.

Closure

Discuss that as students mature, certain changes will occur in their body. Ask students what changes they can expect as a result of puberty.

- Get taller, heavier, and stronger.
- Increase in sweating (which will also increase body odor, making it time for deodorant).
- Skin will get oilier (which could cause pimples).
- Increase in body hair.

Emphasize that these changes are natural as students' bodies grow into their adult form. Recommend that students ask a parent or trusted adult for more information if they have questions or concerns.

Flossing Teeth and Basketball Dribbling

GRADE LEVEL: 3

INTRODUCTORY INFORMATION

SHAPE America Outcomes

- S1.E17.3 Dribbles and travels in general space at slow to moderate jogging speed, with control of ball and body.
- S4.E4.3a Works cooperatively with others.
- S4.E4.3b Praises others for their success in movement performance.

National Health Education Performance Indicators

- 1.5.4 Describe ways to prevent common childhood injuries and health problems.
- 4.5.1 Demonstrate effective verbal and non-verbal communication skills to enhance health.
- 4.5.3 Demonstrate non-violent strategies to manage or resolve conflict.

Lesson Objectives

Students will be able to do the following:

- Demonstrate effective problem-solving skills.
- Communicate effectively with all members of their group.
- Demonstrate correct basketball dribbling technique.

Learning Materials and Technology

- 4 50-foot (15 m) ropes
- 40 poly spots (or cones)
- 1 basketball per student
- 4 bowling balls (optional)
- 1 roll of dental floss
- 1 floss pick
- 1 bowling pin, beanbag, or foam cylinder per student
- 1 roll of twine (cut into 30 segments, each 18 inches [46 cm])
- 1 tablet playing a video that models skills, pictures of each skill on laminated cards, braille instructions, or MP3 player with verbal instructions (as needed for UDL)
- Resource handout from HK*Propel*
  - Resource 1: 1 printout per 2 students

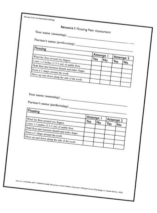

Skill Cues

Problem-Solving

- Make sure you understand the problem and the rules.
- Allow group members to share ideas freely.
- Make sure everyone who wants to be involved can be.
- Do not try to dominate the problem-solving process.

- Discuss options with the group and come to an agreement.
- Along with the group, follow the established plan.

Effective Communication

- Use a tone of voice, facial expressions, and words that are respectful.
- Listen to others without interrupting.
- Convey all the information needed (completeness).
- Make sure message is concise (to the point).

Basketball Dribble

- Use the fingertips (not the palm).
- Push down gradually on the ball (don't slap).
- Keep the bounce hip high or slightly lower.
- Keep the ball approximately a forearm's length from the body.
- Keep the head up (glancing down occasionally is OK).

Basketball Spin Dribble

- Step toward the defender.
- Spin in the opposite direction from the stepping leg (e.g., if you step with the right foot, spin left).
- Switch the dribbling hand midspin.
- Move in a different direction from the original pathway.

Wheelchair Basketball Backspin Dribble

- Complete two rim pushes with the ball on the lap.
- Hold the ball in both hands.
- Toss the ball in front of the chair with backspin so it returns to the dribbler.
- Put the ball on the lap again.
- Complete two additional pushes.

LEARNING ACTIVITIES

Lesson Introduction

- **WHAT** are we learning today? Students will learn how to effectively floss their teeth, solve problems using effective communication, and dribble a basketball using the correct cues.
- **WHY** are we learning this? Flossing is an important but sometimes overlooked part of caring for teeth. Flossing can help teeth remain healthy if it is done often and with correct technique. Problem-solving and effective communication are important skills when working with other people, which is most of the time. It is vital for group projects, athletic teams, friendships, and, in the future, jobs. Basketball dribbling is one of the sport's most fundamental skills; it is needed to move the ball around the court and to maintain possession.
- **HOW** will learning be measured? Students will complete a peer assessment on flossing technique (resource 1).

Activity 1: Floss Practice (10 minutes)

Ask students what flossing is and how it is beneficial. Flossing is the movement of floss (like a string or thin cord) between the teeth to remove plaque and food particles. Flossing helps prevent cavities, tooth decay, and gingivitis (sore, red, and puffy gums).

Show students a roll of dental floss and a floss pick. Pass around an example of each. Both are commonly used to floss. Place two pieces of PE equipment that resemble teeth close together. Demonstrate how to floss using the following technique:

1. Break off 18 to 24 inches (about 45-50 cm) of floss (if using a roll).
2. Wind the floss around a finger (middle or index usually) on either hand, leaving 1 to 2 inches (2.5-5 cm) of usable floss.
3. Hold the floss taut using the thumb and index finger on each hand.
4. Position the floss between two teeth.
5. Curve the floss around a tooth in a C shape and glide it up and down, cleaning the side of the tooth.
6. Clean the floss if it becomes dirty.

Universal Design for Learning: Alternate Means of Demonstration

- Use descriptive wording.
- On a tablet, play a video on loop that models the activity.
- Students who cannot see the demonstration use tactile modeling with their hands over the teacher's hands.
- Give priority seating to students who need to be close.

Students form pairs and get one piece of twine and two pieces of equipment such as foam cylinders, bowling pins, or cones to simulate teeth. Students place their two pieces of equipment against each other. Students practice flossing for 3 to 5 minutes and then they take turns conducting the peer assessment (resource 1).

Universal Design for Learning: Alternate Means of Practice

- Employ a peer buddy to assist a student.
- Use multiple demonstrations and cue words.
- Break task into one part at a time and provide one- or two-step commands to complete the task.
- Use a reinforcement such as praise or other socially positive behavioral support after each step of the task.

Universal Design for Learning: Alternative to Assessment

- Student puts individual photos of each step into the correct order.
- Student points to or circles pictures on a worksheet in the correct order.
- Student accesses this assessment on a BrailleNote or MP3 player.
- The assessment is read aloud as the student performs the skills.

Activity 2: Pick Play (15 minutes)

Create groups of eight students. Give each group a long rope. Position students around a circle with a 10-foot (3 m) diameter made of poly spots or cones. In the middle, place a ball approximately the size of a soccer ball to represent an errant food particle lodged between two teeth. The objective is for students to use their rope to remove the ball without entering the circle. Students must pick up the ball, they cannot roll it. Allow students time to plan. If successful, students show the teacher their successful technique.

Processing

- Problem-solving: Read the cues for effective problem-solving (and ask how well the group was able to demonstrate them). Give specific examples.

- Communication: Read the statement, "Say what you mean; don't say it mean." Ask students how it applies to the activity and cite specific examples.

Universal Design for Learning: Alternate Means of Movement or Game Play

- Make a group smaller if eight is overwhelming to a student.
- Provide a buddy to work closely with a student.
- Use a beeping foam ball as the errant food particle.
- Use a foam noodle for students who are not able to control a loose rope.
- Teach the group the American Sign Language for "Say what you mean; don't say it mean."
- Allow students who need communication support to point, use a thumbs-up, or raise a hand when the correct phrase is spoken.

Activity 3: Gate Challenge (15 minutes)

Demonstrate the proper technique for basketball dribbling, both standing and sitting versions.

Students begin by dribbling in general space to music at a walking, wheeling, or crutch-walking pace that incrementally increases to jogging speed, pushing quickly, or walking quickly. Add extensions depending on student skill level, such as nondominant hand, dominant to nondominant and back, or spin dribble. Demonstrate all extensions used.

Universal Design for Learning: Alternative Means of Participation

- Students who sit can remain in a stationary position or sit on a scooter and move.
- Students who cannot use their hands for dribbling due to crutches or a walker can simulate the movement while stationary.
- Have an adult assistant support the student while sitting in a chair
- The student punches or pushes a beach ball through the gates.
- Change the goal to walking or wheeling in general space without dribbling or to reaching out to touch a suspended basketball in a net bag.

Set up several gates throughout the general space; gates are two cones about three feet (1 m) apart. On the go signal, students have 90 seconds to pass through as many gates as possible. They must use a C-shaped pathway to represent the path floss should take while moving around teeth. They should move as close to the near cone as possible.

Universal Design for Learning: Alternative Means of Participation

- Make gates 4 feet wide (121 cm) if students need more room.
- Students follow a pattern made with floor tape.
- Students bounce and catch the ball then take two steps forward.
- Use wheelchair basketball backspin dribble.
- The student points in the desired direction of travel and an adult helper pushes them there.
- The student holds the elbow of a human guide while dribbling with the other hand.
- Preteach the skill individually.

If there is extra time, play dribble tag. Each student tries to touch the basketball of another player while maintaining possession of their own. Count the number of touches.

Closure

Students get a partner. One student explains the steps for flossing teeth. The other fills in any missing information and then they switch roles.

Universal Design for Learning

The following are additional universal design for learning considerations for all learners:

- Consider a grouping of two students for those who need more individual attention and less distraction.
- Improve representation by using photos of children in the class performing the basketball dribble and bounce-and-catch photos of the activities and assessment.
- When assessing, consider students who need alternative assessment such as pictures and videos. Use detailed description and a more detailed breakdown of skills or adaptations for holding the string.
- Provide additional means to check for understanding by asking yes or no questions, having students say or use sign language cue words, or perform the movement for the teacher before being assessed.
- Use floor tape, dome cones, or other soft barriers to help designate an area of play for students who need additional information.
- On a tablet, play a video model of each skill, pretend flossing, and playing the game with errant food particles.
- Change the goal of the activity to include looking in the desired dribble direction, pointing to the correct motor skill on a tablet or worksheet, or using the arms only for the motion of dribbling without a ball.
- Provide paraeducators and classroom teachers with specific actions they should use to support students.
- Use peer buddies for students who might need additional demonstrations or motivation to stay on task.
- Use a 3D doll or figure to demonstrate the hand position when dribbling, or use tactile modeling in which a student puts their hands on the teacher's hand or arm to feel the dribbling motion.

Food Labels and Soccer Dribbling

GRADE LEVEL: 3-4

INTRODUCTORY INFORMATION

SHAPE America Outcomes

- S1.E18.4 Dribbles with the feet in general space with control of ball and body while increasing and decreasing speed.
- S1.E19.3 Passes and receives a ball with the insides of the feet to a stationary partner, "giving" on reception before returning the pass.
- S1.E20.4 Dribbles with hands or feet in combination with other skills (e.g., passing, receiving, shooting).

National Health Education Performance Indicators

- 7.5.2 Demonstrate a variety of healthy practices and behaviors to maintain or improve personal health.
- 7.5.3 Demonstrate a variety of behaviors that avoid or reduce health risks.

Lesson Objectives

Students will be able to do the following:

- Correctly perform soccer dribbling, a sole trap, and an inside-of-the-foot pass.
- Describe the basic components of a food label and correctly answer related questions on a food label worksheet.
- Define "added sugar" and provide a rough estimate of the amount of physical activity required to burn those calories.

Learning Materials and Technology

- 1 soccer ball per student
- 40 cones
- 1 sugar cube
- Resource handouts from HK*Propel*
  - Resource 1: 1 printout per 2 students
  - Resource 2: 1 printout per student

Skill Cues

Maintaining Possession

- Shield the ball with your body.
- If appropriate, dribble away using a random or zigzag pattern.
- Use the sole of the foot to pull back or initiate a dribble.

Passing

- Step next to the ball.
- Contact the ball on the inside or outside of the foot.
- Contact at the middle point of the ball or below and keep the ball on the ground.

- Swing the leg in a pendulum motion.
- Follow through low toward the target.

Dribbling

- Tap the ball forward gently using the inside or the outside of the feet.
- Keep the ball within the distance of an arm extended straight out.
- Keep the head up as much as possible. It's OK to glance down to monitor the ball.
- Match the speed of travel to the skill level.

Sole Trap

- Position the body in front of the incoming ball.
- Place the sole of the foot on top of the ball.
- Use enough force so that the ball stays in the same place.

LEARNING ACTIVITIES

Lesson Introduction

- **WHAT** are we learning today? Students will learn about food labels, how to read them correctly, and how physical activity relates to calorie burned. Students also will learn how to dribble and pass in soccer.
- **WHY** are we learning this? "You are what you eat." It important to put the correct fuels into the body so it can operate at its highest level. Being able to dribble and pass in soccer is important to maintaining possession and moving the ball down the field.
- **HOW** will learning be measured? Learning will be assessed through a worksheet (resource 2) that requires students to answer questions about a food label.

Activity 1: Worksheet (10 minutes)

Students get a partner and one copy of the food label handout (resource 1) and find a quiet location in the gym. Students take turns reading different parts of resource 1 to their partner. When students return to the larger group, they highlight important aspects of the resource they just read. Ask students to define the following terms: serving size, servings per container, calories, and % daily value. Next, each partner group answers the questions on resource 2. Beforehand, show them a sugar cube so they have a size reference for question five. A can of soda has eight teaspoons (cubes) of added sugar, while an apple has zero grams of added sugar.

Activity 2: Dribble Warm-Up (5 minutes)

Tell students they will be working on soccer skills to help burn calories. Ask how long they'll need to be physically active to use the calories from one can of soda.

Demonstrate the correct technique for soccer dribbling and how to perform a sole trap. Students get a soccer ball and dribble at a slow pace. On your cue, students must trap the ball. After a few minutes, increase the speed to jogging. Remind students to keep control of the ball and to trap it if they are losing control. After a few minutes have students freeze and trap their soccer ball. Now, each time you yell, "change," students leave their ball and find a new one and resume dribbling.

Differentiations

- Challenge task: Dribble with the nondominant foot or use the bottom of the foot to dribble.
- Simplified task: Continue to dribble at a walking pace.

Activity 3: Dribble Knockout (10 minutes)

Demonstrate how to maintain possession against a defender.

Students spread out with a soccer ball in general space. On go, students try to knock other soccer balls outside the boundary while maintaining possession of their own ball. Any student whose ball is knocked out must dribble along two sides of a boundary and then may return to the game. Students must stay in close proximity to their soccer ball; they cannot leave it alone.

Differentiations

- Challenge task: Alternate using the inside and outside of the foot.
- Simplified task: Dribble along one side of a boundary instead of two before returning.

Activity 4: Keep the Cone (25 minutes)

Divide the class into two teams on opposite sides of the playing space and set up 15 cones randomly on each side. There are multiple rounds to this game. In each round, when a player knocks down a cone of the other team, they pick it up and place it upright on their side. Cones placed down by students should be scattered and not clumped together or positioned only along the boundary.

Round 1

Each student dribbles their own soccer ball to the other side, attempting to knock over a cone. Players may not steal balls from the other team. After 1 to 2 minutes, stop to see which side has more cones. Play multiple rounds. Change the dribbling pattern—inside of foot only, outside of foot only, alternate inside and outside, and sole of foot.

Round 2

This activity is similar to round 1, except that the ball is passed instead of dribbled. Students get a partner and return one ball to the cart or bin. The student with the soccer ball may not move; the student without the ball can move freely. The ball is passed back and forth. If the ball is not successfully trapped or passed, both partners must return to their side before continuing (if in the other team's territory) or do 15 jumping jacks (in their own territory). A trap is considered unsuccessful if the trapper must take two steps to control it after first contact. After a minimum of five passes, players may use a pass to knock a cone over. If they miss the cone, they must try on a different cone. Play multiple rounds. Vary the type of pass: inside of foot, outside of foot, and instep.

Round 3

Players pass from their own territory, trying to knock down cones on the other side. Passes must stay on the floor and be made using the inside of the foot. If successful, they cross the center line, pick up the cone, and place it on their side.

Closure

Students turn to a partner and explain the critical elements of maintaining possession when being pressured by a defender. Look at resource 2 to determine which students had the closest guess to 8 cubes of sugar. Each cube is 16 empty calories, which equals 128 calories. A 12-ounce can of soda contains 140 calories. Students just participated in roughly 30 minutes of soccer. Have students guess how many calories were burned. The answer depends on body weight but should be roughly 60 to 80 calories or half the calories of the soda.

Healthy Eating and Striking

INTRODUCTORY INFORMATION

SHAPE America Outcomes

- S1.E25.4 Strikes an object with a long-handled implement while demonstrating three of the five critical elements of a mature pattern for the implement (grip, stance, body orientation, swing plane, and follow through).
- S4.E3.3 Accepts and implements specific corrective feedback from the teacher.

National Health Education Performance Indicators

- 5.5.3 List healthy options to health-related issues or problems.
- 7.5.2 Demonstrate a variety of healthy practices and behaviors to maintain or improve personal health.

Lesson Objectives

Students will be able to do the following:

- Identify attributes of healthy eating.
- Determine if a food item is healthy or not.
- Correctly perform a forehand striking pattern.
- Accept and attempt to implement corrective partner feedback.

Learning Materials and Technology

- 1 racket per student
- 1 foam tennis ball, trainer tennis ball, or regular tennis ball per student (recommend foam)
- 10 hoops
- 10 cones
- 10 poly spots
- Printouts of food items (available from many websites)
- Resource handouts from *HKPropel*
  - Resource 1: 1 printout per student
  - Resource 2: 1 printout per 2 students

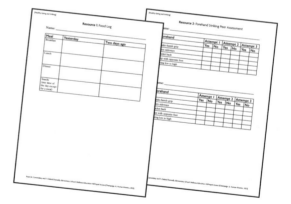

Skill Cues

Forehand Strike

- Take a handshake grip on the racket handle.
- Turn sideways with the nondominant shoulder pointing towards the incoming ball.
- Pull the racket back in preparation for striking.
- Step with the opposite foot.
- Follow through.

LEARNING ACTIVITIES

Lesson Introduction

- **WHAT** are we learning today? Students will learn about striking by performing a tennis forehand. Students will also learn about tips for healthy eating, selecting healthy foods, and how physical activity equates to calories burned.

- **WHY** are we learning this? Students in third grade are beginning to get some autonomy in picking what foods to eat at home. The ideas presented will help them pick healthier foods. Being able to control a ball struck with a racket is critical in multiple sports, including tennis and badminton.

- **HOW** will learning be measured? Student learning will be measured by completing the food log (resource 1) and the forehand striking peer assessment (resource 2).

Activity 1: Food Log (10 minutes)

Distribute one copy of resource 1 per student. Students write into the food log everything they ate over the past two days. They also indicate their favorite meal. Collect the logs, which will be used later. Students may also use photos glued into the log, a typed log, an oral version of the log, or a video of the foods eaten.

Ask students what healthy eating looks like. Students should not answer with actual meals or individual food items. Write student responses on a whiteboard and read them aloud. If any student lip-leads, avoid speaking while facing the board. Include the following points, but write all acceptable responses on the whiteboard.

1. Eat a variety of foods.
2. Eat plenty of fruits and vegetables.
3. Limit excess fat and sugar.
4. Choose natural foods and limit processed foods.
5. Avoid overeating (be mindful of portions).

Activity 2: Warm-Up (10 minutes)

All students perform the following:

- Ball carrying: Walk or wheel around with a tennis ball on the forehand side of the racket (palm facing up), on the palm of the hand, on a racket affixed to a wheelchair armrest, or in a stationary position for several seconds. Change the pathways, speeds, and directions. Incorporate harder movement patterns like the gallop and skip. Repeat while using the other side of the racket.

- Dribbling: Bounce the ball down to the floor and back up with the racket repeatedly. See how many times students can do this without the ball bouncing twice. Repeat while walking.

- Keep it up: Bounce the ball on the racket, but not above head height. Provide a hanging ball or a small beach ball, or have student use their hand instead of a racket if needed.

- Partner volley: One student underhand tosses the ball to a partner, who uses a volley stroke to hit it back. See how many times the thrower can catch the return without taking more than one step. Partners switch roles. In necessary, strike the ball off a tee or hanging from a basketball net.

- Partner strike: The tossed ball bounces once and then is struck gently back to the thrower. See how many times the thrower can catch the return. Then, toss the ball slightly to the side so the striker must move before contacting the ball. Switch roles. Allow multiple bounces; encourage peer buddies to provide support in a triple-partner group.

Activity 3: Food Fight (15 minutes)

Cut out pictures of food items (available from many websites) and face them down in the center of the gym surrounded by cones. Braile labels should be used on the items. Demonstrate with verbal explanations how to execute a tennis forehand against a wall so the ball rebounds back.

Pairs of students get one hoop, one poly spot, one racket, and one tennis ball. They place the poly spot 10 to 20 feet from the wall and the hoop 10 feet behind the poly spot. The partner with the racket stands on the poly spot, and the partner without the racket stands in or near the hoop. The student with the racket does a drop-and-hit toward the wall using correct tennis forehand technique from the location of the poly spot and catches the rebound. Alternatives include performing the skill without the ball, hitting off a tee, or hitting a ball suspended on a string. The nonhitting partner stands in or near the hoop and retrieves any balls that get past the hitter. Switch after two minutes.

In the next progression, students attempt to rally the ball off the wall three consecutive times or five times total nonconsecutively. The ball must strike the wall in the air and not bounce twice to count. If successful, students give their racket to their partner and run to the center circle to pick up a facedown food item printout. The food item area should have a sound device for students with visual impairments. Students must take the first item they touch; there are no put backs. The returning student puts the food item in their hoop. Students are permitted three self-drops before they must give the racket to their partner. After five minutes, students separate the food items into healthy and unhealthy categories based upon the guidelines in activity 1. Ask students to share with the class some of their food items and discuss why they are healthy or not. Next, students build a healthy meal that follows the MyPlate guidelines taught in an earlier class. Ask one or two groups of students to share their meal with the class. Provide accommodations to the rules to allow for multiple practice tries, alternative equipment, and a variety of ways to strike (or throw) the ball.

Repeat the activity a second time, but the partner completes the peer assessment instead of retrieving errant balls. In this round, students do not collect food items.

Differentiations

- Challenge task: Hit five backhands off the wall.
- Simplified task: Allow fewer hits before retrieving a food item.

Activity 4: Discussion (5 minutes)

Pass back the food logs and use the criteria established in activity 1 to determine whether the overall meal was healthy or not. Students put an arrow up if the meal was mostly healthy, an arrow sideways if it had healthy and unhealthy components, and an arrow down if it was mostly unhealthy. Other options include orally saying the words; writing the words; typing them; or doing a thumbs-up, thumbs-sideways, or thumbs-down. Start with breakfast the day before and progress to lunch, dinner, and snacks. If there is time and student recall is adequate, discuss two days before.

Closure

Students turn to a partner and explain why each meal was marked with an up, sideways, or down arrow, and then switch. Ask students what the five characteristics of healthy eating are without looking at their papers. If time allows, one partner stands up and physically demonstrates the cues for forehand striking while the partner checks for accuracy.

Universal Design for Learning

The following are additional universal design for learning considerations for all learners:

- Provide a wide range of rackets, including foam, light weight, large heads, small grip size, colors, and a hand racket for students who cannot grip a racket.
- Use auditory devices at areas where students might need to go to or behind targets.

- Consider using a raised representation of where someone stands to perform an activity, such as rope under two-inch-wide (5 cm) floor tape, or cones with jump ropes strung from one to another.
- Provide additional means to check for understanding by asking yes or no questions or having students say or use sign language cue words when requested.
- On a tablet, play a video model of the forehand strike and how to perform each of the activities in the lesson plan.
- Change the goal of the activity to include performing the striking motion without the ball, using a hand to strike a larger ball, dropping or throwing the ball without striking it, or holding a racket for a certain number of seconds.
- Provide individual cards with the forehand cues represented by words, pictures, and braille descriptions.
- Work with the American Sign Language interpreter, if there is one, for vocabulary words directly related to this lesson, such as the forehand strike cues and healthy meals.
- Pre-teach the forehand strike to students who might be in adapted physical education or who need extra support to be able to successfully participate in the lesson.
- Provide multiple means of expression by encouraging pointing to the cues that are on a display; allowing the use of communication devices or one-word answers; or posing questions that require only a yes or no answer, a nod of the head, or thumbs-up or thumbs-down.
- Consider equipment accommodations such as larger ball size, a tee to put the ball on, a ball suspended on a string, or a tennis ball with bells or BBs inside. Provide a chair for students who use crutches or canes or need to sit. Incorporate wheelchair tennis rules and drills.

Immune System, Open Space, and Person-to-Person Defense

GRADE LEVEL: 3-4

INTRODUCTORY INFORMATION

SHAPE America Outcomes

- S1.E16.3 Catches a gently tossed hand-size ball from a partner, demonstrating four of the five critical elements of a mature pattern.
- S2.E1.3 Recognizes the concept of open spaces in a movement context.
- S2.E1.4b Applies the concept of closing spaces in small-sided practice tasks.

National Health Education Performance Indicators

- 1.5.1 Describe the relationship between healthy behaviors and personal health.
- 2.5.1 Describe how the family influences personal health practices and behaviors.
- 7.5.3 Demonstrate a variety of behaviors that avoid or reduce health risks.

Lesson Objectives

Students will be able to do the following:

- Effectively move to open space.
- Correctly demonstrate person-to-person defense.
- Describe the three major defense levels of the immune system.
- Identify steps for keeping skin healthy at the beach and preventing acne.

Learning Materials and Technology

- 50 cones
- 1 scooter per student
- 10 scarves
- 10 hoops
- 10 pinnies of any color
- 5 bath towels
- 1 bucket
- 1 beanbag per six students
- Resource handout from HK*Propel*
  - Resource 1: 1 printout

Skill Cues

Open Space

- Be ready to receive the pass.
- Keep space between you and the defenders; none should be close to you (proximity).
- Check to see if the passing lane is open.
- If you must change position, move toward the goal if possible.
- If you are covered, move (reposition).

Person-to-Person Defense

- Remain close to the person defending.
- Make sure you can see the opponent and the ball.
- Stay between the person and the ball.

LEARNING ACTIVITIES

Lesson Introduction

- **WHAT** are we learning today? Students will learn about the immune system, which keeps us healthy by protecting us against germs. They will learn about its three lines of defense, especially its outermost layer: the skin. Students will also learn about moving to open space and guarding in a person-to-person defense.
- **WHY** are we learning this? It is important to understand the immune system and keep it healthy. The skin is part of the critical first line of defense. Finding open space and effectively executing a person-to-person defense are integral to successful offensive and defensive strategies.
- **HOW** will learning be measured? Learning will be measured using an assessment of moving to open space and person-to-person defense (resource 1).

Activity 1: Ninja Warm-Up (5 minutes)

Students choose partners and stand facing one another approximately an arm's length apart. The objective of the game is to move a hand quickly so that it contacts the hand of their partner. One of the partners says, "3-2-1 ninja!" at which time they both strike a pose. One partner moves first, attempting to contact their partner's hand. If contact is made, that person wins. If not, the hand stops moving at a natural ending position; it may not return to the original position. After one person moves and freezes, the partner has two options: (1) move to form a different stationary position, or (2) attempt to contact their partner's hand. They may not do both. Here is an example. After saying "3-2-1 ninja", partner 1 moves both hands in front of their body. Partner 2 moves their right hand, attempting to touch partner 1's left hand. Partner 1 is able to move their hand away and avoid contact. Partner 1 then quickly moves their right hand and is able to contact partner 2's hand, meaning partner 1 wins that round. Play to the best of three and then find a new partner.

Activity 2: Level Three (15 minutes)

Separate the gym into three sections marked by lines of cones. The lines represent the immune system's three levels of defense. Everyone is seated on a scooter. Some students are germs (pathogens) who attempt to ride their scooters across the three lines of defense and reach the host, their teacher. Other students represent the three lines of defense whose job it is to prevent as many pathogens from reaching the host as possible.

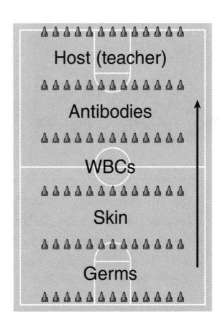

- The first line of defense is the skin. Two or three players represent the skin. The skin players try to tag invading pathogens while staying connected (holding hands or a small object). The skin is an effective defender only when it is connected and there are no openings into the body. A tagged pathogen stands up, holds their scooter like a suitcase, returns to the start, and tries again.

- The second line of defense is the white blood cells (WBC). The WBCs are represented by students in pairs, who each hold a corner of a bath towel and move inside the boundary to envelop or gently touch the invading germs.
- The third and final line of defense is antibodies. Put a bucket of scarves in the middle of the third zone. Each antibody carries a scarf. When an antibody touches a germ with a scarf, that marks the germ, who then walks back to the start holding the scarf above their head.

Meanwhile, one player is the vaccine and can move freely throughout any level. Any pathogen touched by the vaccine must stand up and walk back to the start. Rotate positions every three to four minutes. Any student walking with a scooter should hold it like a suitcase.

Adapted by permission from PE Central, *Invasion of the Microbes* (Colchester, CT: PE Central). www.pecentral.org/lessonideas/ViewLesson.asp?ID=12191#.X_qWL9hKhnJ

Activity 3: Discussion (10 minutes)

Explain that the skin needs to be taken care of to function well over time. One of the most common threats to the skin is the sun. Show students the following pictures (or other pictures of your choice). Have students get with a partner and discuss how these children could better protect themselves. The answers are to wear sunscreen, wear a sun shirt, put on a hat, play under an umbrella, and avoid the sun during peak hours. Some of these factors are not under the students' control, but they can bring these health issues to the attention of their parents or caregivers.

Discuss with students the recommendations for using sunscreen:

- Use sunscreen with a sun protection factor (SPF) of 15 or higher for adequate protection.
- Reapply every two hours, sooner if you're sweating or in the water.
- Make sure sunscreen is no more than three years old. It typically expires after three years.
- It takes approximately 15 minutes for your skin to absorb the sunscreen and protect you, so apply it before going outside.

Another skin-related issue for upper-elementary students is acne. Pimple frequency starts to increase around this age. Ask students what steps work to reduce pimples.

- Wash your face twice a day with warm water and a mild soap.
- Avoid touching your face with your fingers or directly touching your face with objects like a phone.
- If you wear glasses or sunglasses, clean them frequently.
- If you get acne on your body, try not to wear tight clothes; loose cotton is better.

Activity 4: Wound Defenders (10 minutes)

Outline a playing space of 10 × 30 feet using cones. Place a hoop at both ends of the playing space. One of the hoops should contain a beanbag. Divide the class into teams of three with two teams in each playing space. Use a demonstration to teach open space and person-to-person defense beforehand. The hoop represents a scrape experienced during a fall. The beanbags represent dirt. One team tries to put a beanbag into the hoop while the other is defending. Three passes are needed before attempting to underhand toss a beanbag into the hoop. If the beanbag hits the floor, a turnover occurs on the spot. Beanbags must only land in the hoop; they do not need to stay in the hoop to count.

Closure

Students get a partner and stand up. Designate one student as the offensive player and the other as the defender. The teacher pretends to be an offensive player holding an imaginary ball, attempting to complete a pass. Instruct the defender to position themselves in an ideal person-to-person defensive position to prevent the pass. Provide feedback based on how well the defensive players demonstrate the person-to-person defensive cues. Next, the offensive player points to an open space. Repeat by the teacher moving to a new location. This will force the defensive player to reposition themselves. Again, check that the defensive players are correctly demonstrating the cues for person-to-person defense.

Inclusion and Batting

INTRODUCTORY INFORMATION

SHAPE America Outcomes

- S4.E4.5 Accepts, recognizes, and actively involves others with both higher and lower skill abilities into physical activities and group projects.
- S4.E2.5a Participates with responsible personal behavior in a variety of physical activity contexts, environments, and facilities.
- S4.E1.5 Engages in physical activity with responsible interpersonal behavior (e.g., peer to peer, student to teacher, student to referee).
- S5.E4.5 Describes the social benefits gained from participating in physical activity (e.g., recess, youth sport).
- S1.E25.4 Strikes an object with a long-handled implement (e.g., hockey stick, golf club, bat, tennis racket, badminton racket), while demonstrating three of the five critical elements of a mature pattern for the implement (grip, stance, body orientation, swing plane, and follow-through).
- S1.E25.5a Strikes a pitched ball with a bat, using a mature pattern.

National Health Education Performance Indicators

- 1.5.3 Describe ways in which a safe and healthy school and community environment can promote personal health.
- 1.5.2 Identify examples of emotional, intellectual, physical, and social health.

Lesson Objectives

Students will be able to do the following:

- Define inclusive practices.
- Identify ways they can promote a healthy school environment through the use of inclusive practices.
- Correctly perform the baseball swing.

Learning Materials and Technology

- 2 beeping foam balls
- 15 poly spots
- 1 foam bat for every 2 students (choice of large, medium, and small)
- 50 fleece balls
- 5 pinnies with jingle bells pinned to them
- 4 hoops or crushed chalk for circles
- 30 blindfolds
- 3 batting tees (The tees may need modifications to accommodate a larger ball. If necessary, cut a gallon milk jug in half and insert the spout end over the batting tee.)
- 1 tactile map
- Resource handout from HK*Propel*
  - Resource 1: 1 printout

Skill Cues

Batting

- Assume an athletic stance with the weight shifted back somewhat and the hands armpit high.
- Step toward the pitcher, or transfer weight from back buttock to forward one if sitting.
- Open the hips and throw the hands toward the ball, or rotate the torso if sitting.
- Keep the eyes on the ball until contact is made, or keep the face, nose, and chin toward the pitcher.
- Keep the swing level.

LEARNING ACTIVITIES

Lesson Introduction

- **WHAT** are we learning today? Students will learn about including all people, especially those who have different abilities. At the same time, students will learn how to bat a pitched ball with proper technique.
- **WHY** are we learning this? People throughout the world are different; therefore, it's important to coexist peacefully and respect differences.
- **HOW** will learning be measured? Student performance will be measured using a psychomotor batting assessment (resource 1) administered by the teacher.

Activity 1: Toss Tag Warm-Up (5 minutes)

Choose three to five students to be it. Have them wear or hold a pinny that has jingle bells pinned to it. Pass out fleece balls to a third of the remaining students. On go, students flee from the taggers. Any student tagged performs 10 jumping jacks, 10 high knees, or 10 pretend jump rope jumps and then may return to the game. Alternatives include jumping jack arms (no legs) or opening and closing the legs if seated. The taggers may not tag anyone with a fleece ball. If chased, students are encouraged to yell, "help," lift a "help" sign, or use the American Sign Language sign for help to alert those with the fleece balls to throw them a ball for safety. If a seated student is unable to see the ball, make sure the ball is placed in the lap or hand. Play rounds of 60 to 90 seconds, calling out the last 10 seconds, and then rotate taggers. Afterward, discuss calling for help when students need it: when they are frustrated with an assignment, are being bullied, or are feeling sad too much. Strong people know it's OK to ask for help.

Activity 2: Batting Practice (10 minutes)

Demonstrate the correct technique for batting a pitched ball. Have students shadow the demonstration, observe, and provide feedback. Next, students get a partner, a poly spot, three fleece balls, and an appropriate bat from the choices provided. The pitcher underhand tosses the ball to the plate (poly spot) from a distance of 10 paces, and the batter use correct technique. After six pitched balls, rotate the batter and pitcher. For safety, the batter should face away from other groups.

Differentiations

- Challenge task: The pitcher can use an overhand throw.
- Simplified task: The pitcher moves closer to the batter, the batter selects a bat with a larger barrel, or the batter uses a batting tee.

Universal Design for Learning: Alternative Movements and Equipment

- Strike with an open hand.
- Use a beeping foam ball. (A beeping ball is larger than a softball and contains a speaker that emits a high-pitched beeping sound.)

- Wear a large oven mitt on the hand to strike with.
- Place the ball on a tee or suspend it from a string held by a buddy.
- Use a foam or lightweight bat.
- Student pushes the ball off their lap or strikes it with their hand out of a buddy's hand.

Activity 3: Beep Baseball (20 minutes)

Show students the YouTube video "How to Play Beep Baseball." (See the lesson plan links file on HK*Propel* for a link to this video.) Verify that descriptive captioning is available for students with a visual impairment and that open or closed captioning is available for students with an auditory impairment.

Ask, "Why do you think the sport of beep baseball was invented?" (Answer: It allows people with a disability to participate in a popular American sport and participate in physical activity with both sighted and blind individuals.)

Duration

A beep baseball game lasts six innings, and each team receives three outs per inning. The batter is allowed three strikes or attempts to hit the ball into fair play.

Design

Two bases are located in approximately the same position as first and third base and are represented by a hoop. Home plate is located in its traditional position. There are six fielding players, numbered one through six. One offensive player is positioned in each hoop, and the batter is positioned at home plate. Hoops also can be used to represent the two buzzing bases.

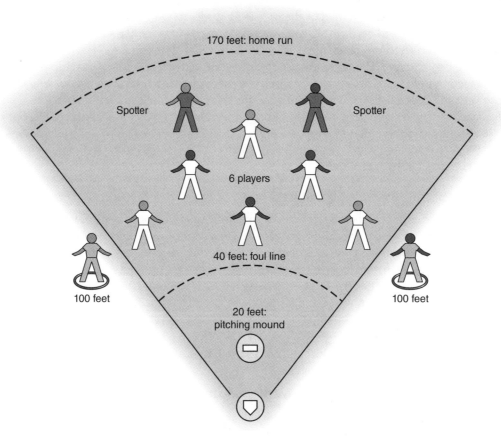

Play

To simulate blindness, have students wear blindfolds. If blindfolds are not available, instruct students to close their eyes. For beginning players, the beeping foam ball is placed on a tee. For more advanced players, the ball is pitched by an offensive player (not the fielding team). After contact is made, the umpire or teacher yells the number of the player best positioned to field the ball. This alerts that player that the ball is coming to them. Meanwhile, the batter runs toward the hoop in the opposite direction of where the ball was struck. The batter is guided by a teammate standing in a hoop yelling their name. (An alternative is to sound a buzzer.) That teammate must always keep at least one foot inside the hoop; they may reach outside the hoop with their hand and one foot. For example, if the ball is struck to player four, the spotter in the position of first base would begin yelling the batter's name. If the batter high-fives this teammate before the ball is controlled by a fielder or fielders, the batter is safe. Conversely, if the fielders collect it first, the batter is out. An alternative to high fives is the runner being contacted by a pool noodle held by the teammate.

Fielders start out standing but are permitted to lie on the ground if necessary to control a ball. The ball must travel at least back to the pitcher's mound and remain between first and third base to be fair. Each batter who reaches first or third base scores one run for their team. Partner each fielder with a sighted classmate for safety and to help the game flow more smoothly. The teacher may pitch, select a student to act as the pitcher, or use a batting tee. If using this activity over multiple lessons, start with one game and progress to two separate games. During game play, complete the batting assessment (resource 1) to measure students' skill levels.

Closure

Before students sit down, have them spread out, and on the count of 3, perform a batting swing without equipment. Repeat once or twice more. After students sit, ask them what it was like to play beep baseball. What are examples of ways other students might be different from them? Why is it important to respect and be kind to differences?

Universal Design for Learning

The following are additional universal design for learning considerations for all learners:

- Consider smaller groupings such as one-on-one for students who need less sensory information.
- Decrease the speed of movements by asking children to walk instead of run.
- Improve representation by using photos of children in the class performing the batting technique, running to a base, or fielding the ball.
- When assessing children whose mobility is different from that of others or who need to perform a closed skill, consider breaking down the task further.
- Consider using a raised representation of the field, called a tactile map, made with waxed pieces of string or pipe cleaners taped or glued to a clipboard to represent the field.
- Provide additional means to check for understanding by asking yes or no questions, having students say or use sign language cue words, or perform the movement for the teacher before being assessed.
- Cover one eye instead of blindfolding both.
- On a tablet, play a video model of batting, fielding, and running.
- Change the goal of the activity to include looking in the direction and pointing to where the student is supposed to run, using assistance or a human guide, having a friend push a wheelchair, or pointing arrows toward the base.
- Provide paraeducators and classroom teachers with the lesson plan and cue cards in advance.
- Use peer buddies for students who might need additional demonstrations or cue words.
- Work with the American Sign Language interpreter, if one is available, for vocabulary words directly related to this lesson.

Muscular System and Fitness

INTRODUCTORY INFORMATION

SHAPE America Outcomes

- S3.E5.5a Analyzes results of fitness assessment (pre and post), comparing results to fitness components for good health.
- S3.E5.5b Designs a fitness plan to address ways to use physical activity to enhance fitness.

National Health Education Performance Indicators

- 5.5.1 Identify health-related situations that might require a thoughtful decision.
- 7.5.2 Demonstrate a variety of healthy practices and behaviors to maintain or improve personal health.

Lesson Objectives

Students will be able to do the following:

- Identify the roles muscles play in the body.
- Correctly perform fitness exercises that require no equipment.
- Identify the names of major muscles and their actions in the body.

Learning Materials and Technology

- Gymnastics mats, yoga mats, or bath towels (enough for half the class)
- Resource handouts from HK*Propel*
  - Resource 1: 1 printout per 2 students
  - Resource 2: 1 printout per 2 students

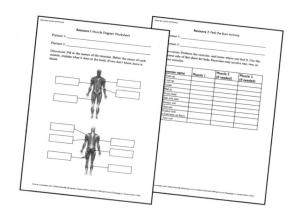

LEARNING ACTIVITIES

Lesson Introduction

- **WHAT** are we learning today? Students will learn about the muscular system and ways to keep it healthy.
- **WHY** are we learning this? Muscles affect students' athletic performance, appearance, injury rates, and body composition.
- **HOW** will learning be measured? Students will complete the feel the burn activity (resource 2) to demonstrate how well they can apply the information from class.

Activity 1: Role of Muscles and Worksheet (10 minutes)

See what students already know about the names of muscles. Point to a muscle and ask students if they can identify its name and action. Write student responses on a whiteboard.

Ask what functions muscles play in the body. Write student responses on the whiteboard. Fill in missed functions from the list below:

- Produce movement of the joints (contract to produce movement)

- Maintain posture (produce tension without movement)
- Move substances around the body (e.g., swallowing)
- Produce heat (shivering)
- Stabilize bones and joints
- Circulate blood
- Allow breathing

Based on all these functions, convey the importance of the muscular system to the body. Like any system in the body, it needs to be maintained for optimal health.

Have students get a partner and distribute the muscle diagram worksheet (resource 1). Students fill in the name of the muscles. Below the name of the muscle, students explain what it does in the body. If students don't know, they may leave the space blank.

Answers

1. Pectoralis major (pecs): Moves the arm horizontally in front of the body.
2. Abdominals (abs): Curls the spine.
3. Triceps brachii: Straightens the arm at the elbow.
4. Gluteus maximus: Moves the leg backward at the hip.
5. Gastrocnemius: Allows you to go up on your tiptoes.
6. Back: Straightens the back or stabilizes it.
7. Latissimus dorsi (lats): Pulls the arm down at the shoulder.
8. Deltoid: Lifts the arm at the shoulder.
9. Quadriceps (quads): Straightens the leg at the knee.
10. Biceps: Bends the arm at the elbow.

Review the correct answers, demonstrate each action, and have students copy them onto their worksheets.

Activity 2: Feel the Burn (15 minutes)

Demonstrates the correct technique for the exercises listed on resource 2. Distribute resource 2 to the partner groups. Both partners perform the exercise and feel which muscle or muscles are activated based on a burning sensation or where the tension is generated. Students follow the order of exercises in the handout.

Answers to Resource 2

Exercise name	Muscle 1	Muscle 2 (if needed)	Muscle 3 (if needed)
1. Push-up	Pectoralis major	Triceps brachii	
2. Curl-up	Abdominals		
3. Lunge	Quadriceps	Gluteus maximus	Gastrocnemius
4. Wall sit	Quadriceps		
5. Front plank	Abdominals	Deltoid	Back
6. Side arm raise	Deltoid		
7. Partner row	Biceps	Latissimus dorsi	
8. Heel-up	Gastrocnemius		
9. Donkey kick (do from knee on floor)	Gluteus maximus		
10. Arm curl	Biceps brachii		

All exercises should be familiar to teachers except possibly the partner row, which is shown here.

Matthew Cummiskey

Differentiations

- Challenge task: perform a full sit-up or a reverse lunge.
- Simplifying task: perform a push up from the knees, use a smaller range of motion for the lunge, or use a greater angle at the knee for the wall sit.

When students are finished, review resource 2 for accuracy by asking students for their responses.

Activity 3: Leonardo (10 minutes)

Form groups of three. One student is the clay, one student is the model, and the other is the artist Leonardo da Vinci. The clay and model stand about three feet (1 m) apart and face opposite directions. The model strikes a pose. The clay cannot turn around to see the model. The artist stands in a location unseen by the clay. The artist uses words only to tell the clay how to move. Each direction must include the name of the muscle and a description of the action. For example, the clay might say "quadriceps straighten" in order to extend the knee or "deltoids up" to raise the arms. Pointing or using nonmuscle terms like *thigh* or *shoulder* are not allowed.

Closure

As students sit down for the closure, ask them to get a partner different from the one they worked with earlier in the lesson. One partner points to the muscles discussed in class and identifies their name. If a student forgets, their partner helps out. When they are finished, they switch roles. Next, have one partner perform two exercises while their partner checks for correct technique, and then they switch.

Peer Pressure

GRADE LEVEL: 4-5

INTRODUCTORY INFORMATION

SHAPE America Outcomes

- S4.E1.4 Exhibits responsible behavior in independent group situations.
- S4.E3.4 Listens respectfully to corrective feedback from others (e.g., peers, adults).
- S5.E4.4 Describes and compares the positive social interactions when engaged in partner, small-group, and large-group physical activities.

National Health Education Performance Indicators

- 2.5.3 Identify how peers can influence healthy and unhealthy behaviors.
- 4.5.3 Demonstrate non-violent strategies to manage or resolve conflict.
- 5.5.1 Identify health-related situations that might require a thoughtful decision.
- 8.5.1 Express opinions and give accurate information about health issues.

Lesson Objectives

Students will be able to do the following:

- Define peer pressure.
- Identify examples of positive and negative peer pressure.
- Identify ways to cope with negative peer pressure.

Learning Materials and Technology

- 1 pool noodle per student
- 1 scarf per student
- 8 tennis balls
- Resource handout from *HKPropel*
  - Resource 1: 1 printout

Skill Cues

Communication

- Use a supportive tone.
- Express ideas clearly.
- Share "airtime."

- Listen without interrupting.
- Use positive body language.

LEARNING ACTIVITIES

Lesson Introduction

- **WHAT** are we learning today? Students will learn about peer pressure and positive communication.
- **WHY** are we learning this? It is important to be able to identify how peer pressure can affect health and how to resist negative types of peer pressure.

• **HOW** will learning be measured? Learning will be measured using the communication assessment (resource 1).

Activity 1: Follow the Crowd? (5 minutes)

Ask for two volunteers; pick students who would not be bothered by the activity described here. The volunteers go the nurse's office and pick up items you have arranged ahead of time. It could be adhesive bandages or something else that would not draw their suspicion. While students are out, tell the remaining students they are going to conduct an experiment. Pass out scarves and have students balance one scarf on top of their head so it stays there without being held. Place the unused scarves in a bin where the volunteers will see them when they return to the gym. Tell students to ignore the volunteers as they return; don't talk, don't giggle, and don't give away the secret. See what the volunteers do. Will they grab a scarf and put it on their head? Will they ask for an explanation? Will they ignore the strange behavior? When finished, ask the volunteers why they did what they did. If they followed the crowd, why did they? Ask how the activity is an example of peer pressure.

Activity 2: Speed Scarf (5 minutes)

Next, students hold the scarf against their chest, begin running, and then take their hand off the scarf. The scarf should stay in place if students are running fast enough. Start with walking, and then increase to a run.

Ask students if the activity made them feel a bit weird or self-conscious. Have them close their eyes and hold up fingers against their chest to rate their level of discomfort. Five is the highest. Discuss the results. Students who are more worried about the perceptions and opinions of others are more at risk from peer pressure because they don't want to stand out. Remind them of the saying, "Be yourself; everyone else is taken."

Activity 3: Entourage (5 minutes)

Form partners and play rock, paper, scissor (best of one or three). The losing person becomes part of the other person's entourage and forms a group of two. The leader of the entourage of two plays rock, paper, scissors against another group of two. The losing group joins the other to form a group of four, one leader and three in the entourage. Continue until one person has the entire class as their entourage. It is important throughout the activity that entourage members loudly praise their leader and clap for them. Students should encourage festivity and support for their entourage leader.

How did the entourage leader experience peer pressure? How did the entourage members experience peer pressure? Did it make anyone do something they wouldn't normally do?

Activity 4: Pipeline (20 minutes)

Divide the class into groups of four. Each person gets a pool noodle, and each group gets one tennis ball. The ball is the Earth, and noodles are the Earth's orbit. By sandwiching two noodles together, the Earth (tennis ball) can roll along its orbit. The job of the participants is to move the Earth from one end of the gym and back to complete one full orbit around the sun (a year). The Earth is rolled from two noodles to two other noodles. The students holding the noodles containing the Earth ball cannot move, but the other two may. If the Earth stops or goes backward, gravity is interrupted, and everyone flies off the Earth. Therefore, the group must start

Matthew Cummiskey

over at the beginning. If the Earth is touched by any of the participants or falls out of its orbit, the entire group must start over. An alternative to starting over is to have the group count out loud to 10 or perform an exercise before resuming. Allow participants to explore using the noodles and the Earth for a few minutes. Line up the groups on one end of the gym and have them race to the other end of the gym and back; this completes one calendar year. During this activity, complete the communication assessment (resource 1).

Discuss with students how peer pressure might influence the race. The following are possible scenarios:

- Positive peer pressure: The competition motivates students to perform their best and stay focused for the duration.
- Negative peer pressure: Excessive pressure causes belittling conversation or put downs, especially when the group performs poorly.

Discuss positive communication during the activity and how it can reduce negative peer pressure. Ask students what positive communication during the activity would look like. Write their responses on the whiteboard; use the skill cues listed earlier as a guide. Play another round. Give students time beforehand to plan strategy, addresses weaknesses, and determine their tolerance for how fast the group should go.

Extensions

- Form one large group with the entire class and try to have one Earth move from one corner of the gym to another corner in the least amount of time (designate one student as the timer). The Earth must land in the teacher's hand. To increase the difficulty, the teacher may stand on a chair or move locations once during the activity.
- Form a square using four cones roughly 15 yards (14 m) across. Equally space each group at a different starting point along the square. On go, each team moves its Earth around the square using the rules from before, except the objective is now to tag other groups. Count the number of times a group tags another. If a group violates any of the rules (e.g., drops Earth, touches it), that group must count to 10 before resuming. That group may be tagged while counting.

Closure

Students sit with a partner and brainstorm one way in which peer pressure can be negative and one way peer pressure can be positive. Next, students identify specific examples of positive communication from the pipeline activity. Ask for volunteers to share their insights.

Physical Activity Pyramid, Goal Setting, and Yard Games

GRADE LEVEL: 3-5

INTRODUCTORY INFORMATION

SHAPE America Outcomes

- S3.E1.5 Charts and analyzes physical activity outside physical education class for fitness benefits of activities.
- S3.E1.4 Analyzes opportunities for participating in physical activity outside physical education class.
- S4.E3.5 Gives corrective feedback respectfully to peers.
- S1.E13.5a Throws overhand using a mature pattern in nondynamic environments (closed skills), with different sizes and types of objects.

National Health Education Performance Indicators

- 2.5.1 Describe how the family influences personal health practices and behaviors.
- 6.5.1 Set a personal health goal and track progress toward its achievement.

Lesson Objectives

Students will be able to do the following:

- Create a physical activity SMART goal.
- Describe how family influences physical activity at home.
- Correctly execute a backhand disc throw.
- Identify five of the seven components of the physical activity pyramid.

This is a two-day lesson.

Learning Materials and Technology

- 4 cornhole boards
- 16 cornhole beanbags or PE equivalent
- 4 Kan Jam cylinders
- 1 fun gripper flying disc per two students
- 16 bocce balls (8 of one color, 8 of another color)

- 2 pallinos (jacks)
- 2 ladder golf sets
- Resource handouts from HK*Propel*
    - Resource 1: 1 printout per student
    - Resource 2: 1 printout per 2 students
    - Resource 3: 1 printout per student

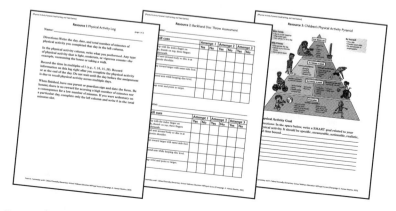

Skill Cues

Backhand Disc Throw

- Hold the disc with the index finger along the side, the thumb on top, and the remaining three fingers curled underneath.
- Curl the arm holding the disc around the body so that the disc is near the opposite shoulder.
- Step toward the target with the same-side foot.
- Extend the arm forward while keeping the disc level.
- Snap the wrist and point to the target.

LEARNING ACTIVITIES

Lesson Introduction

- **WHAT** are we learning today? The class will track progress toward meeting their physical activity goals. In addition, students will learn activities they can participate in outside of school and that contribute to the physical activity pyramid.
- **WHY** are we learning this? Physical activity is critical to maintaining one's health. It is important to be active throughout the day and accrue 60 minutes of total physical activity through a mixture of low-, moderate-, and high-intensity activities.
- **HOW** will learning be measured? Learning will be measured through a peer assessment of the backhand disc throw (resource 2).

Activity 1: Physical Activity Discussion (10 minutes)

Start by asking students the benefits of physical activity. Write all responses on the whiteboard. Fill in the following benefits if they are not stated:

- Makes muscles and bones stronger
- Elevates mood
- Gives you energy
- Reduces the likelihood of illness (e.g., heart disease, certain cancers, diabetes)
- Controls weight
- Boosts the immune system

Next, ask students how their family influences physical activity. What kinds of activities do they do together? Do parents send them outside to play? Do families tell them that physical activity is important?

Tell students they are old enough now to influence their amount of physical activity. Today's lesson focuses on teaching yard games they can play with family and friends. Yard games are simple activities that require little equipment and few participants and can be played in small spaces. They are conveniently located just outside the back door or in the courtyard of many homes.

Activity 2: Disc Tag Warm-Up (5 minutes)

One student is the tagger (wears a pinny), one student is the saver (has the disc), and the remaining students are escapers trying not to get tagged. On go, the tagger tags other students. If tagged, those students must do high knees or jumping jacks. For tagged students to be freed, they must successfully catch the disc thrown to them by the saver and throw it back without it being dropped. The savers must throw from a distance of 10 feet (3 m) or greater; demonstrate this distance. As the game progresses, vary the type of throw required (forehand, backhand), the type of catch (one hand or two), and add another disc if warranted. Play the first minute at walking speed only, and then allow students to run.

Activity 3: Demonstration (10 minutes)

Demonstrate to students how to perform the backhand disc throw. Have students practice throwing back and forth with a partner using the backhand throw. After 2 to 3 minutes, have them keep track of the number of consecutive catches. If two partners catch five passes in a row, one person takes a step back. This may be repeated up to five times.

Differentiations

- Challenge task: Throw with the nondominant hand.
- Simplified task: Move one or two steps closer together.

Yard Game Stations (60 minutes, two class periods)

Each yard game is played at a different station. Explain the rules for each. Limit students to eight per station for 12 to 15 minutes per rotation.

Station 1: Cornhole

Bags are tossed from the side of the platform called the pitcher's box. The bottom of the platform forms the foul line; players may not step over the foul line while pitching. Cornhole matches are broken into innings of play. During each inning, the players at one platform alternate throwing all four bags. After all eight bags have been thrown, players walk to the other platform and pick up the bags. The player who scored in the preceding inning pitches first in the next inning. If neither pitcher scored the previous inning, the last player to score pitches first. If playing doubles cornhole, four players split into two teams. Members of the same team are at separate platforms. Players do not change platforms after each inning as they do in singles.

A bag that lands and stays on the platform is worth 1 point, one that passes through the hole is worth 3 points. The bag can be tossed directly into the hole, slide into the hole, or be knocked into the hole by another bag. If a bag touches the ground and comes to rest on the board, it is removed before the next throw. Cancellation scoring is used where points cancel each other out. For example, if one team lands two bags in the hole and one on the board for 7 points, and the other team lands one in the hole and two on the board for 5 points, the first team's score would be 2, and the second team's would be 0. The first player or team to reach 21 points wins. The winning team does not need to win by 2 or more points. One scoring variation requires one team to earn exactly 21 points to win. If a team's score exceeds 21 after any inning, they return to 15 points.

Station 2: Kan Jam

Play consists of four players divided into teams of two. Members of the same team (partners) stand at opposite goals. One partner throws the disc and, when necessary, the other partner redirects (deflects) it toward or into the can. All throws must originate from behind an imaginary line at the front of the can called the release line. Both players from the same team throw one time, then the disc is passed to the opposing team. Players can score in one of three ways:

1. The disc is redirected and it hits the side of the can: 1 point, called a *dinger*
2. The disc hits the can directly: 2 points, called a *deuce*
3. The disc is pushed down or slammed into the can: 3 points, called a *bucket*

An instant win is when the disc enters the slot in the front without being touched. Deflectors may not catch or carry the disc, stop the disc so it falls directly down, or use two hands on either side of the disc.

Kan Jam games are played to 21 points. A team must achieve an exact score of 21 points to win, and teams must complete an equal number of turns (except when an instant win is scored). If one team reaches 21 first, the other team has an opportunity to equalize. Because a team must score exactly 21 points, if a given throw results in points that raise a team's score above 21, the points from that play are deducted from their current score and play continues. For example, if a team has 19 points and dunks a bucket (3 points), their score is reduced to 16 points (current score of 19 points – 3 points = 16 points).

At the Kan Jam station, one student completes resource 2 while their partner plays a singles game. After the assessment is complete, players switch.

Station 3: Bocce Ball

Each group gets eight balls (four of each color) and one small ball (golf-ball sized) called a pallino, or jack. Teachers may substitute tennis balls, softballs, or other appropriate balls for bocce balls. Bocce may be played between two players or two teams of up to four players. The team that wins the coin toss tosses the pallino into an open area not less than 10 yards (9 m) and not more than 25 yards (23 m) away. The team that tossed the pallino bowls first from behind the bowling line, followed by alternating bowls thereafter. The objective is to roll the bocce balls so that they come to rest as close to the pallino as possible. The toss must be underhand and may not be lofted into the air above shoulder height. After the eighth ball has been bowled, teams examine the bocce balls to determine who is closest; tape measures may be provided to measure close distances. The team with the closest ball scores 1 point; the first team to 12 wins. If the two closest balls from opposing teams are equidistant to the pallino, no point is awarded. The winner of each round may score multiple points depending on how many balls are closest before a ball belonging to the opposition. For example, if the three green balls are closer than a red one, green scores 3 points to none for red. The last team to score tosses the pallino to begin each new round. According to official rules, the bocce balls are bowled in one direction and then back again. In physical education, you may allow, depending on space available, the pallino to be tossed in any direction.

Station 4: Ladder Golf

Ladder golf is played using two sets of ladders and six bolas (three of each color). The ladders are set up 15 feet (4.5 m) or five paces apart. The objective is to throw bolas from one ladder and land it on the rungs of the opposite ladder. A coin toss is used to determine who throws first. Players throw all three bolas consecutively; throws are not alternated. However, you may choose to alternate throws. Players must throw from behind the ladder, not its footers.

The top rung is worth 3 points, the middle is worth 2, and the bottom is worth 1. Participants may score one additional point by landing all three bolas on the same rung or one bola on each rung. The first player to score exactly 21 points wins. If a player earns more than 21 points, all the points from that round are negated. For example, if a player has 18 points and scores 5 additional points, the player's score remains at 18 for the next round. Official rules dictate that scores per round do not cancel; however, you may choose this option if you wish. Players may knock the bolas of their opponent off the ladder. After each round, players walk to the opposite end and retrieve their bolas. If using four players, there are two teams of two, and each player remains at the same ladder throughout.

Activity 4: Physical Activity Log (10 minutes)

At the end of the first day of this lesson, distribute a copy of resource 1 to each student. Explain that students will track the amount of physical activity they accrue in and outside of school. Describe how the log should be completed. Students write down any form of physical activity between lesson 1 and lesson 2. Ask if anyone knows the recommended number of minutes per day. Tell students the answer if no one knows (60 minutes). At the second lesson, students turn in their completed physical activity logs. Ask how many students achieved 60 minutes three times, four times, five times, and so on. Lead a discussion of how effectively students were able to meet their daily goal of 60 minutes. Discuss what activities they used, how their families may have affected their physical activity, whether they made changes to their routines, and what barriers they encountered.

Distribute and discuss resource 3—the children's physical activity pyramid. Emphasize that physical activity comes in many forms, not just sports, and can take place in all manner of intensities, not just high intensity. The most important point is to accrue 60 minutes total. For example, the yard games played in class are less intense physical activity. At the bottom of the resource, have students write one SMART goal related to physical activity. Students may use the physical activity pyramid for ideas to incorporate into the goal.

Closure

Challenge students to meaningfully implement their SMART goal and achieve 60 minutes of physical activity per day. Remind them to involve their family and friends. Students get a partner and share their physical activity log. Next, they discuss ways to incorporate more physical activity into their day. Lastly, demonstrate an incorrect backhand disc throw. Students turn to their partner and analyze the performance in light of the cues.

Skeletal System and Fitness

INTRODUCTORY INFORMATION

SHAPE America Outcomes

- S3.E2.4 Engages actively in the activities of physical education class, both teacher-directed and independent.
- S3.E2.5 Engages actively in all of the activities of physical education.

National Health Education Performance Indicators

- 1.5.4 Describe ways to prevent common childhood injuries and health problems.
- 7.5.2 Demonstrate a variety of healthy practices and behaviors to maintain or improve personal health.

Lesson Objectives

Students will be able to do the following:

- Identify the names of major bones in the body.
- Describe healthy practices to maintain bone health.
- Identify movements of the bones in the body

Learning Materials and Technology

- 1 laptop
- 1 pair of scissors per 2 students
- 1 cone per 2 students
- 1 pencil or marker

- Resource handouts from HK*Propel*
  - Resource 1: 1 printout per 2 students
  - Resource 2: 1 printout per 4 students
  - Resource 3: 1 printout

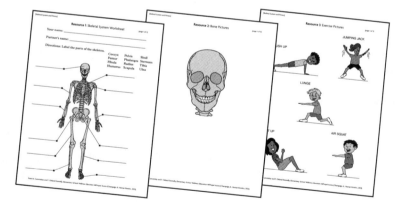

LEARNING ACTIVITIES

Lesson Introduction

- **WHAT** are we learning today? In this lesson, students will learn about the major bones and how they work.
- **WHY** are we learning this? The bones can be cared for just like the other organs and systems of the body. People tend to take them for granted unless they get broken.
- **HOW** will learning be measured? Students will complete the skeletal system worksheet (resource 1).

Activity 1: Video (10 minutes)

Play the YouTube video "Bones: The Dr. Binocs Show." (See the lesson plan links file on *HKPropel* for a link to this video.) After the video is over, do the following:

- Ask students, "What do you think your bones are made of?"
- Ask students to turn to someone seated next to them and see if they can come up with the names of five bones. Afterward, have students volunteer the names of bones and write them on the whiteboard.
- Ask students, again with a partner, to come up with two facts from the video besides the names of bones. Write responses on the whiteboard.

Activity 2: Worksheet (10 minutes)

In pairs, students complete the worksheet (resource 1). Remind students that the worksheet is double sided. Review the correct answers when students are finished.

Activity 3: Create Your Own Skeleton (15 minutes)

Form groups of four and pass out bone pictures (resource 2) to each group. Students use the scissors to take turns cutting out the bones. Students use the cutouts to create an accurate skeleton on the floor. Have them label each bone with a pencil or marker. When finished, have the class walk around and observe each group's skeleton.

Activity 4: Personal Trainer Activity (15 minutes)

Before class, cut the exercise pictures in resource 3 into eight separate cards. Demonstrate each exercise or ask for a volunteer who believes they can perform it correctly. Students get back with their partner from activity 2. One partner picks a card that is facedown. When they return to their partner, partner 1 guides partner 2 through the exercise using the names of bones. For example, partner 1 says, "Move the humerus up." Partner 2 can only move if the correct name of the bone is used. Students must complete one full repetition of the exercise. For example, in a push-up, partner 2 lowers and then pushes up to the starting position. After each exercise, students return the card to you, get a new card, and switch roles. Do a brief demonstration of a non-pictured exercise as an example.

Differentiation

- Challenge task: Students immediately give the card back to the you after viewing it. They may not keep it.

Activity 5: Discussion (5 minutes)

Have a discussion with the students about how to keep bones healthy. Explain that students will gain most bone density in childhood and during the teen years. Tell them that there are three easy ways to keep bones healthy and strong: Consume plenty of calcium, eat foods with vitamin D, and exercise. Ask students the following questions:

- What foods contain calcium? Contain vitamin D? (Answer: milk, cheese, green leafy vegetables, bread with fortified flour)
- How can exercise keep bones healthy? (Answer: build bone density and reduce fractures)
- Are all exercises the same or are some better than others for your bones? Give examples. (Answer: load-bearing exercises like running or soccer are better than non-load-bearing exercises like swimming or bike riding)

Closure

With a partner, students see how many bones they can name. Ask who can name the most. Have that group repeat all the bones they know while pointing to their location.

Stress, Coordination, and Heart Rate

GRADE LEVEL: 3-4

INTRODUCTORY INFORMATION

SHAPE America Outcomes

- S1.E16.2 Catches a self-tossed or well-thrown large ball with hands, not trapping or cradling against the body.
- S2.E2.4 Combines movement concepts with skills in small-sided practice tasks, gymnastics, and dance environments.
- S3.E1.3b Identifies physical activity as a way to become healthier.

National Health Education Performance Indicators

- 1.5.2 Identify examples of emotional, intellectual, physical, and social health.
- 5.5.3 List healthy options to health-related issues or problems.
- 7.5.2 Demonstrate a variety of healthy practices and behaviors to maintain or improve personal health.

Lesson Objectives

Students will be able to do the following:

- Describe how different physical activity intensities affect heart rate.
- Perform activities that reduce stress levels.
- Demonstrate eye–hand coordination while catching a self-tossed ball.
- Identify ways to decrease stress in their lives.

Learning Materials and Technology

- 60 fleece balls
- 1 pencil per 4 students
- 1 die per 4 students
- 1 blank sheet of paper per student
- Resource handout from HK*Propel*
  - Resource 1: 1 printout per student

Skill Cues

Eye–Hand Coordination of a Tossed Ball

- Toss the ball underhand to the appropriate height.
- Track the ball with the eyes without taking the eyes off the object.
- Move the hands to the correct intercept position.
- Give with the ball to gradually absorb force (soft hands).
- Close the hands around the object.

LEARNING ACTIVITIES

Lesson Introduction

- **WHAT** are we learning today? Students will learn how to measure their pulse, what factors affect heart rate, and how to reduce stress.

- **WHY** are we learning this? Accurately measuring heart rate enables students to monitor the intensity of physical activity and identify factors that can increase or decrease it. Sometimes it's OK to have a higher rate; other times it is not.

- **HOW** will learning be measured? Student learning will be measured using the pulse chart handout (resource 1).

Activity 1: Heart Rate and Stress Game (10 minutes)

As students enter the gym, have them form groups of four. Each student should also get a copy of resource 1 and a pencil. Ask students if they know what their pulse is. It is their heart rate, or the number of times their heart beats in one minute. There are two common locations to determine one's pulse, at the wrist (radial pulse) and at the neck (carotid pulse). Ask students to find their pulse in either location. When you say go, students count their pulse for 15 seconds. Afterward, ask how they would convert that number to their heart rate over 60 seconds (answer: multiply by four). Next, students count for 30 seconds and multiply the result by 2.

Students will now play the stress game. Each group of four forms a small circle on the gym floor. Each student has a blank piece of paper, one student has a pencil, and the student one position clockwise has a die. On go, the student with the paper begins writing numbers 1, 2, 3, 4, and so on. The student with the die rolls furiously, trying to roll a six. When a six is rolled, the die and pencil are passed one position clockwise. The procedure repeats until one person reaches 100 to win. At that point, students in the group take their pulse.

Compare the heart rates between when students entered the gym and following the stress game. Discuss with students the factors that affect heart rate. Convey the message that it's not just physical activity; it can be social and emotional factors too. Even though no one was running around, heart rates and breathing rates increased. These effects mirror stress. Elevated and uncontrolled stress can lead to heart disease, high blood pressure, anxiety, depression, and other negative outcomes.

Activity 2: Toss and Catch (10 minutes)

Heart rate can also be affected by physical activity. Physical activity will increase heart rate and make the heart stronger. Enough physical activity reduces heart rate and stress when a person is not active. The class will examine how low to moderate physical activity affects heart rate. To do so, have students get one fleece ball and perform the following:

- Toss the ball up and catch it with both hands.
- Toss and catch the ball with the right hand.
- Toss and catch the ball with the left hand.
- Toss the ball, clap, and catch it.
- Toss the ball, clap twice, and catch it.
- Toss the ball, spin, and catch it.

Students get a second ball and do the following:

- Toss both balls and catch them.
- Toss one ball from each hand and catch them in the other hand.
- Toss the balls in a two-ball juggling configuration.

Immediately after the last progression, students take their pulse for 15 seconds. Record the information on resource 1.

Activity 3: Creepy Crawlers (10 minutes)

Every student starts as a runner on their feet with a fleece ball. Runners try to roll their fleece ball at the feet of other students. If hit, the student becomes a crawler and drops to their hands and knees. Crawlers attempt to roll fleece balls at runner's feet. If they are successful, the crawler becomes a runner again. Runners may only touch stationary fleece balls and can only take two steps before rolling. Modification: When the number of runners equals crawlers, yell that runners can't roll at other runners anymore.

When you yell, "freeze," students sit down and take their pulse for 15 seconds. Record the information on the sheet.

Activity 4: Meditation (8 minutes)

Students spread out in the gym, and the lights are dimmed if possible. Play a meditation video from YouTube or a peaceful song. The video may or may not include narration and imagery. Remind students to clear their minds; take deep, slow breaths; and relax their bodies. At the end, have students record their heart rate a final time.

Closure

Stress is a part of everyone's life. Excessive stress, however, can lead to physical and emotional problems. Ask students these questions: "What are ways to reduce undue stress and anxiety?" "Did anyone's heart rate during the different activities surprise them?" Students turn to a partner and discuss this question, "If someone is more fit, will their heart rate be higher or lower and why?" (Answer: lower because the heart is able to pump more blood with each beat).

In pairs, student 1 takes their carotid pulse for 15 seconds while their partner takes the radial pulse of student 1 at the same time. Repeat with student 1 taking their radial pulse while their partner takes the carotid pulse of student 1. Partners switch and measure the pulse of student 2. Log all results in resource 1 and compare the results when finished. The measurements for a student should be identical or one beat off.

Valid Health Information and Body Weight Fitness

GRADE LEVEL: 5

INTRODUCTORY INFORMATION

SHAPE America Outcomes

- S3.E2.5 Engages actively in all of the activities of physical education.
- S3.E4.5 Identifies the need for warm-up and cool-down relative to various physical activities.
- S4.E6.5 Applies safety principles with age-appropriate physical activities.

National Health Education Performance Indicators

- 2.5.5 Explain how media influences thoughts, feelings, and health behaviors.
- 3.5.1 Identify characteristics of valid health information, products, and services.
- 3.5.2 Locate resources from home, school, and community that provide valid health information.
- 6.5.2 Identify resources to assist in achieving a personal health goal.

Lesson Objectives

Students will be able to do the following:

- Demonstrate correct technique for dynamic flexibility, body weight, and static stretching exercises.
- Critically evaluate websites for valid health information.
- Identify five criteria for assessing valid health information.

Learning Materials and Technology

- 1 device (e.g., Chromebook, laptop, tablet) per 3 students

- Resource handouts from *HKPropel*
  - Resource 1: 1 printout per 3 students
  - Resource 2: 1 printout

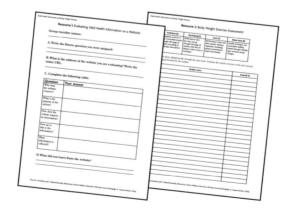

LEARNING ACTIVITIES

Lesson Introduction

- **WHAT** are we learning today? Students will learn how to evaluate health information to determine whether it is accurate and valid. Students also will learn how to perform fitness activities that require little or no equipment.
- **WHY** are we learning this? Following bad advice can lead to negative health consequences. Learning to improve muscular strength and endurance with little to no equipment allows students to exercise from anywhere without needing access to a fitness center.
- **HOW** will learning be measured? Students will complete a worksheet on evaluating valid health information on a website (resource 1), and the teacher will complete the body weight exercise assessment (resource 2).

Activity 1: Websites Evaluation (15 minutes)

Ask students where they would turn if they wanted to learn information about a new topic. For most of them, the answer is Google. The Internet provides an astounding array of information and services; however, buyer beware. It can be difficult to sort out fact from fiction. It is important to use only valid health information that can positively affect overall wellness. Following the wrong advice can potentially cause injury. Ask students what questions they should ask of a website to determine whether the information is valid. Write the responses on the board, but narrow the list to these questions:

- Who runs the website (source)? Is it from a business (.com), college (.edu), organization (.org), or the government (.gov)? The latter three are the most valid. For example, the Centers for Disease Control and Prevention provides a government-run website focused on health information. If unsure, look for an "about us" link.
- What is the purpose of the website? Is it to provide information or to sell products and services? Websites looking to sell can be more biased.
- How does the website support its information? Ideally, it will be based on proven facts and figures and link to trustworthy websites and true experts. It should not be based on opinions or testimonials from a limited number of people.
- How up to date is the information? Look for the date the website was last reviewed or updated. Be careful if the date is not recent or not listed.
- What information is collected? The website should not ask you to provide personal information or to subscribe or become a member.

To practice accessing valid health information, students will research fitness topics on the Internet. Divide students into groups of three, give them one device per group, and assign them to answer one of the following questions:

1. What is the best way to lose body fat?
2. How can you improve your flexibility?
3. How can you improve your abdominal strength?
4. How can I get quicker and faster?
5. How can I get healthy?
6. What are the keys to a longer life?

Students must use KidRex or Kiddle as the search engine and pick a result on the first page. Once on the website, they will use resource 1 to evaluate the information.

Activity 2: Body Weight Exercises (25 minutes)

Students will learn how to correctly perform body weight exercises they can do at home or anywhere. To practice, students will rotate through the following stations. Each station consists of a dynamic flexibility exercise and a muscular strength exercise. Demonstrate each exercise and provide task cards at each station. Rotate every three minutes.

Station 1

- Dynamic flexibility: open gate
- No-equipment exercise: push-up

Station 2

- Dynamic flexibility: arm swing (forward and back)
- No-equipment exercise: lunge

Station 3

- Dynamic flexibility: hamstring scoop
- No-equipment exercise: plank (bent arms, straight arms)

Station 4

- Dynamic flexibility: butt kick
- No-equipment exercise: curl-up, crunch kick, or sitting twist

Station 5

- Dynamic flexibility: carioca
- No-equipment exercise: side-lying hip abduction

Station 6

- Dynamic flexibility: close gate
- No-equipment exercise: calf raise

Station 7

- Dynamic flexibility: Frankenstein
- No-equipment exercise: contralateral limb raise

Station 8

- Dynamic flexibility: glute walk
- No-equipment exercise: burpee or air squat

Closure

Students get a partner who was not from the group of three formed earlier. Students take turns answering the five questions about the website they chose. Afterwards, one student will share their group's answers with the entire class. Next, one partner correctly performs a dynamic flexibility exercise, and the other partner correctly performs an exercise that doesn't require any equipment. Partners should give corrective feedback if needed.

References

PREFACE

Centers for Disease Control and Prevention (CDC). (2021). CDC Healthy Schools. www.cdc.gov/healthyschools/wscc/index.htm

CHAPTER 1

Allensworth, D.D., & Kolbe, L.J. (1987). The Comprehensive School Health Program: Exploring an expanded concept. *Journal of School Health, 57*, 409-412.

Amin, S.A., Wright, C.M., Boulos, R., Chomitz, V.R., Chui, K., Economos, C.D., & Sacheck, J.M. (2017). The physical activity environment and academic achievement in Massachusetts schoolchildren. *Journal of School Health, 87*, 932-940.

Baghurst, T. (2014). Assessment of effort and participation in physical education. *Physical Educator, 71*(3), 505-513.

Bartee, R.T., Heelan, K.A., & Dority, B.L. (2018). Longitudinal evaluation of aerobic fitness and academic achievement among schoolchildren. *Journal of School Health, 88*(9), 644-650.

Basch, C.E. (2011). Healthier students are better learners: A missing link in school reforms to close the achievement gap. *Journal of School Health, 81*, 593-598.

Beale, A. (2015). Physical education is part of public health. *Journal of Physical Education, Recreation and Dance, 86*(6), 3-4.

Brewer, H.J., Nichols, R., Leight, J.M., & Clark, G.E. (2017). Preparing physical and health education teacher candidates to create a culture of wellness in schools. *Journal of Physical Education, Recreation and Dance, 88*(9), 15-20.

Buns, M.T., & Thomas, K.T. (2015). Impact of physical educators on local school wellness policies. *Physical Educator, 72*(2), 194-316.

Centers for Disease Control and Prevention (CDC). (n.d.). *Physical activity prevents chronic disease.* www.cdc.gov/chronicdisease/resources/infographic/physical-activity.htm

Centers for Disease Control and Prevention (CDC). (2014, May). *Health and academic achievement.* www.cdc.gov/healthyyouth/health_and_academics/pdf/health-academic-achievement.pdf

Centers for Disease Control and Prevention (CDC) & ASCD. (2014). *Whole school, whole community, whole child (WSCC): A collaborative approach to learning and health.* https://files.ascd.org/staticfiles/ascd/pdf/siteASCD/publications/wholechild/wscc-a-collaborative-approach.pdf

Centers for Disease Control and Prevention (CDC). (2015). *School health policies and practices study 2014.* www.cdc.gov/healthyyouth/data/shpps/pdf/shpps-508-final_101315.pdf

Cheak-Zamora, N., & Thullen, M. (2016). Disparities in quality and access to care for children with developmental disabilities and multiple health conditions. *Maternal and Child Health Journal, 21*, 36-44.

Ciotto, C.M., & Gagnon, A.G. (2018). Promoting social and emotional learning in physical education. *Journal of Physical Education, Recreation and Dance, 89*(4), 27-33.

Corbin, C.B., Welk, G.J., Richardson, C., Vowell, C., Lambdin, D., & Wikgren, S. (2014). Youth physical fitness: Ten key concepts. *Journal of Physical Education, Recreation and Dance, 85*(2): 24-31.

DeLong, M., & Winters, D. (2002). *Learning to teach and teaching to learn mathematics.* Mathematical Association of America.

Dictionary.com. (n.d.). Wellness. In *Dictionary.com.* www.dictionary.com/browse/wellness

Donnelly, J.E., Hillman, C.H., Castelli, D., Etnier, J.L., Lee, S., Tomporowski, P., Lambourne, K., & Szabo-Reed, A.N. (2016). Physical activity, fitness, cognitive function, and academic achievement in children: A systematic review. *Medicine and Science in Sports and Exercise, 48*(6), 1197-1222. https://doi.org/10.1249/MSS.0000000000000901

Evans, R.R., & Sims, S.K. (2015). *Health and physical education for elementary classroom teachers: An integrated approach.* Human Kinetics.

Global Wellness Institute. (n.d.). *What is wellness?* https://globalwellnessinstitute.org/what-is-wellness

Gray, S., MacIsaac, S., & Jess, M. (2015). Teaching 'health' in physical education in a 'healthy' way.' RETOS: *Nuevas Tendenies en Educacion Fisica Deportes y Recreacion, 28*, 165-172. http://recyt.fecyt.es/index.php/retos/article/view/34950/19218

Hinckson, E.A., Dickinson, A., Water, T., Sands, M., & Penman, L. (2013). Physical activity, dietary habits and overall health in overweight and obese children and youth with intellectual disability or autism. *Research in Developmental Disabilities, 34*, 1170-1178.

Hivner, E., Hoke, A., Francis, E., Ricci, T., Zurlo. C., & Kraschnewski, J. (2019). When a "one size" model doesn't fit all: The building healthy schools program. *Journal of Physical Education, Recreation and Dance, 90*(2), 8-16. https://doi.org/10.1080/07303084.2018.1546629

Holmes, E.A., O'Connor, R.C., Perry, V.H., Tracey, I., Wessely, S., Arseneault, L., Ballard, C., Christensen, H., Silver, R.C., Everall, I., Ford, T., John, A., Kabir, T., King,

K., Madan, I., Michie, S., Przybylski, A., Shafran, R., Sweeney, A., . . Bullmore, E. (2020). Multidisciplinary research priorities for the COVID-19 pandemic: A call for action for mental health science. *The Lancet Psychiatry, 7*(6), 547– 60. https://doi.org/10.1016/S2215-0366(20)30168-1

Kohl III, H.W., & Cook, H.D. (2013). *Educating the student body: Taking physical activity and physical education to school.* Institute of Medicine. www.ncbi.nlm.nih.gov/books/NBK201500

Lavizzo-Mourey R., Dorn J.M., Fulton J.E., Janz, K.F., Lee, S.M., McKinnon, R.A., Pate, R.R., Pfeiffer, K.A., Young, D.R., & Troiano, R.P. (2012). *Physical activity guidelines for Americans mid-course report: Strategies to increase physical activity among youth.* U.S. Department of Health and Human Services. https://health.gov/sites/default/files/2019-09/pag-mid-course-report-final.pdf

Lohrmann, D.K., Vamos, S., & Yeung, P. (2011). *Creating a healthy school using the healthy school report card* (2nd ed.). ASCD.

Mahar, M.T., Murphy, S.K., Rowe, D.A., Golden, J., Shields, A.T., & Raedeke, T.D. (2006). Effects of a classroom-based program on physical activity and on-task behavior. *Medicine & Science in Sports & Exercise, 38,* 2086-2094.

Merriam-Webster. (n.d.). Wellness. In *Merriam-Webster.com dictionary*. Retrieved August 4, 2020, from www.merriam-webster.com/dictionary/wellness

Michael, S.L., Merlo, C.L., Basch, C.E.,Wentzel, K.R., & Wechsler, H. (2015). Critical connections: Health and academics. *Journal of School Health, 85,* 740-758.

Moljord, I.E., Moksnes, U.K., Espnes, G.A., Hjemdal, O., & Eriksen, L. (2014). Physical activity, resilience, and depressive symptoms in adolescence. *Mental Health and Physical Activity, 7*(2),79-85.

Murray, N.G., Low, B.J., Hollis, C., Cross, A.W., & Davis, S.M. (2007). Coordinated school health programs and academic achievement: A systematic review of the literature. *Journal of School Health, 77,* 589-600.

National Physical Activity Plan Alliance. (2018). *The 2018 United States Report Card on Physical Activity for Children and Youth.* https://paamovewithus.org/for-transfer/reportcard

O'Brien L.M., Polacsek, M., MacDonald, P.B., Ellis, J., Berry, S., & Martin, M. (2010). Impact of a school health coordinator intervention on health-related school policies and student behavior. *Journal of School Health, 80,* 176-185.

Rasberry, C.N., Lee, S.M., Robin, L., Laris, B.A., Russell, L.A., Coyle, K.K., & Nihiser, A.J. (2011). The association between school-based physical activity, including physical education, and academic performance: A systematic review of the literature. *Preventive Medicine, 52*(Suppl 1), S10-S20. https://doi.org/10.1016/j.ypmed.2011.01.027

Rasberry, C.N., Slade, S., Lohrmann, D.K., & Valois, R.F. (2015). Lessons learned from the whole child and coordinated school health approaches. *Journal of School Health, 85,* 759-765.

Rosner, D., & Fried, L.P. (2010). Traditions, transitions, and transfats: New directions for public health. *Public Health Reports, 125,* 3-7.

Sanetti, L.M.H. (2017). Increasing equitable care for youth through coordinated school health. *Psychology in the Schools, 54,* 1312-1318.

Shimon, J.M. (2020). *Introduction to teaching physical education: Principles and strategies* (2nd ed). Human Kinetics.

SHAPE America. (n.d.a). *Alliance history.* www.shapeamerica.org/about/upload/Alliance_History.pdf

SHAPE America. (n.d.b). *Fact sheet.* www.shapeamerica.org//about/upload/2017-SHAPE-America-Fact-Sheet-final.pdf

SHAPE America. (2016). *2016 Shape of the nation: Status of physical education in the USA.* www.shapeamerica.org/shapeofthenation

SHAPE America. (2017). Can we bridge the gap between health and physical education? *Journal of Physical Education, Recreation and Dance, 88*(2), 62-64.

Sullivan, R.A., Kuzel, A.H., Vaandering, M.E., & Chen W. (2017). The association of physical activity and academic behavior: A systematic review. *Journal of School Health, 87,* 388-398.

Sundaresan, N., Dashoush, N., & Shangraw, R. (2017). Now that we're "well rounded," let's commit to quality physical education assessment. *Journal of Physical Education, Recreation and Dance, 88*(8), 35-38.

Trudeau, F., & Shephard R. (2008). Physical education, school physical activity, school sports and academic performance. *International Journal of Behavioral Nutrition and Physical Activity, 5*(1), 10.

U.S. Department of Health and Human Services (USDHHS). (2018). *2018 Physical Activity Guidelines Advisory Committee Scientific Report.* https://health.gov/our-work/physical-activity/current-guidelines/scientific-report

Valois, R.F., & Hoyle, T.B. (2000). Formative evaluation results from the Mariner Project: A coordinated school health pilot program. *Journal of School Health, 70*(3), 95-103.

Weiler, R.M., Pigg Jr., R.M., & McDermott, R.J. (2003). Evaluation of the Florida coordinated school health program pilot schools project. *Journal of School Health, 73*(1), 3-8.

Westrich, L., Sanchez, M., & Strobel, K. (2015). Coordinated school health and the contribution of a district wellness coordinator. *The Journal of School Health, 85,* 260-266.

CHAPTER 2

Allensworth, D., & Kolbe, L. (1987). The comprehensive school health program: Exploring an expanded concept. *Journal of School Health, 57*(10), 409-412.

Association for Supervision and Curriculum Development (ASCD), Centers for Disease Control and Prevention (CDC). (2014). *Whole School, Whole Community, Whole Child: A collaborative approach to learning and health.* https://files.ascd.org/staticfiles/ascd/pdf/siteASCD/publications/wholechild/wscc-a-collaborative-approach.pdf

Consortium for Academic, Social, and Emotional Learning (CASEL). (2020, December). *SEL: What are the core competence areas and where are they promoted?* https://casel.org/sel-framework

Centers for Disease Control and Prevention (CDC). (2013). *Comprehensive school physical activity programs: A guide for schools.* www.cdc.gov/healthyschools/professional_development/e-learning/cspap/_assets/FullCourseContent- CSPAP.pdf

Centers for Disease Control and Prevention (CDC). (2014). *Health and academic achievement.* www.cdc.gov/healthyschools/health_and_academics/pdf/health-academic-achievement.pdf

Centers for Disease Control and Prevention (CDC). (2015). *Components of coordinated school health.* www.cdc.gov/healthyyouth/cshp/components.htm.

Centers for Disease Control and Prevention (CDC). (2019). *Youth Risk Behavior Surveillance System (YRBSS).* www.cdc.gov/healthyyouth/yrbs/index.htm.

Hunt, P., Barrios, L., Telljohann, S., & Mazyck, D. (2015). A whole school approach: Collaborative development of school health policies, processes, and practices. *Journal of School Health 85*(11), 802-809.

Lewallen, T.C., Hunt, H., Potts-Datema, W., ZaZa, S., & Giles, W. (2015). The Whole School, Whole Community, Whole Child Model: A new approach for improving educational attainment and healthy development of students. *Journal of School Health, 85*(11), 729-739. Wiley Periodicals.

Rooney, L.E., Videto, D., & Birch, D. (2015). Using the Whole School, Whole Community, Whole Child model: Implications for practice. *Journal of School Health, 85*(11), 817-823.

SHAPE America. (2014). *National standards & grade-level outcomes for K-12 physical education* (3rd ed.). Human Kinetics.

U.S. Department of Health and Human Services (USDHHS). (2018). *Physical activity guidelines for all Americans,* (2nd ed.). https://health.gov/sites/default/files/2019-09/Physical_Activity_Guidelines_2nd_edition.pdf

U.S. Department of Health and Human Services (USDHHS) & U.S. Dietary Association (USDA). (2015). *Dietary guidelines for Americans 2015-2020* (8th ed.). https://health.gov/sites/default/files/2019-09/2015-2020_Dietary_Guidelines.pdf

U.S. Department of Health and Human Services (USDHHS). (2021.) *Healthy people 2030.* https://health.gov/healthypeople

CHAPTER 3

Bell, L.A. (2016). Theoretical foundations for social justice education. In M. Adams, L.A. Bell, & P. Griffin (Eds.). *Teaching for diversity and social justice* (pp. 3-26). Routledge.

Benes, S. & Alperin, H. (2019). Health education in the 21st century: A skills-based approach. *Journal of Physical Education, Recreation and Dance, 90*(7), 29-37.

Brame, C. (2016). *Active learning.* Vanderbilt University Center for Teaching. https://cft.vanderbilt.edu/active-learning

Butler, J. (2004) *Precarious life: The powers of mourning and violence.* Verso.

CAST (2018). Universal Design for Learning Guidelines version 2.2. http://udlguidelines.cast.org

Centers for Disease Control and Prevention (CDC). (2013). *Comprehensive school physical activity programs: A guide for schools.* U.S. Department of Health and Human Services.

Centers for Disease Control and Prevention (CDC). (2019a). *Standard 1.* https://www.cdc.gov/healthyschools/sher/standards/1.htm

Centers for Disease Control and Prevention (CDC). (2019b). *Standard 7.* www.cdc.gov/healthyschools/sher/standards/7.htm

Centers for Disease Control and Prevention (CDC). (2019c). *National Health Education Standards.* www.cdc.gov/healthyschools/sher/standards/index.htm

Chandler, M.A. (2015, September 23). All D.C. public school students will learn to ride a bike in second grade. *Washington Post.* www.washingtonpost.com/local/education/all-dc-public-schools-students-will-learn-to-ride-a-bike-in-second-grade/2015/09/23/22a0b356-6203-11e5-b38e-06883aacba64_story.html

Cleland Donnelly, F. & Millar, V. (2019). Moving green, going green: An interdisciplinary creative dance experience. *Journal of Physical Education, Recreation and Dance, 90*(8), 20-3.

Cleland Donnelly, F., Mueller, S., & Gallahue, D. (2017). *Developmental physical education for all children: Theory into practice* (5th ed.). Human Kinetics.

Collaborative for Academic, Social, and Emotional Learning. (2022). *Fundamentals of SEL.* https://casel.org/fundamentals-of-sel/

Dewey, J. (1938). *Experience and education.* Macmillan.

Goodway, J., Ozmun, J., & Gallahue, D. (2019). *Understanding motor development: Infants, children, adolescents, adults* (8th ed.). Jones & Bartlett.

Gutek, G. (2014). *Philosophical, ideological, and theoretical perspectives on education* (2nd ed.). Pearson.

Hellison, D. (2011). *Teaching personal and social responsibility through physical activity* (3rd ed.). Human Kinetics.

Landi, D., Lynch, S., & Walton-Fusett, J. (2020). The A-Z of social justice physical education: Part 2. *Journal of Physical Education, Recreation and Dance, 91*(5), 20-27.

Lieberman, L.J. (2017). The need for universal design for learning. *Journal of Physical Education, Recreation and Dance 88*(3), 5-7. https://doi.org/10.1080/07303084.2016.1271257

Lynch, S., Sutherland, S., & Walton-Fusette, J. (2020). The A-Z of social justice physical education: Part 1. *Journal of Physical Education, Recreation and Dance, 91*(4), 8-13.

Rose, D.H., & Meyer, A. (2002). *Teaching every student in the digital age: Universal design for learning.* ASCD.

SHAPE America. (2014). *National standards & grade-level outcomes for K–12 physical education* (3rd ed.). Human Kinetics.

SHAPE America. (2021). *Literacy in PE + HE.* www.shapeamerica.org/events/healthandphysicalliteracy.aspx

Sorenson, K., Van den Brouks, S., Fullam, J., Doyle, G., Pelikan, J., Slonska, Z., & Brand, H. (2012). Health literacy and public health: A systematic review and integration of definitions and models. *BMC Public Health, 12*(80), 1-13.

Teaching and Learning Team International. (2020). *Active learning.* https://www.cambridgeinternational.org/Images/271174-active-learning.pdf

Teaching Tolerance. (2016). *Social justice standards the teaching tolerance anti-bias framework. Project of Southern Tolerance Law Center.* https://www.learningforjustice.org/sites/default/files/2017-06/TT_Social_Justice_Standards_0.pdf

CHAPTER 4

Albion. (2011). *The core rules of netiquette.* www.albion.com/netiquette/corerules.html

Bakia, M., Shear, L., Toyama, Y., & Lasseter, A. (2012). *Understanding the implications of online learning for educational productivity.* U.S. Department of Education, Office of Educational Technology.

Beseler, B., & Plumb, M.S. (2019). 10 tips for using video analysis more effectively in physical education. *Journal of Physical Education, Recreation and Dance, 90,* 51-56.

Bouchrika, I. (2021, May 13). *Best LMS for schools in 2021: Key features of the top learning management systems.* https://research.com/education/best-lms-for-schools

Brooks, C., & Schneider, M. (2020). *Health Education* [PowerPoint slides]. OAHPERD Think Tank.

Bryan, C., & Solmon, M.A. (2012). Student motivation in physical education and engagement in physical activity. *Journal of Sport Behavior, 35*(3), 267-285.

Bumgardner, W. (2020, July 27). *The best ways to measure how far you have walked.* Verywell Fit. www.verywellfit.com/how-to-measure-how-far-youre-walking-3975561

Buschner, C. (2006). Online physical education: Wires and lights in a box. *Journal of Physical Education, Recreation and Dance, 77*(2), 3-8. https://doi.org/10.1080/07303084.2006.10597818

Casey, A., & Jones, B. (2011). Using digital technology to enhance student engagement in physical education. *Asia-Pacific Journal of Health, Sport and Physical Education, 2*(2), 51-65.

Centers for Disease Control and Prevention (CDC) & ASCD. (2014). *Whole School, Whole Community, Whole Child (WSCC): A collaborative approach to learning and health.* www.cdc.gov/healthyschools/wscc/index.htm

Cummiskey, M. (2011). There's an app for that: Smartphone use in health and physical education. *Journal of Physical Education, Recreation and Dance, 82*(8), 24-29.

Darby, F. (2019, April 17). How to be a better online teacher. *The Chronicle of Higher Education.* www.chronicle.com/article/how-to-be-a-better-online-teacher

Dartmouth. (n.d.). *Remote teaching good practices: Beyond the tech.* https://sites.dartmouth.edu/teachremote/remote-teaching-good-practices

Daum, D.N. (2020). Thinking about hybrid or online learning in physical education? Start here! *Journal of Physical Education, Recreation and Dance, 91*(1), 42-44. https://doi.org/10.1080/07303084.2020.1683387

Daum, D.N., & Buschner, C. (2012). The status of high school online physical education in the United States. *Journal of Teaching in Physical Education, 31,* 86-100.

Daum, D.N., & Buschner, C. (2018). Research on teaching blended and online physical education. In R.E. Ferdig & K. Kennedy (Eds.), *Handbook of research on K-12 online and blended learning* (2nd ed.) (pp. 321-334). ETC Press.

Daum, D.N., & Woods, A.M. (2015). Physical education teacher educator's perceptions toward and understanding of K-12 online physical education. *Journal of Teaching in Physical Education, 34,* 716-724. http://dx.doi.org/10.1123/jtpe.2014-0146

Digital Learning Collaborative. (2019). *Snapshot 2019: A review of K-12 online, blended, and digital learning.* https://static1.squarespace.com/static/5a98496696d4556b01f86662/t/5df14341d5d15f7ed7bf8c93/1576092485377/DLC-KP-Snapshot2019.pdf

Florida Virtual School. (n.d.). *Module 2 wellness plan.* https://learn.flvs.net/educator/common/Course/HOPEv14/HelpSite/ModuleTwoSampleWellnessPlan.pdf

Friedrick, M. (2020). Team building through a pandemic [PowerPoint slides]. www.shapeamerica.org/publications/resources/downloads-lessons-curriculum.aspx

Gaudreault, K.L. (2014). "Cool PE" and confronting the negative stereotypes of physical education. *Strategies, 27*(3), 32-35.

Gemin, B., & Pape, L. (2016). *Keeping pace with K-12 online learning.* Evergreen Education Group. https://files.eric.ed.gov/fulltext/ED576762.pdf

Gemin, B., Pape, L., Vashaw, L., & Watson, J. (2015). *Keeping pace with K-12 digital learning.* Evergreen Education Group. https://static1.squarespace.com/static/59381b9a17bffc68bf625df4/t/5949b64bb11be1ad7855fb51/1498003034517/KeepingPace%20+2015.pdf

Goad, T., & Jones, E. (2017). Training online physical educators: A phenomenological case study. *Education Research International.* https://doi.org/10.1155/2017/3757489

Goad, T., Towner, B., Jones, E., & Bulger, S. (2019). Instructional tools for online physical education: Using mobile technologies to enhance learning. *Journal of Physical Education, Recreation and Dance, 90*(6), 40-47.

Gunnell, M. (2020, April 10). *What is Zoombombing, and how can you stop it?* How-to-Geek. www.howtogeek.com/667183/what-is-zoombombing-and-how-can-you-stop-it

Harris, F. (2009). Visual technology in physical education using Dartfish video analysis to enhance learning: An overview of the Dartfish project in New Brunswick. *Physical and Health Education Journal, 74*(4), 24-25.

Harvard. (n.d.). *Build community in your online course.* https://canvas.harvard.edu/courses/72996/pages/build-community-in-your-online-course

Hastie, P.A., Casey, A., & Tarter, A.M. (2010). A case study of wikis and student-designed games in physical education. *Technology, Pedagogy, and Education, 19*(1), 79-91. https://doi.org/10.1080/14759390903579133

Hughes, J. (2020, November 9). *Zoom vs Microsoft Teams vs Google Meet: Top video conferencing apps compared.* www.codeinwp.com/blog/zoom-vs-microsoft-teams-vs-google-meet

Joint Committee on National Health Education Standards (JCNHES). (2007). *National health education standards: Achieving excellence* (2nd ed.). The American Cancer Society. www.cdc.gov/healthyschools/sher/standards/index.htm

Juniu, S. (2011). Pedagogical uses of technology in physical education. *The Journal of Physical Education, Recreation and Dance, 82*(9), 41-49.

Kennedy, K., & Archambault, L. (2012). Offering preservice teachers field experiences in K-12 online learning: A national survey of teacher education programs. *Journal of Teacher Education, 63*(3), 185-200.

Krause, C. (2020). *How to forge a strong community in an online classroom.* Edutopia. www.edutopia.org/article/how-forge-strong-community-online-classroom

Laughlin, M.K., Hodges, M., & Iraggi, T. (2019) Deploying video analysis to boost instruction and assessment in physical education. *Journal of Physical Education, Recreation and Dance, 90*(5), 23-29. https://doi.org/10.1080/07303084.2019.1580637

Leeb, R.T., Bitsko, R.H., Radhakrishnan, L., Martinez, P., Njai, R., & Holland, K.M. (2020). Mental health–related emergency department visits among children aged <18 years during the COVID-19 pandemic — United States, January 1–October 17, 2020. *Morbidity and Mortality Weekly Report, 69*, 1675-1680. http://dx.doi.org/10.15585/mmwr.mm6945a3

Lynch, M. (n.d.) Dimensions of wellness project journal [PowerPoint slides]. www.shapeamerica.org/publications/resources/downloads-lessons-curriculum.aspx

Martin, M.R., Melnyk, J., & Zimmerman, R. (2015). Fitness apps: Motivating students to move. *Journal of Physical Education, Recreation and Dance, 86*(6), 50-54.

McElrath, K. (2020, August 26). *Nearly 93% of households with school-age children report some form of distance learning during COVID-19.* U.S. Census Bureau. www.census.gov/library/stories/2020/08/schooling-during-the-covid-19-pandemic.html

McNamara, J.M., Swalm, R.L., Stearne, D.J., & Covassin, T.M. (2008). Online weight training. *Journal of Strength and Conditioning Research, 22*, 1164-1168.

Mellon, J. (2020). Manipulative skills – striking [Word document].

Miller, M. (2020, September 2). *How to use Jamboard in the classroom: 20+ tips and ideas.* Ditch That Textbook. https://ditchthattextbook.com/jamboard/

Mohnsen, B. (2012). Implementing online physical education. *Journal of Physical Education, Recreation and Dance, 83*(2), 42-47.

Molnar, M. (2019). U.S. K-12 market for mobile devices remains flat; only 2% growth in 2018. Editorial Projects in Education. https://marketbrief.edweek.org/marketplace-k-12/u-s-k-12-market-mobile-devices-remains-flat-2-percent-growth-2018/

Mosier, B., & Lynn, S. (2012). An initial exploration of a virtual personal fitness course. *Online Journal of Distance Learning Administration, 15*(3).

National Association for Sport and Physical Education (NASPE). (2004). *Moving into the future: National standards for physical education* (2nd ed.). Author.

National Association for Sport and Physical Education (NASPE). (2006). *Shape of the nation: Status of physical education in the USA.* Author.

National Association for Sport and Physical Education (NASPE). (2007). *Initial guidelines for online physical education.* Author.

National Association for Sport and Physical Education (NASPE). (2012). *Shape of the nation: Status of physical education in the USA.* Author.

National Association for Sport and Physical Education (NASPE) & American Heart Association (AHA). (2010). *Shape of the nation: Status of physical education in the USA.* https://www.shapeamerica.org/advocacy/son/2012/upload/2012-Shape-of-Nation-full-report-web.pdf

Niedzwiecki, N. (2020a). Remote health and PE expectations [PowerPoint slides].

Niedzwiecki, N. (2020b). Catching [Word document].

O'Hara, K. (n.d.). Code of conduct for online discussion boards [Word document].

Papadopoulou, A. (2020). *How to build an online learning community (in 2021)*. LearnWorlds. www.learnworlds.com/build-online-learning-community

Persia, N. (2020). Underhand throw and toss [Word document].

Persky, A.M., & McLaughlin, J.E. (2017). The flipped classroom – from theory to practice in health professional education. *American Journal of Pharmaceutical Education, 81*(6), 1-11.

Quality Matters and Virtual Learning Leadership Alliance. (2019). *National standards for quality online teaching* (3rd ed.). www.nsqol.org

Ransdell, L.B., Rice, K., Snelson, C., & Decola, J. (2008). Online health-related fitness courses. *The Journal of Physical Education, Recreation and Dance, 79*(1), 45-52.

Raygoza, M., León, R., & Norris, A. (2020). *Humanizing online teaching*. St. Mary's College Digital Commons. https://digitalcommons.stmarys-ca.edu/school-education-faculty-works/1805

Rhea, D.J. (2011). Virtual physical education in the K–12 setting. *Journal of Physical Education, Recreation and Dance, 82*(1), 5-6, 50. https://doi.org/10.1080/07303084.2011.10598551

Schroeder, B. (2019, August 14). Disrupting education. The rise of K-12 online and the entrepreneurial opportunities. *Forbes*. www.forbes.com/sites/bernhardschroeder/2019/08/14/disrupting-education-the-rise-of-k-12-online-and-the-entrepreneurial-opportunities/?sh=5c0fb61248a2

SHAPE America. (2009). *Appropriate instructional practice guidelines, K-12: A side-by-side comparison*. www.shapeamerica.org/uploads/pdfs/Appropriate-Instructional-Practices-Grid.pdf

SHAPE America. (2013). *Grade-level outcomes for K-12 physical education*. www.shapeamerica.org/standards/pe/upload/Grade-Level-Outcomes-for-K-12-Physical-Education.pdf

SHAPE America. (2016). *Shape of the nation. Status of physical education in the USA*. www.shapeamerica.org/advocacy/son/2016/upload/Shape-of-the-Nation-2016_web.pdf

SHAPE America. (2018). *Guidelines for K-12 online physical education*. www.shapeamerica.org/uploads/pdfs/2020/guidelines/Online-PE-Guidance-Document.pdf

SHAPE America. (2020). *Teacher's toolbox activity calendars*. www.shapeamerica.org/publications/resources/teachingtools/teachertoolbox/activity-calendars.aspx

Siegelman, A. (2019). *Blended, hybrid, and flipped courses: What's the difference?* Temple University. https://teaching.temple.edu/edvice-exchange/2019/11/blended-hybrid-and-flipped-courses-what%E2%80%99s-difference

Solano. (n.d.). Rules of netiquette. http://bcs.solano.edu/workarea/mfracisc/Word/Homework%20Solutions/Unit%202%20Ch%206-10/U2PA/PDF-Annotated/U2-PA12-Netiquette-Anno.pdf

Surdin, J. (2018). *Zoom: Allow participants to record breakout rooms during a meeting*. Penn State. https://pennstate.service-now.com/kb?id=kb_article_view&sysparm_article=KB0012039

Trent, M. (2016). Investigating virtual personal fitness course alignment with national guidelines for online physical education [Unpublished doctoral dissertation]. Georgia State University. https://scholarworks.gsu.edu/kin_health_diss/16

UOTP Marketing. (2020). *Online etiquette: 14 netiquette rules online students should know*. https://potomac.edu/netiquette-rules-online-students

UTEP Connect. (n.d.). *10 rules of netiquette for students*. www.utep.edu/extendeduniversity/utepconnect/blog/october-2017/10-rules-of-netiquette-for-students.html

We and Me. (2020). *We! Connect cards*. https://weand.me/product/we-connect-cards/

Williams, L. (2013). *A case study of virtual physical education teachers' experiences in and perspectives of online teaching* [Doctoral Dissertation, University of South Florida]. Scholar Commons. https://scholarcommons.usf.edu/etd/4962

Williams, M.R., & Ritter, S. (2020, April 27). *Could remote teaching end snow days after COVID-19?* Center for Digital Education. www.govtech.com/education/k-12/Could-Remote-Teaching-End-Snow-Days-After-COVID-19.html

Yu, H., Kulinna, P.H., & Lorenz, K.A. (2018). An integration of mobile applications into physical education programs. *Strategies, 31*(3), 13-19. https://doi.org/10.1080/08924562.2018.1442275

Index

Note: The italicized *f* and *t* following page numbers refer to figures and tables, respectively.

About the Authors

Matthew Cummiskey

MATTHEW CUMMISKEY, PHD, is an associate professor at West Chester University (WCU) in West Chester, Pennsylvania, where he trains future school wellness educators. He taught K-12 health and physical education for five years and has taught within higher education for 13 years. Dr. Cummiskey helped develop the wellness-centric teacher education program at WCU in collaboration with Dr. Frances Cleland Donnelly. He is codirector of the WCU adventure education program. He is the editor for the SHAPE Pennsylvania journal and the Mid-Atlantic adventure education journal. Dr. Cummiskey has formed collaborations with the School District of Philadelphia to promote quality urban wellness education. He has numerous articles and conference presentations to his credit. Dr. Cummiskey enjoys implementing technology in his classes. He contributed a chapter to *Technology for Physical Educators, Health Educators, and Coaches,* published in 2021 by Human Kinetics.

Courtesy of Caroline Shorey.

FRANCES CLELAND DONNELLY, PED, is a professor in the department of kinesiology at West Chester University. She served on the SHAPE America's board of directors (2016-2019) and is a former president of SHAPE America (2017-2018). Dr. Cleland has also been president of the National Association for Sport and Physical Education and SHAPE Pennsylvania. Cleland Donnelly has numerous articles in refereed publications and chapters in books to her credit. She has made many dozens of presentations at the international, national, district, and state levels. In 2020 she received the SHAPE America Eastern District Tilia Fantasia Service Award, and in 2016 she was awarded the SHAPE America Margie R. Hanson Elementary Physical Education Distinguished Service Award. In 2014, she was inducted into the North American Society of HPERSD Professionals, and she has received numerous awards for teaching and service throughout her career. She was the lead author on *Developmental Physical Education for All Children, Fifth Edition,* published in 2017 by Human Kinetics.

HUMAN KINETICS

Books

Ebooks

Continuing Education

Journals ...and more!

US.HumanKinetics.com
Canada.HumanKinetics.com